Tourism in Brazil

Since the 1990s, tourism has become a major driver of economic activity and community development in Brazil. New policies and approaches, growing expertise and investment in tourism have brought significant transformation in tourism products, destination development and community involvement. In addition, Brazil will be hosting two major sporting events in the years ahead: the FIFA World Cup, in 2014, and the Olympic Games in Rio de Janeiro, in 2016. Brazil offers many cultural and natural attractions but, similarly to many other developing countries, it still struggles with keeping up levels of infrastructure, product development and accessibility, service quality, market access and workforce training.

This book provides an in-depth examination of tourism in Brazil, critically reviewing its development and management. The social, economic, political and environmental contexts of this emerging global power provide an intriguing backdrop. The book considers important development issues such as the changing policy context, community benefit tourism and indigenous tourism. It explores the impacts of tourism on the environment, changing community attitudes towards tourism, transport infrastructure and sustainability issues in events, as well as backpacker tourism, sensual tourism, adventure tourism and ecotourism, and the implications for tourism research and education are examined. The book draws from theoretical foundations and practical insights, and gives voice to Brazilian researchers who are actively engaged in researching tourism.

Drawing from cutting-edge cross-cultural research, this original and timely book will be of interest to students, researchers and academics in the areas of tourism, geography and related disciplines.

Gui Lohmann is a lecturer at the School of Tourism and Hospitality Management, Southern Cross University (Australia).

Dianne Dredge is Associate Professor in the School of Tourism and Hospitality Management, Southern Cross University (Australia).

Contemporary Geographies of Leisure, Tourism and Mobility

Edited by C. Michael Hall
Professor at the Department of Management, College of Business and Economics, University of Canterbury, Christchurch, New Zealand

The aim of this series is to explore and communicate the intersections and relationships between leisure, tourism and human mobility within the social sciences.

It will incorporate both traditional and new perspectives on leisure and tourism from contemporary geography, e.g. notions of identity, representation and culture, while also providing for perspectives from cognate areas such as anthropology, cultural studies, gastronomy and food studies, marketing, policy studies and political economy, regional and urban planning, and sociology, within the development of an integrated field of leisure and tourism studies.

Also, increasingly, tourism and leisure are regarded as steps in a continuum of human mobility. Inclusion of mobility in the series offers the prospect to examine the relationship between tourism and migration, the sojourner, educational travel, and second home and retirement travel phenomena.

The series comprises two strands:

Contemporary Geographies of Leisure, Tourism and Mobility aims to address the needs of students and academics, and the titles will be published in hardback and paperback. Titles include:

1. The Moralisation of Tourism
Sun, sand … and saving the world?
Jim Butcher

2. The Ethics of Tourism Development
Mick Smith and Rosaleen Duffy

3. Tourism in the Caribbean
Trends, development, prospects
Edited by David Timothy Duval

4. Qualitative Research in Tourism
Ontologies, epistemologies and methodologies
Edited by Jenny Phillimore and Lisa Goodson

5. The Media and the Tourist Imagination
Converging cultures
Edited by David Crouch, Rhona Jackson and Felix Thompson

6. Tourism and Global Environmental Change
Ecological, social, economic and political interrelationships
Edited by Stefan Gössling and C. Michael Hall

7. Cultural Heritage of Tourism in the Developing World
Edited by Dallen J. Timothy and Gyan Nyaupane

8. Understanding and Managing Tourism Impacts
An integrated approach
C. Michael Hall and Alan Lew

9. An Introduction to Visual Research Methods in Tourism
Edited by Tijana Rakic and Donna Chambers

10. Tourism and Climate Change
Impacts, adaptation and mitigation
C. Michael Hall, Stefan Gössling and Daniel Scott

Routledge Studies in Contemporary Geographies of Leisure, Tourism and Mobility is a forum for innovative new research intended for research students and academics, and the titles will be available in hardback only. Titles include:

1. Living with Tourism
Negotiating identities in a Turkish village
Hazel Tucker

2. Tourism, Diasporas and Space
Edited by Tim Coles and Dallen J. Timothy

3. Tourism and Postcolonialism
Contested discourses, identities and representations
Edited by C. Michael Hall and Hazel Tucker

4. Tourism, Religion and Spiritual Journeys
Edited by Dallen J. Timothy and Daniel H. Olsen

5. China's Outbound Tourism
Wolfgang Georg Arlt

6. Tourism, Power and Space
Edited by Andrew Church and Tim Coles

7. Tourism, Ethnic Diversity and the City
Edited by Jan Rath

8. Ecotourism, NGOs and Development
A critical analysis
Jim Butcher

9. Tourism and the Consumption of Wildlife
Hunting, shooting and sport fishing
Edited by Brent Lovelock

10. Tourism, Creativity and Development
Edited by Greg Richards and Julie Wilson

11. Tourism at the Grassroots
Villagers and visitors in the Asia-Pacific
Edited by John Connell and Barbara Rugendyke

12. Tourism and Innovation
C. Michael Hall and Allan Williams

13. World Tourism Cities
Developing tourism off the beaten track
Edited by Robert Maitland and Peter Newman

14. Tourism and National Parks
International perspectives on development, histories and change
Edited by Warwick Frost and C. Michael Hall

15. Tourism, Performance and the Everyday
Consuming the Orient
Michael Haldrup and Jonas Larsen

16. Tourism and Change in Polar Regions
Climate, environments and experiences
Edited by C. Michael Hall and Jarkko Saarinen

17. Fieldwork in Tourism
Methods, issues and reflections
Edited by C. Michael Hall

18. Tourism and India
A critical introduction
Kevin Hannam and Anya Diekmann

19. Political Economy of Tourism
A critical perspective
Edited by Jan Mosedale

20. Volunteer Tourism
Theoretical frameworks and practical applications
Edited by Angela Benson

21. The Study of Tourism
Past trends and future directions
Richard Sharpley

22. Children's and Families' Holiday Experience
Neil Carr

23. Tourism and National Identity
An international perspective
Edited by Elspeth Frew and Leanne White

24. Tourism and Agriculture
New geographies of consumption, production and rural restructuring
Edited by Rebecca Torres and Janet Momsen

25. Tourism in China
Policy and development since 1949
David Airey and King Chong

26. Real Tourism
Practice, care, and politics in contemporary travel culture
Edited by Claudio Minca and Tim Oakes

27. Last Chance Tourism
Adapting tourism opportunities in a changing world
Edited by Raynald Harvey Lemelin, Jackie Dawson and Emma Stewart

28. Tourism and Animal Ethics
David A. Fennell

29. Actor Network Theory and Tourism
Ontologies, methodologies and performances
Edited by René van der Duim, Gunnar Thór Jóhannesson and Carina Ren

30. Liminal Landscapes
Travel, experience and spaces in-between
Edited by Hazel Andrews and Les Roberts

31. Tourism in Brazil
Environment, management and segments
Edited by Gui Lohmann and Dianne Dredge

32. Slum Tourism
Edited by Fabian Frenzel, Malte Steinbrink and Ko Koens

33. Medical Tourism
Edited by C. Michael Hall

Forthcoming:

Tourism and War
Edited by Richard Butler and Wantanee Suntikul

Sexuality, Women and Tourism
Susan Frohlick

Gender and Tourism
Social, cultural and spatial perspectives
Cara Atchinson

Backpacker Tourism and Economic Development in the Less Developed World
Mark Hampton

Adventure Tourism
Steve Taylor, Peter Varley and Tony Johnson

Dark Tourism and Place Identity
Elspeth Frew and Leanne White

Scuba Diving Tourism
Kay Dimmcock and Ghazali Musa

Travel, Tourism and Green Growth
Min Jiang, Terry DeLacy and Geoffrey Lipman

Tourism in Brazil

Environment, management and segments

Edited by Gui Lohmann and Dianne Dredge

Routledge
Taylor & Francis Group
LONDON AND NEW YORK

First published 2012
by Routledge
2 Park Square, Milton Park, Abingdon, Oxon, OX14 4RN

Simultaneously published in the USA and Canada
by Routledge
711 Third Avenue, New York, NY 10017

First issued in paperback 2017

Routledge is an imprint of the Taylor & Francis Group, an informa business

British Library Cataloguing in Publication Data
A catalogue record for this book is available from the British Library

Library of Congress Cataloging-in-Publication Data
Lohmann, Guilherme Masella
Tourism in Brazil: environment, management and segments/
Gui Lohmann and Dianne Dredge. -- 1st ed.
p. cm. -- (Contemporary geographies of leisure, tourism and mobility)
Includes bibliographical references and index.
ISBN 978-0-415-67432-4 (hardback)
1. Tourism--Brazil. 2. Tourism--Economic aspects--Brazil.
I. Dredge, Dianne. II. Title.
G155.B7P26 2012
338.4′79181--dc23

2011042693

ISBN 13: 978-1-138-08149-9 (pbk)
ISBN 13: 978-0-415-67432-4 (hbk)

Typeset in Times New Roman by Deerpark Productions

Contents

Illustrations

Figures

Tables

Contributors

Lindemberg Medeiros de Araujo has a PhD in Tourism Management from Sheffield Hallam University, England. He teaches Geography of Tourism and Environmental Analysis at the Universidade Federal de Alagoas (UFAL) in Brazil. He has written and contributed to a number of books and has published papers in tourism and geography-related journals. His current tourism research activities focus on coastal zones, environmental management, territory dynamics, internationalization of developing regions, participation, partnerships and sustainable development. He is a member of ABRATUR, the International Academy for the Development of Tourism Research in Brazil.

Sandro Carnicelli-Filho is Lecturer in Events Management at the University of the West of Scotland. Sandro has presented over 20 papers in international conferences and has published in peer-reviewed journals such as *Tourism Management*, *World Leisure Journal*, *Annals of Leisure Research*, and the *Brazilian Journal of Physical Education and Sport*. Altogether, Sandro has gained five grants in Brazil and New Zealand to fund his research in adventure tourism and leisure, including the 2009 Skills Active Outdoor Recreation Research Scholarship (New Zealand). He is a member of ABRATUR, the International Academy for the Development of Tourism Research in Brazil.

Lamartine Pereira DaCosta, PhD, is a Professor in the Physical Education Department, Universidade Gama Filho, Rio de Janeiro, Brazil, and visiting Professor at the Technical University of Lisbon and the University of East London. Lamartine is a member of the Research Council of the Olympic Studies Centre, and the Education and Ethics Committee of the World Anti-Doping Agency (WADA). He acted as International Chair in Olympism from 2004 to 2005 for the International Olympic Committee and the Universidad Autonoma de Barcelona, and is a consultant for research policy and grants within the Brazilian national government (CAPES and CNPq) and São Paulo State government (FAPESP). Lamartine has published 39 books and book chapters and over 90 research articles in national and international peer-reviewed journals in the areas of physical education and sports.

Dianne Dredge is Associate Professor in the School of Tourism and Hospitality Management, Southern Cross University. She has 20 years' experience as a tourism planner in Queensland, New South Wales, Canada, Mexico and China. Her work has included conceptual design and site analysis of large-scale integrated resort proposals; integration of tourism considerations in strategic and local area plans; comparative analyses of competitive destinations; studies into the re-imaging of destinations in crisis; and the assessment of the environmental impacts of tourism. She has also been involved in tourism capacity-building activities in local governments and tourism organizations, including stakeholder audits and community consultation. Dianne has an active research agenda exploring and publishing in local government tourism management, place-based planning and management of tourism places, tourism organisations, tourism planning and policy.

Paulo Jordão de O.C. Fortes teaches business management at Universidade Federal do Piauí (UFPI), Brazil. He completed a master's degree in Business Administration from Fundação Getúlio Vargas (EBAPE/FGV), Brazil, and a BA in Business Administration from the University of Nebraska at Omaha (UNO), USA. Currently, he researches innovative ways to alleviate poverty and to create business opportunities in Brazilian semi-arid regions in the sectors of tourism, agriculture and industry.

José Manoel Gândara is a senior lecturer in the Tourism Department, Universidade Federal do Paraná. He has a Masters in Tourism Management from SSCTS in Milan and a PhD in Tourism and Sustainable Development from Las Palmas de Gran Canária University. He has taught at the Universities of Málaga, Valencia, Las Palmas and Alicante in Spain. His main research areas are in marketing and service quality in destinations. He is a member of ABRATUR, the International Academy for the Development of Tourism Research in Brazil.

Rodrigo de Azeredo Grünewald is an Associate Professor in Anthropology at the Universidade Federal de Campina Grande, Brazil. He is a member of CULTUS (Tourism, Culture and Society group) based at the Universidade Federal do Rio Grande do Sul, Brazil, and of the Tourism Studies Working Group (TSWG) at the University of California at Berkeley, USA. His major research area explores indigenous cultural change under tourism.

Sergio Rodrigues Leal has a PhD in Tourism from the University of Surrey and a Masters degree in Tourism from James Cook University. He is currently a Senior Lecturer at the Department of Hotel Management and Tourism at Universidade Federal de Pernambuco (UFPE). Sergio has authored the book *Quality in tourism higher education in Brazil: the voices of undergraduate students* and several book chapters, conference papers and journal articles in Brazil, Argentina and the UK. He is also the founding editor of the academic journal *Boletim de Estudos em Hotelaria e Turismo*. He is a member of ABRATUR, the International Academy for the Development of Tourism Research in Brazil.

Gui Lohmann is Lecturer in the School of Tourism and Hospitality Management, Southern Cross University. He has taught and undertaken research in several universities around the world, including the University of Waikato, New Zealand, Universidade de São Paulo, Brazil, and the University of Hawaii at Manoa, USA. He has authored several books and peer-reviewed journal articles both in English and Portuguese. He has worked as a consultant for the Brazilian Ministry of Tourism, the World Tourism Organization, the United Nations Environmental Program, and the Abu Dhabi Tourism Authority. Gui is the founder and currently executive director of ABRATUR, the International Academy for the Development of Tourism Research in Brazil.

Eduardo Jorge Costa Mielke has a PhD in Tourism Management and Sustainable Development (University of Malaga, Spain). Currently, he is the Director of Studies at the Faculty of Tourism, Universidade do Estado do Rio de Janeiro (UERJ). He is an expert in tourism development, with extensive experience in tourism destination management, community-based tourism (CBT) and cooperative tourism. He has 12 years experience as a lecturer in both graduate and undergraduate programmes. He has authored the book *Desenvolvimento Turístico de Base Comunitária (Community-based tourism development: a practice approach)*. He also has eight years of consulting experience, developing more than a dozen CBT projects in Brazil, Colombia and Argentina.

Miguel Moital has a PhD in Tourism from the School of Tourism, Bournemouth University, where he currently is a Senior Lecturer in Events Management. His areas of research include the consumer experience of leisure, tourism and events and event and leisure marketing and management. He has published in a number of journals, including *The Service Industries Journal*, *Tourism & Hospitality Planning & Development*, *The Tourist Review*, the *International Journal of Contemporary Hospitality Management* and *Visão e Ação* (Brazil). He has also presented more than 20 papers in international conferences. Miguel is a member of ABRATUR, the International Academy for the Development of Tourism Research in Brazil.

Alexandre Panosso Netto is a lecturer in Leisure and Tourism at the Escola de Artes, Ciências e Humanidades at Universidade de São Paulo. He has a PhD in Communication Sciences from the same university. He has published several book chapters and journal articles and 16 books on tourism. He is the author of *Filosofia do turismo: teoria e epistemologia* published both in Portuguese and Spanish; *Teoria do turismo: conceitos, modelos e sistemas* (with Gui Lohmann); and *Epistemología del turismo: estúdios críticos*, with

Marcelino Castillo Nechar. He is a member of ABRATUR, the International Academy for the Development of Tourism Research in Brazil.

José Antonio Puppim de Oliveira is Assistant Director and Senior Research Fellow at the United Nations University Institute of Advanced Studies (UNU-IAS) in Yokohama, Japan. He has academic interests in the political economy of sustainable development, and the links between economic activities and environmental protection in several sectors, including tourism, mining and agriculture. Before joining UNU-IAS, he worked at the University College London, the Brazilian School of Public and Business Administration (EBAPE) of the Getúlio Vargas Foundation (FGV), and at the University of Santiago de Compostela, Spain. He is editor of the journal *Public Administration and Development* (PAD, Wiley-Blackwell).

Fernanda de Vasconcellos Pegas has a PhD in Recreation, Parks and Tourism Sciences from Texas A&M University, USA, and a Masters in Forest Social Science from Oregon State University, USA. She currently holds a position as a Research Fellow at the International Centre for Ecotourism Research at Griffith University, Gold Coast Campus. Fernanda has undertaken research in the United States and in Brazil, publishing in English peer-reviewed journals. She has assisted in research and worked as an instructor at the Ecotourism Department at Texas A&M University, where she taught classes on tourism, leisure, and outdoor recreation. She is a member of ABRATUR, the International Academy for the Development of Tourism Research in Brazil.

Bruce Prideaux is a Professor of Marketing and Tourism Management and Director of Centre for Tropical Tourism Studies at James Cook University, Cairns, Australia. He has authored over 230 journal articles, book chapters and conference papers on a range of issues related to tourism. He has authored or co-authored seven books, the most recent of which is titled *Drive tourism: trends and emerging markets*. He has guest-edited special issues of journals on themes including cybertourism, drive tourism, crisis management, crisis recovery, war and tourism and more recently on climate change. He has a diverse range of research interests including climate change issues, tourism transport (including drive tourism, low-cost carriers and rail), heritage, destination development, seniors, Korean tourism issues, backpackers, crisis management, marine and rainforest tourism.

Arianne Carvalhedo Reis has a PhD in Tourism from the University of Otago, New Zealand. In Brazil she worked for two years as a project manager for the Ceará State Department of Sports and subsequently as a Lecturer in Physical Education at Ceará State University, Brazil. While in New Zealand, she worked as a casual lecturer for the Department of Tourism, University of Otago, and as a research fellow for the Centre for Recreation Research in the same university. Currently, she is a Postdoctoral Research Fellow with the School of Tourism and Hospitality Management, Southern Cross University. Arianne has published on the topics of sport and nature-based tourism and has acted as a consultant in numerous tourism research projects for government and private businesses in New Zealand and Australia. She is a member of ABRATUR, the International Academy for the Development of Tourism Research in Brazil.

Cristina Rodrigues is a PhD candidate in Tourism at James Cook University. She has several years experience as a lecturer teaching undergraduate tourism courses in two private universities in Brazil. She completed her Master in Human Geography at the University of Campinas, Brazil. Her areas of interest include tourism impacts, backpacker tourism and local communities.

Luiz Gonzaga Godoi Trigo is a Professor in the Leisure and Tourism Programme and at the Masters of Cultural Studies at Escola de Artes, Ciências e Humanidades at Universidade de São Paulo, Brazil. He graduated in philosophy and tourism, has a Masters degree in Philosophy from PUC-Campinas, Brazil, and a PhD in Education from Unicamp, Brazil. Luiz has published several book chapters, journal articles and 18 books about tourism, entertainment and education. He is a member of ABRATUR, the International Academy for the Development of Tourism Research in Brazil.

Jakob Trischler is a PhD candidate in the Southern Cross Business School, Southern Cross University, Australia. He has a background in tourism studies undertaken at the Management Center Innsbruck, Austria, and Högskolan Dalarna, Sweden. His practical background is in the tourism and hospitality industry as well as in marketing. His areas of research are service marketing, destination management and entrepreneurship in tourism.

Preface

The idea of this book occurred to me (Gui) a few weeks after I returned to Australia from a trip to São Paulo in September 2010. On that occasion, I attended the seventh ANPTUR (Brazilian Tourism Research Association) conference, giving a keynote address and participating in a round-table about research internationalization. My point was very much about the need to expose to overseas audiences the depth and breadth of research about tourism in Brazil. Brazil is becoming increasingly relevant on the global stage and international audiences are getting more and more interested in learning about Brazil.

In order to 'walk the talk', and considering that there had been no attempt as yet to publish a book in English dealing with different aspects of tourism in Brazil, an edited book seemed like the perfect opportunity to contribute in this area. I then sold the idea to Dianne Dredge to collaborate as co-editor and to other key Brazilian and international colleagues to participate as authors. We were both astonished by the huge interest expressed by colleagues and the publisher towards this project.

One of the major appeals of this book is the simple fact that English academic literature on tourism in Brazil is scarce. A search on Amazon's bookstore website with the keywords 'tourism' and 'Brazil' in May 2011 would have shown a total of 64 results, of which only a couple were academic books dealing with specific issues about tourism in Brazil, including tourism in protected areas in the northeast region of Brazil[1] and *Quality in Tourism Higher Education in Brazil* (Leal 2010).[2] Hence, this current book is the first to address tourism in Brazil from a broader and more general perspective. From a larger geographical perspective, *Tourism in South America* (Santana 2001)[3] was published with only one chapter dealing with tourism and HR issues in the State of Bahia.[4] Apart from books, journal articles and book chapters dealing with tourism in Brazil are more evident in English literature, with some incipient studies published between the 1970s and 1990s,[5–10] but with the bulk of publications taking place during the 2000s. This reflects both the recent and growing interest shown by international academics in publishing about tourism in Brazil, as well as Brazilian academics publishing in international fora.

Some of the more recurrent topics in recent articles and book chapters include sustainable/environmental/ecotourism related studies[11–13], tourism development[14–19], events[20–22], transport and supply chain issues[23–26], and tourism education[27]. To a lesser degree, other topics have also been covered, including adventure tourism[28], crises[29], gastronomy[30], image[31], human resources[32], safety[33] and regional studies[34]. Not surprisingly, some of these topics are included in this book.

Other initiatives have followed as a consequence of this book, including the creation of ABRATUR – Academia Internacional para o Desenvolvimento da Pesquisa em Turismo no Brasil (International Academy for the Development of Tourism Research in Brazil). It is our sincere hope that this book will open up other opportunities for increased international scholarship on tourism in Brazil, but also for Brazilian scholars to engage more fully in the international arena.

Gui Lohmann and Dianne Dredge
Southern Cross University
Gold Coast campus, Australia
April 2012

Notes

1 Puppim de Oliveira, J.A. (2008) *Implementation of environmental policies in developing countries: a case of protected areas and tourism in Brazil.* Albany: State University of New York Press.
2 Leal, S. (2010) *Quality in Tourism Higher Education in Brazil: The Voices of Undergraduate Students.* Cologne: LAP Lambert Academic Publishing.
3 Santana, G. (2001) *Tourism in South America.* Binghamton: The Haworth Hospitality Press.
4 Bécherel, L. (2001) A framework for human resources development strategy at the macro-level: A situational analysis of tourism human resources in Bahia, Brazil, in G. Santana (ed.) *Tourism in South America.* Binghamton: The Haworth Hospitality Press.
5 Aspelin, P.L. (1977) The anthropological analysis of tourism: indirect tourism and political economy in the case of the mamainde of Mato Grosso, Brazil, *Annals of Tourism Research*, 4: 135–60.
6 Belfort, M., Lang, H.R. and Teuscher, H. (1980) The importance of inland tourism for regional planning and development. With special reference to Minas Gerais, Brazil. *Applied Geography and Development*, 16: 92–104.
7 Robben, A.C.G.M. (1984) Tourism and change in a Brazilian fishing village. *Contours*, 1: 408–57.
8 Ruschmann, D.V.D.M. (1992) Ecological tourism in Brazil. *Tourism Management*, 13: 125–28.
9 Wagner, J.E. (1997) Estimating the economic impacts of tourism. *Annals of Tourism Research*, 24: 78–89.
10 Wallace, G.N. and Pierce, S.M. (1996) An evaluation of ecotourism in Amazonas, Brazil, *Annals of Tourism Research*, 23: 843–73.
11 Kim, H., Borges, M.C. and Chon, J. (2006) Impacts of environmental values on tourism motivation: the case of FICA, Brazil. *Tourism Management*, 27: 957–67.
12 Oliveira, J.A.P. (2005) Tourism as a force for establishing protected areas: The case of Bahia, Brazil, *Journal of Sustainable Tourism*, 13: 24–49.
13 Storni, A., Paiva, P.M.V., Bernal, R. and Peralta, N. (2007) Evaluation of the impact on fauna caused by the presence of ecotourists on trails of the Mamirauá Sustainable

Development Reserve, Amazonas, Brazil. *Tourism and Hospitality: Planning and Development*, 4: 25–32.
14 Green, C. and Green, A. (2009) Global service learning through green mapping tourism development in the Brazilian Atlantic rainforest, *Journal of Hospitality and Tourism Education*, 21: 43–54.
15 Hoeffel, J.L., Fadini, A.A.B. and Suarez, C.F.S. (2009) The nature we all want. Influences of São Paulo Metropolis on tourism development in the Bragantina Region, São Paulo, Brazil. *Tourism and Hospitality: Planning & Development*, 6: 191–205.
16 Nobre, E.A.C. (2002) Urban regeneration experiences in Brazil: Historical preservation, tourism development and gentrification in Salvador da Bahia. *Urban Design International*, 7: 109–24.
17 Oliveira, J.A.P. (2003) Governmental responses to tourism development: three Brazilian case studies. *Tourism Management*, 24: 97–110.
18 Ros-Tonen, M.A.F. and Werneck, A.F. (2009) Small-scale tourism development in Brazilian Amazonia: the creation of a 'tourist bubble'. *European Review of Latin American and Caribbean Studies*, 86: 59–79.
19 Santana, G. (2000) An overview of contemporary tourism development in Brazil. *International Journal of Contemporary Hospitality Management*, 12: 424–30.
20 Flecha, A.C., Lott, W., Lee, T.J., Moital, M. and Edwards, J. (2010) Sustainability of events in urban historic centers: The case of Ouro Preto, Brazil. *Tourism and Hospitality: Planning and Development*, 7: 131–43.
21 Gaffney, C. (2010) Mega-events and socio-spatial dynamics in Rio de Janeiro, 1919–2016. *Journal of Latin American Geography*, 9: 1–29.
22 Greenfield, G. (2010) Reveillon in Rio de Janeiro. *Event Management*, 14: 301–08.
23 Costa, T.F., Lohmann, G. and Oliveira, A.V. (2010) A model to identify airport hubs and their importance to tourism in Brazil. *Research in Transportation Economics*, 26: 3–11.
24 Lohmann, G., Santos, G. and Allis, T. (2011) 'Los hermanos' visiting the south region of Brazil: a comparison between drive tourists and coach tourists from Argentina, Paraguay and Uruguay in B. Prideaux and D. Carson (eds) *Drive tourism: trends and emerging markets*. London: Routledge.
25 Martins, R.S., Labegalini, L., Lobo, D.S. and Carrieri, A.P. (2008) Logistics managers' stated preferences for supply management attributes for the case of inns in Brazil. *Anatolia: An International Journal of Tourism and Hospitality Research*, 19: 323–39.
26 Turolla, F.A., Vassallo, M.D. and Oliveira, A.V.M.D. (2008) Intermodal competition in the Brazilian interstate travel market. *Revista de Análisis Económico*, 23: 21–33.
27 Knowles, T., Teixeira, R.M. and Egan, D. (2003) Tourism and hospitality education in Brazil and the UK: a comparison. *International Journal of Contemporary Hospitality Management*, 15: 45–51.
28 Carnicelli-Filho, S., Schwartz, G.M. and Tahara, A.K. (2010) Fear and adventure tourism in Brazil. *Tourism Management*, 31: 953–56.
29 Santana, G. (2003) Crisis management and tourism: beyond the rhetoric. *Journal of Travel and Tourism Marketing*, 15: 299–321.
30 Fajans, J. (2006) Regional food and the tourist imagination in Brazil. *Appetite*, 47: 389.
31 Rezende-Parker, A.M., Morrison, A.M. and Ismail, J.A. (2003) Dazed and confused? An exploratory study of the image of Brazil as a travel destination. *Journal of Vacation Marketing*, 23: 243–59.
32 Bécherel, L. (2001) A framework for human resources development strategy at the macro-level: A situational analysis of tourism human resources in Bahia, Brazil. *International Journal of Hospitality and Tourism Administration*, 1: 73–97.

33 Tarlow, P.E. and Santana, G. (2002) Providing safety for tourists: a study of a selected sample of tourist destinations in the United States and Brazil. *Journal of Travel Research*, 40: 424–31.
34 Araújo, L.M. and Bramwell, B. (2002) Partnership and regional tourism in Brazil. *Annals of Tourism Research*, 29: 1138–64.

Acknowledgments

The editors would like to thank each of the contributors for the commitment, dedication and enthusiasm they showed in the development of this book. Thank you for accepting the challenge. The editors are also grateful for the support received from Daniela Alvares, Gisele Pereira, Rosana Mazaro, Glauber Santos and Rivanda Teixeira. Jakob Trischler warrants special mention for his timely and valuable assistance. Cindy Wirick, once more, has been an asset with her cartographic skills.

Gui and Dianne acknowledge support from the School of Tourism and Hospitality Management, Southern Cross University, in bringing this book to fruition. Thanks particularly to John Jenkins, Kevin Markwell and Diana Sims. We also thank the Routledge team, in particular Carol Barber, Faye Leerink and Emma Travis for their interest and patience, the proposal reviewers for their useful comments and Michael Hall, editor of the Contemporary Geographies of Tourism, Leisure and Mobility series, for supporting this book.

Gui acknowledges the support of many international colleagues who have inspired and trusted him over the years, in particular Dianne Dredge, David Duval, Larry Dwyer, Tay Koo, Alison McIntosh, Andreas Papatheodorou, Doug Pearce, Bruce Prideaux, Mondher Sahli, Frank Scrimgeour, Pauline Sheldon, Davina Stanford and Anne Zahra. From Brazil he is indebted to Mariana Aldrigui, Marco Ávila, Débora Braga, Gustavo da Cruz, Betty Fromer, José Gândara, Sandra Molina, Alexandre Panosso, Adriano Piazzi, Mirian Rejowski, Luiz Trigo and Ricardo Uvinha.

Dianne would also like to thank the colleagues who inspire, motivate and challenge her: David Airey, Caryl Bosman, Bill Bramwell, Pierre Benckendorff, Alison Gill, Michael Gross, Tazim Jamal, John Jenkins, Bernard Lane, Gui Lohmann, Johanna Rosier, Pauline Sheldon, Michelle Whitford, Paul Whitelaw, Paul Williams and Peter Williams.

On a personal level, Gui is grateful to the 'crew' – Pissu, Petito, Pepolo and Petulo – for holding the ropes during the many times we have 'rounded Cape Horn', in the search for smooth waters either in the Atlantic or the Pacific. Dianne would like to thank 'hideous' and 'awesome'. They know who they are.

1 Introduction

Gui Lohmann and Dianne Dredge

Brazil: a land of contrasts

Since the beginning of the twenty-first century, there has been a spotlight shining on Brazil. Once the only Portuguese colony in South America (hence the only country in the South American subcontinent in which Spanish is not the official language), Brazil is one of the largest countries in the world, both in terms of land mass and population. It will host the FIFA World Cup in 2014 and the Summer Olympic Games in 2016. São Paulo and Rio de Janeiro are two of the world's largest megacities and the country has one of the largest gross domestic products (GDPs) in the world. Moreover, how the Brazilian government addresses environmental management, and manages the pressures on the Amazon rainforests in particular, are central issues in international climate-change debates.

Not only is it an emerging powerhouse, Brazil is also a land of stark contrasts. The extraordinary economic growth witnessed in recent decades has not been translated into the alleviaton of poverty and equality for its population. In the major metropolises, state-of-the-art hospitals that serve the country's elite are found adjacent to *favelas*, or slums in which houses are poorly constructed of bricks or wood and are characterized by inadequate levels of basic services, such as sewage, water, telephone and garbage collection. Brazil has a network of more than 60 public federal universities, some of which are equipped with cutting-edge, expensive laboratories but have bathrooms that lack bathroom tissue and having leaking roofs. One can stay at a five-star resort and, within metres, find garbage, prostitution, drug users and beggars. Essentially, one can experience elements of both Switzerland and Somalia within the same country.

Inequalities in Brazil can be identified at both the interpersonal and interregional levels (Bar-El 2008). For example, in 2008, six state capital cities accounted for a quarter of the country's GDP: São Paulo (11.8 per cent), Rio de Janeiro (5.1 per cent), Brasília (3.9 per cent), Belo Horizonte (1.4 per cent), Curitiba (1.4 per cent) and Manaus (1.3 per cent). The state of São Paulo alone represents a third of the country's GDP. On the interpersonal level, inequity is even greater. The Gini coefficient, which measures the degree of inequality in the distribution of family income in a country, was 56.7 for Brazil in 2005 (with a score of 100 indicating that no inequality exists). For this measure, Brazil had the tenth lowest score in the world, meaning that inequity is firmly entrenched.

This book explores tourism in Brazil. Although a vast number of books and academic publications about tourism in Brazil have been published in Portuguese, English-language literature that addresses tourism in Brazil remains scarce. Hence, this book aims to contribute to filling this gap by providing the international audience with an opportunity to become familiar with various trends and issues relating to tourism in Brazil, particularly since 2000. However, this book does not attempt to provide a comprehensive review of the variety of issues that are associated with the transformation of tourism in Brazil during this time frame. Rather, this book provides a snapshot of current research on tourism in Brazil produced by both Brazilian and international scholars.

This introductory chapter describes the Brazilian economy, society and geography and discusses some key issues and data pertaining to tourism in Brazil. The aim is to provide the international audience, who may not be familiar with Brazil, with the opportunity to develop a basic understanding of the country and its tourism context as background to the remaining chapters.

People

According to the 2010 census, Brazil is the fifth most populous country in the world, with a population that totals 190.7 million people, 84 per cent of whom live in cities (IBGE 2011). In comparison with the population reported in the 2000 census, the population in 2010 increased by nearly 21 million inhabitants. Despite this population growth, birth rates have decreased dramatically from 6.3 births per female in 1960 to 1.9 births per female in 2009, a rate that is similar to Australia, Sweden and the UK (Gorney 2011). Nevertheless, geographically, the southeast and northeast regions of Brazil (see Figure 1.1) remain the most populous regions, with 80.4 million (42.1 per cent of the total population) and 53.1 million (27.8 per cent of the total population) inhabitants, respectively, whereas the population of the central-west and north region of Brazil is 29.1 million (15.3 per cent of the total population). Among the 26 federal states, São Paulo is the most populous, with 41.3 million (21.7 per cent) inhabitants (IBGE 2011).

Brazil is characterized as a melting pot of ethnic groups with varied origins and backgrounds, and the indigenous population of Brazil accounts for a marginal 0.9 per cent of the total population. Although there are longstanding debates regarding ethnic and racial grouping, the 2008 National Survey of Sampling of Households (PNAD) identified the following ethnic groups in Brazil (Portal Brasil 2010a): First, the 'white' group, at 48.4 per cent of the population, represents the largest group, resulting from the colonial migrations from Portugal from the 1550s to the present. Based on these colonial migrations, Portuguese became Brazil's official language. Furthermore, during the nineteenth century and the first half of the twentieth century, European nationals from Italy,

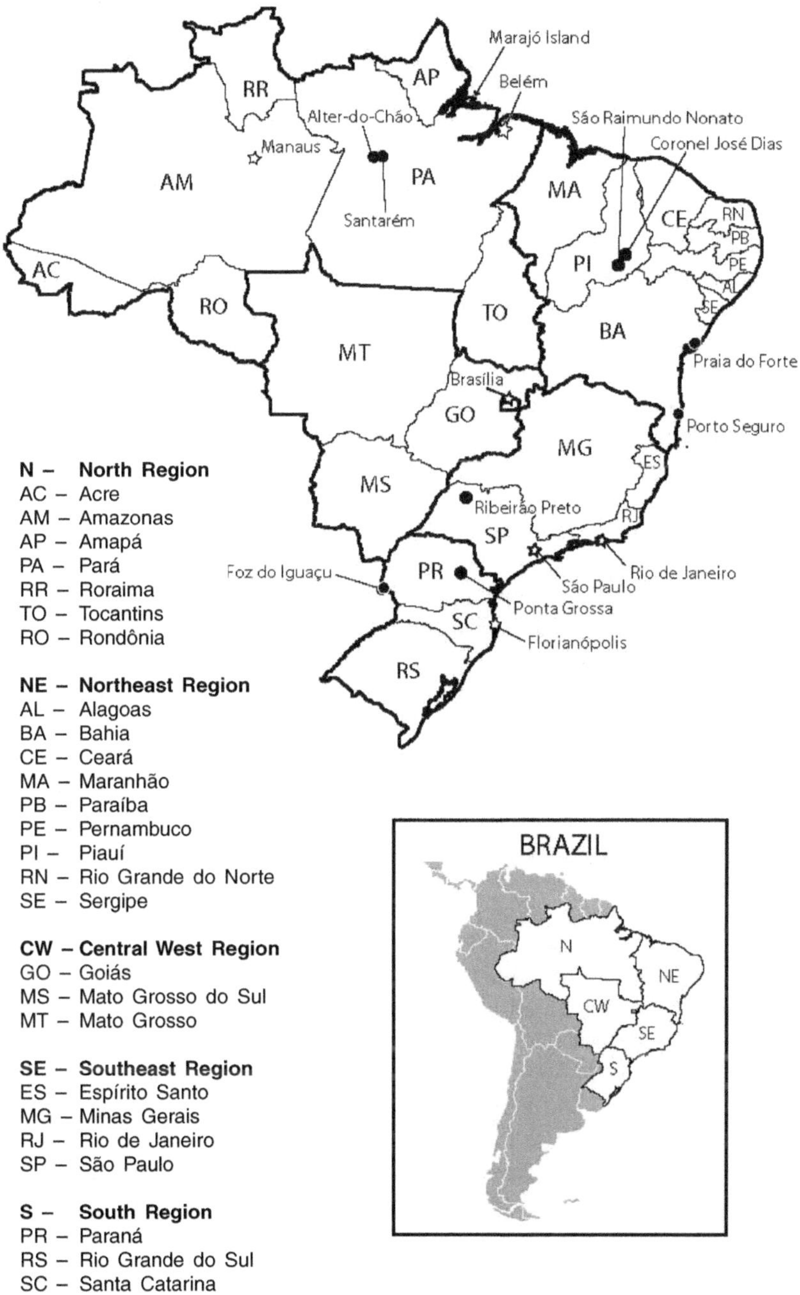

Figure 1.1 Location map of Brazil, its five macro-regions and 26 states

Germany and Spain migrated to Brazil, primarily because of political upheaval and wars in the 'Old World'. These immigrants tended to settle in the southern and southeast regions of the country, drawn by the climate, which is similar to that in Europe. Second, the 'coloured' group accounts for 43.8 per cent of the population and includes *mulattoes*, *caboclos* and *cafuzos*. The origins of these three groups can be traced to the early nineteenth century, when Brazil was primarily composed of people of three different backgrounds: indigenous, Portuguese and Africans. Since that time, three varying degrees of racial mixture have emerged, including the *mulatto* (mixed ancestry of black African and white European), *caboclo* (mixed ancestry of Amerindians and white European) and *cafuzos* (mixed ancestry of black African and native Brazilian). Third, the 'black' group represents 6.8 per cent of the population and originates from African migration movements that occurred in the early nineteenth century and the African slave trade from the 1550s to the nineteenth century. Fourth, native Brazilians account for 0.9 per cent of the population and are referred to as Indians. Indigenous, full-bloodied Indians primarily inhabit the northern and western border regions and the upper Amazon Basin. Their numbers are declining as a result of increasing commercial expansion and contact with the outside world. Finally, during the late 1920s and the early 1930s, there was a notable wave of migration from Japan, and these immigrants tended to settle in the states of São Paulo and Paraná. Although Japanese descendents account for only 0.7 per cent of the Brazilian population, Brazil hosts the largest Japanese community outside of Japan, and these immigrants and their descendants are well integrated into Brazilian society.

During Brazil's military dictatorship (1964–85), immigration generally decreased. However, there were some significant influxes of immigrants during this period, including Lebanese immigrants in the 1970s, immigrants from the former republics of Yugoslavia in the 1990s, and immigrants from Afghanistan and West Africa, particularly Angola. On a smaller scale, Latin Americans from Argentina and Bolivia migrated to Brazil in the 2000s (Durand and Massey 2010) as a result of economic crises and wars in those countries.

These immigration movements from starkly different countries have had many implications for Brazil. One of the key implications for tourism has been the contribution of these people to the easy-going, friendly and hospitable image of Brazilians. Despite the great power discrepancy that exists between the social, educational and financial 'elite' and the remainder of the population, levels of racism are low, and Brazilians interact without regard to ethnic differences. Another attraction of Brazil for tourists is the celebrative spirit of Brazilians, which is represented by festivals such as Carnivals, *Réveillon* parties and religious events. All these characteristics, in addition to the diversity and richness of ethno-cultures, enable Brazil to generate a particular appeal for tourists.

Culture

As a result of its multi-ethnic population from different parts of the globe, Brazil has developed a rich and distinctive culture. The primary components of Brazilian culture are derived from Portuguese culture: Portuguese is the spoken language, and three-quarters of all Brazilians belong (at least theoretically) to the Roman Catholic Church, a religion that was brought from Europe by the Portuguese colonizers. However, the Portuguese culture has been strongly influenced by the Native American, Amerindian and African cultures; the cultures of other European countries, such as Germany, Italy and Spain; and the Japanese and Lebanese cultures.

Brazil has a strong folklore tradition, which has been influenced by the cultures of Native Americans, Africans and Portuguese. This tradition includes stories, legends, dances, superstitions and religious rituals that are inspired by traditions from a variety of cultural backgrounds (Portal Brasil 2010a). These diverse backgrounds and a strong sense of rhythm and vocal styles have produced a distinctive culture of music and dance in Brazil. The most popular music and dance forms are the *bossa nova*, which originated from the styles of samba and jazz, and the various modifications of the famous samba (Neto 2001). With its Afro-Caribbean influence, axé music evolved as the multicultural music style of Brazil. The best known folklore event is the annual Carnival, which is held 64 days before Easter and staged in various ways throughout the regions of Brazil. As will be discussed later by Moital and Gândara (Chapter 10), *micaretas*, or off-season carnivals, are derived from this carnival. *Micaretas* provide a clear example of how festivity and music are combined by Brazilians to express their emotions.

Brazil's cuisine and gastronomy are further examples of the strong multicultural integration of the country's various ethnicities. Brazilian cuisine varies greatly from region to region. For example, the southern regions are known for their *churrascos*, which are simply barbecues that are specifically influenced by the *gaúcho* culture of the *pampas*, large treeless plains in South America. Food festivals, such as the *Oktoberfest* in Blumenau in the south of Brazil, are clear examples of the influence of German gastronomy, particularly its beer, and this festival attracts a surge in tourists to this part of the country during the month of October. Further north, São Paulo is famous for its international restaurants, including Italian, German, Japanese, Lebanese and Spanish establishments, which have emerged as a result of the city's multicultural population of 11 million people (Un-habitat 2010). The northeast region is predominantly characterized by African cuisine: for example, in Bahia, dishes such as *accarajé* and *vatapá* are common. *Acarajé*, which originated in Nigeria, is a deep-fried, ball-shaped dish made from peeled black-eyed peas. *Acarajé* is often served with *vatapá*, which is a type of a soup or creamy paste made from mashed bread, shrimp, coconut milk and palm oil. Although this topic is beyond the scope of this book, food plays a key role in attracting tourism to various regions of Brazil (Fajans 2006).

Although less well known, Brazilian art is highly regarded in certain sectors. Pre-Columbian art was overtaken in importance by the European Renascentist movement and later by the Modernist schools. The Baroque movement was thoroughly explored in Brazilian architecture due to the Catholic influence and the richness of the country in terms of gold and other natural resources; some magnificent architectural examples of Baroque churches can be found particularly in the states of Rio de Janeiro, Minas Gerais and Bahia. Modern Brazilian architects and urbanists, such as Oscar Niemeyer and Lúcio Costa, who in the 1950s designed Brasília, the nation's capital city, exemplify this urbanistic approach. Later in this book (Chapter 6) Jordão Fortes and Puppim de Oliveira present an example of how pre-Columbian arts are incorporated into contemporary tourism products and souvenirs to assist in developing protected areas in the Northeast region.

The Brazilian culture, including its music, sports (particularly football), the lifestyle associated with '*havaianas*' thongs or flip-flops, and the sensuality of the Brazilian women and their tradition of wearing bikinis, has been exported to many parts of the world. In many aspects, these features create and shape an image of the country that attracts leisure tourists to Brazil.

Social development

Inequalities in the social sphere are among the major issues that inhibit Brazil's development process. Strong economic growth in recent decades has generated extreme spatial and social inequalities, which are reflected in overall quality-of-life indicators for the population (Neto 2001). As a whole, Brazil presents social indicators that are similar to or below those of other developing countries, including those regarding life expectancy (average 72.3 years), infant mortality (average 16/1,000), education (87.2 per cent of children enrolled in schools) and literacy rates (90 per cent for those 15 years old and older) (IBGE 2010). The wealthier segments of society present significantly higher scores for these indicators. More than one-third of all children live in poverty, lack proper housing and health-care access and suffer from malnutrition. The social inequalities in health and the ways in which health-care services are organized favour high-income groups (de Souza Noronha and Andrade 2002). Disparities are particularly evident among the different regions of Brazil: the south and southeast regions show social indicators of well-being, social inclusion and education that are similar to those of developed countries, whereas these indicators in the north and northeast regions of Brazil resemble those of developing regions of the world (Azzoni 2001).

With a GDP that exceeded US$1.572 trillion in 2009, Brazil is among the world's largest economies, although the socioeconomic inequalities within the country are vast. According to Forbes (2011), Brazil ranks eighth in the world in the number of billionaires, which is significantly higher than for other Latin

American countries and is even higher than Japan (Forbes 2011). For example, although nine per cent of the population survived on less than one US dollar per day in 2000, 46.7 per cent of the national income was made by only 10 per cent of the population (Neto 2001). Nevertheless, the proportion of extremely poor people (with an average monthly wage of US$48) and poor people (US$94 per month) has consistently decreased since 2001. This result has been achieved through the introduction of numerous government initiatives designed to address regional and social inequalities, such as minimum wage and income programmes, rural pensions, scholarships for poor students and agrarian reform (Maluf and Burlandy 2007).

Another significant challenge for Brazil's social development lies in its education system (Gomes 2002). Brazilian education levels are lower than those of undeveloped countries. Consistent with the situation in other developed countries, Brazilian education lacks funding and development (World Bank 2011). In 2006, 4.3 per cent of GDP was invested in education; however, the federal government aims to increase this proportion to 7 per cent. In 2006, the average level of formal education was 7.2 years; the subgroup of 'white people' had completed 8.4 years of education, and 'black people' had completed 6.1 years of education. From a regional perspective, people from the northeast and south regions had completed an average of 5.1 years and 6.1 years of education respectively, whereas the southeast region was identified as the most educated, with an average of 7.2 years of schooling. The literacy rate of people aged 15 and older was 90.2 per cent in 2006 and increased to 92 per cent in 2008 (World Bank 2011). Although public primary and secondary education in Brazil is generally the responsibility of local councils and state governments, schools are generally underfunded. Higher education is increasingly composed of both public and private institutions, and public institutions are free and completely subsidized by the federal state governments. During the 1990s, efforts were undertaken to increase the participation of lower socioeconomic groups and this resulted in private providers establishing higher education degrees in predominantly teaching institutions with little or no research components. Tourism is one sector that has experienced an increase in the number of courses and degrees available (see Chapter 12).

Social inequities, unemployment and low rates of educational achievement contribute to high crime rates and violence in major developed cities, such as Rio de Janeiro and São Paulo, and in rural and isolated areas. The homicide rate per 100,000 inhabitants among young males between the ages of 15 and 24 years increased from 54.4 to 128 in São Paulo, and from 148.9 to 275.3 in Rio de Janeiro between 1981 and 1995, respectively (de Mendonca *et al.* 2003). Drug abuse and crimes committed by children and teenagers are the consequence of increasing desperation and inaccessibility of educational and social support (de Mendonca *et al.* 2003; Maluf and Burlandy 2007). International movies, such as *City of God* and *Elite Squad*, have exposed these realities and have impacted upon the image of Brazil as a tourism destination. Mortality rates are also high on Brazilian roads with such deaths accounting for 18.9 fatalities per

100,000 inhabitants in 2004. According to Modelli *et al.* (2008), reckless driving behaviour, causes 70 per cent of fatalities and is often associated with alcohol consumption.

Government and democracy

Brazil is a federal republic with a presidential system that consists of 26 states, one federal district and 5,565 self-governing municipalities. The federal level consists of the legislative, executive and judiciary branches. All states and municipalities have autonomous administrations. The most recent manifestation of Brazil's political organization is derived from the 1988 constitution developed following the country's return to democracy after more than 20 years under a military dictatorship (Burton and Steven 2011; Souza 2002). The new constitution included the following key objectives: to decentralize the balance of power within the federal system, to improve the role of local government, to allocate fiscal resources more efficiently, and to empower local communities (Souza 2002). As will be discussed in Chapter 2, this change had implications for tourism development at the local level, particularly during the 1990s. The challenges in implementing the new constitution and the ongoing process of decentralization effectively divided resources across an already uneven and diverse country. As demonstrated previously, Brazil suffers from marked regional and social inequalities, and these imbalances negatively affect the capacity of municipal governments to develop their regions in a federal system in which fiscal resources are transferred to local councils. Unfortunately, mechanisms that are designed to overcome these regional inequalities, such as fiscal transfers from economically stronger states and municipalities to poorer regions, have failed (Souza 2002).

In response to excessive public-sector spending and inflation, privatization reforms were introduced in state-owned sectors such as energy, telecommunications and transport during the mid-1990s. Social security and taxation reforms were also introduced to counter inflation and socioeconomic imbalances (Estache 2001; Power 1998). In the 2000s, the national political goals were to eradicate extreme poverty, foster economic growth, enhance the country's competitiveness and implement sustainable development initiatives (World Bank 2011).

Nature and natural resources

As the largest tropical country in the world, Brazil features a variety of landscapes, such as the *cerrado* (low brush lands), *caatinga* (vegetation adapted to dry lands), the Atlantic Forest and the Mato Grosso Pantanal (swamp) (Neto 2001). The distinctive climate and diversity of natural resources offer Brazil various economic opportunities, ranging from farming and agriculture in the central-west and southeast regions to mining and hydroelectric plants in the north and south regions. Consequently, the country has high biodiversity and hosts 25 per cent of the world's known plant species. The Amazon is home to more than 300,000 identified flora species, and an estimated 20,000 species remain undiscovered. In addition, Brazil offers a wide range of fauna that include iconic avifauna, such as macaws, toucans and parrots; various types of tropical snakes and crocodiles; and 57 endangered distinctive animals, such as the Brazilian tiger, the jaguar, the armadillo, the sloth and the tapir (Greenpeace 2011). Brazil's natural resources are a major advantage in attracting tourists, and the country was ranked first in the world in terms of its natural resource attractions in the 2011 Travel and Tourism Competitiveness Index (World Economic Forum 2011b).

As the Earth's main biodiversity reserve and largest tropical rainforest, the Amazon rainforest covers nearly half of Brazil's territory. The Amazon Basin is the largest freshwater reservoir in the world and approximately one-fifth of all the running water on the planet flows through the Amazon (Greenpeace 2011). Chapter 4 presents a case study that examines tourism transport issues in the Amazon. To protect this unique ecosystem, the government has prohibited deforestation, although it is difficult to enforce this regulation because of the lack of resources and the size of the Amazon region. With increasing global concern over climate change, Brazil's global reputation in the battle against deforestation and global warming is at risk. The Amazon has an international appeal to the overseas audience, but Brazil has been unable to exploit its full potential in terms of tourism development opportunities. As one possible response to this dilemma, Chapter 10 explores the potential for backpacker tourism in the Amazon, particularly in the gateway cities of Manaus and Belém.

Most of the northeast coastal area of Brazil is pristine, and the area is an increasingly popular tourist destination because of its untouched beaches and pleasant climate. The development of infrastructure and the increased operation of cruise ships in recent years improved the accessibility and attractiveness of this area for tourists (Neto 2001; Seatrade 2011). Accordingly, with its unique and mainly intact ecosystems, Brazil has enormous potential for tourism development in the future, particularly in terms of small-scale ecotourism programmes and sustainable tourism projects (Fennell 2008). Nevertheless, the lack of planning, infrastructure investment or sustainable practices poses risks for the development of the industry. This book presents two case studies that examine protected areas in the northeast of Brazil: Chapter 7 discusses a cluster of small and medium enterprises (SMEs) surrounding the Serra da Capivara National Park in southern Piauí, and Chapter 9 describes community environmental management initiatives at Praia do Forte, which is a seaside resort on the coast of Bahia.

Economic growth

Brazil is one of the world's fastest growing economies and was ranked the world's seventh largest economy in 2010 (World Bank 2011). During the global financial downturn, Brazil was among the last nations to fall into recession in 2008 and was among the first nations to resume growth in 2009, with an increase in the GDP of 7.5 per cent in 2010 (World Bank 2011). Furthermore, in 2007, Brazil launched a growth acceleration plan (Plano de Aceleração do Crescimento,

PAC) to increase investment in infrastructure and to provide tax incentives for rapid and robust economic growth. In 2010, this plan was followed by PAC-2, which was similar to the first phase of the programme and emphasized the following five objectives: urban infrastructure; safety and social inclusion; housing, sanitation and access to electricity; renewable energy, oil and gas; and investment in highways, railways and airports (Portal Brasil 2010b). These programmes were necessary for Brazil to confront the infrastructure challenges associated with its growing economy. Specifically, the transportation network remains deficient and costly (see Chapter 4). Brazil's infrastructure development generally slowed, particularly in the 1980s and the 1990s, as a result of ongoing but partly ineffective privatization programmes (Estache 2001). Road and rail networks lacked investment in upgrades and maintenance, which subsequently affected the reliability and cost of transportation. This is significant because 90 per cent of the country's goods are transported by road or railway (World Bank 2005).

Among the so-called BRIC economies (Brazil, Russia, India, China), Brazil overtook Russia for the first time and partially closed the gap with India and China in the global competitiveness index for 2010 (Schwab 2010). However, Brazil's overall competiveness remains mixed, consisting of both significant strengths (for example, the positive perception of its large market size, dynamic business sector, technological adoption and innovation) and significant weaknesses. Among its weaknesses are its low rates of saving, high interest rates (at 31.1 per cent in 2010, one of the highest rates in the world), high levels of public debt, and overall low quality of basic services provided by public institutions and education system (Schwab 2010). The Global Competitiveness Report 2011–2012, which was produced by the World Economic Forum (2011a), states that Brazil is characterized by low levels of competitiveness, including low participation in exports and imports in the GDP. Thus, the country remains largely closed to international trade and relies primarily on its internal markets. The report also documents a high level of wasteful government spending and burdensome government regulation, the long process required to start a business, including a high number of necessary procedures (15 in total), and high taxation (taxation in Brazil is considered to be the highest in the world, according to the WEF rank).

Brazil's strengths are in its technological adoption and innovation (ranked 44th and 42nd, respectively), reflecting the country's involvement in a number of projects, ranging from submarines to aircraft and even space research (Schwab 2010; US Department of State 2011). Some of Brazil's pioneering research projects include biotechnology development (Brazil is one of the largest soybean producers and exporters in the world), deep-water oil research (73 per cent of its reserves are extracted offshore), the aircraft manufacturer Embraer, and space research (including a satellite launching centre by the Aeronautic Technology Centre) (Cassiolato *et al.* 2003).

Regional development

In geopolitical and economic terms, Brazil is divided into five macro-regions: the north, consisting of seven states and seven million square kilometres of the Amazon rainforest; the northeast, which consists of nine states and is known as the poorest region; the central-west, which consists of three states and the capital, Brasília, and includes the country's last farming frontier; the southeast, which consists of four states and is the most developed and industrialized region; and the south, which consists of three states and has strong European influences (see Figure 1.1). Because of differences in their immigration and geographical characteristics, these regions contrast in terms of their cultural, economic and social development. In fact, the Brazilian Inter-Regional Economic Imbalance divided Brazil into two separate countries: 'Brazil One', which encompasses the south region, the southeast region and parts of the central-west region, contains 63 per cent of the Brazilian population and produces 76 per cent of the GDP; and 'Brazil Two', the poor and underdeveloped area that encompasses 74 per cent of the national territory and 37 per cent of the Brazilian population (Neto 2001).

Southeast region

Encompassing the states of Espírito Santo, Minas Gerais, São Paulo and Rio de Janeiro, the southeast region is the most populated and accounts for more than half of the national GDP (Azzoni 2001). In addition to the automotive industry, steel mills and oil refineries, agriculture also plays an important role in the economy in this region (e.g. coffee, sugar cane and citrus fruits). The southeast region contains 42.5 per cent of the Brazilian population and contributes 60 per cent of the national GDP (Neto 2001). However, high population densities, unemployment, social marginalization and poverty in this region contribute to increasing urban violence (de Mendonca *et al.* 2003).

South region

The south region includes the states of Paraná, Santa Catarina and Rio Grande do Sul. This region has one of the highest rates of participation in education and health care. As a result of its growing partnerships with neighbouring countries, such as Argentina, Paraguay and Uruguay, this region's economy has shown strong growth in the industrial sector (de Souza Noronha and Andrade 2002; Neto 2001). In addition to the contribution of its industry sector, the south region also contributes to Brazil's energy supply by having one of the world's largest hydroelectric plants, Itaipú Dam, which is located in the Paraná River (Neto 2001). Moreover, agriculture and farming play important roles in the regional economy, as this region is one of the main producers of soybeans, rice and apples. The economy of the south region represents approximately 20 per cent of the national GDP.

Central-west region

Formed by the states of Goiás, Mato Grosso, Mato Grosso do Sul and the Federal District, including the capital, Brasília, the central-west region is characterized by farming and agriculture (Neto 2001). In addition to the south region, the central-west region is a major producer of soybeans, rice, corn and cotton, as well as cattle. Subject to intense urbanization since the 1990s, the region's urban infrastructure and services are underdeveloped and struggle to serve the growing population. Consequently, the social and life quality indicators of the central-west region remain below the Brazilian average.

North region

Comprising the states of Acre, Amapá, Amazonas, Pará, Rondônia, Roraima and Tocantins, the north region represents more than 45 per cent of the Brazilian territory but only 7.3 per cent of the country's population. In addition to possessing natural resources, such as latex, açaí and wood, the north region is rich in minerals and contributes significantly to the country's mining industry. The energy supply from the north region plays an important role in the Brazilian economy because of the region's hydroelectric plants on the Tocantins and Solimões rivers. Because this region's economic activities are almost exclusively limited to extractive industries on native flora, its participation in Brazil's GDP is marginal, at approximately 2 per cent (Neto 2001).

Northeast region

Finally, the northeast region, which includes the nine states of Alagoas, Bahia, Ceará, Maranhão, Paraíba, Piauí, Pernambuco, Rio Grande do Norte and Sergipe, is the poorest region in the country (Azzoni 2001). More than half of the population in this area reported a monthly family income that is equal to half of the minimum wage, which was approximately US$325 in 2011. Because of the scarcity of natural resources (60 per cent of the northeast region is located in the semi-arid area of the country and is characterized by periodic droughts) and the large population (47 million people), this region has the highest rates of infant mortality and malnutrition and the lowest life expectancy rates (Neto 2001). In addition to the mining industry, agriculture and farming are important, although agricultural productivity suffers from extended drought periods. However, since the 1990s, with the beautiful beaches and sunny climate of the region's coastal areas, the construction of infrastructure and hotel complexes has helped to increase tourism's contribution to the regional economy (Fennell 2008).

Tourism demand

From the early 1970s to the present, international tourism in Brazil has undergone four main stages of development (see Figure 1.2). The 1970s represents the period during which visitor numbers increased from nearly a

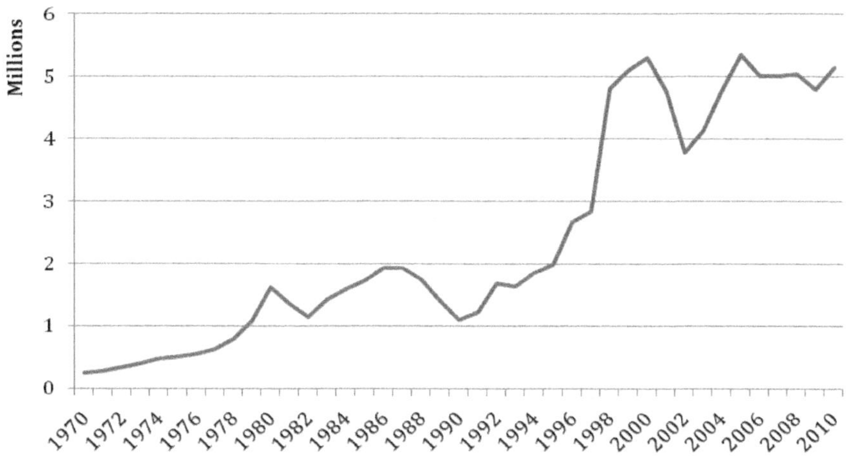

Figure 1.2 Arrivals of international tourists in Brazil, 1970–2010
Source: Ministério do Turismo 2011

quarter of a million in 1970 to slightly more than one million tourists in 1979. Despite the dictatorship that ruled the country, there was an effort to promote the country overseas, particularly through the campaigns initiated by Embratur (Brazilian Tourism Institute). The political and economic instability in the 1980s made it difficult to boost international tourism, and the decade concluded with international tourist numbers that were lower than those of 1980. Brazil attracted more than five million tourists in 1999, representing nearly a five-fold increase in international visitors over the decade. This growth can be attributed to the end of the dictatorial regime and efforts to open the country to international investors and trade through, for example, international hotel chains establishing in major cities and in tourist destinations. Despite the creation of the Ministry of Tourism, and the refocus of Embratur to market Brazil exclusively to overseas audiences, the country was unable to attract a significantly higher number of international tourists during the 2000s. This suggested that Brazil had reached its international demand peak at approximately five million tourists based on current attractions and marketing approaches and that new stimulus was needed. With the unique opportunity of hosting at least two large events in the next decade (the 2014 Soccer World Cup and the 2016 Summer Olympic Games), Brazil has a significant opportunity to develop its international tourism appeal and to eventually begin operating at a new level within the international tourism arena.

The major international tourist markets to Brazil are neighbouring South American countries, the USA and Europe. In 2010, the top ten markets to Brazil included (in order of importance) Argentina (27.1 per cent), the USA (12.4 per cent), Italy, Uruguay, Germany (4 to 5 per cent), Chile, France, Paraguay, Portugal and Spain (3 to 4 per cent), which totalled 71.8 per cent of international tourists. These countries were consistently among the top ten markets for tourism in Brazil during the period from 2006 to 2010, with only minor changes in the order of ranking throughout this period (Ministério do Turismo 2011).

In 2010, air transport accounted for 70 per cent of international arrivals in Brazil, and road transport represented 27.1 per cent of arrivals. An annual survey commissioned by the Brazilian Ministry of Tourism showed that in 2009 international demand in Brazil primarily consisted of leisure (45.5 per cent) and business, convention and event (22.9 per cent) tourists. The main reasons that leisure tourists cite for travelling to Brazil included its sunny weather and beaches (61.5 per cent); nature, ecotourism or adventure (23.3 per cent); and culture (9.7 per cent). International tourists spend an average of 17.5 days in Brazil, and two-thirds of tourists have visited Brazil previously. International tourists spend an average of US$58.19 per day, and business tourists spend almost twice this amount (US$106.14). The types of accommodation that travellers use include hotels or serviced apartments (51.6 per cent), homes of friends and relatives (28.2 per cent) and rented accommodations (9.2 per cent) (Ministério do Turismo 2011).

Domestic demand differs significantly from international tourism demand. Although there are no precise data regarding actual domestic tourism demand in Brazil, a survey commissioned by the Ministry of Tourism in 2006 provides some indication (FIPE 2007). First, domestic trips are made predominantly by road transport, with private cars (45.7 per cent), coaches (25.5 per cent) and charter coaches (7.9 per cent) accounting for eight of ten trips and air transport representing 12.1 per cent of domestic travel. Second, the main types of accommodation that domestic travellers use are the homes of friends and relatives (60.2 per cent), hotels or private accommodation providers (25.1 per cent) and rented accommodation (6.4 per cent). The average spending by domestic tourists is lower than that of international visitors. Interestingly, higher spending occurs in the north and central-west regions, which are the less developed regions of Brazil, as a consequence of the visits by tourists predominantly from the southeast and south of Brazil. Finally, the duration of stays by domestic tourists is shorter than that of international visitors, with domestic tourists spending an average of nine nights in 2005 (FIPE 2007). These domestic travel patterns are a result of the lower income of the average domestic traveller in comparison with the average international tourist.

In the chapters that follow, the geographical, social, cultural, environmental and economic characteristics of Brazil described above play out in different ways to influence tourism. What becomes clear is that not only are there enormous opportunities for developing tourism in Brazil, but there are also significant challenges that are not easily addressed simply by policy or by investment. In what follows, these opportunities and challenges are brought to light through cases and stories that convey the wicked problems and conundrums of tourism development in Brazil.

References

Azzoni, C. R. (2001) Economic growth and regional income inequality in Brazil. *The Annals of Regional Science*, 35, 133–52.
Bar-El, R. (2008) *Regional Development and Conflict Management: A Case for Brazil*, Bingley: Emerald Group Publishing.
Cassiolato, J. E., Lastres, H. M. and Maciel, M. L. (2003) *Systems of Innovation and Development: Evidence from Brazil*. Cheltenham: Edward Elgar Publishing.
de Mendonça, M. J., Loureiro, P. R. and Sachsida, A. (2003) *Criminality and Social Inequality in Brazil*. Brasília: Instituto de Pesquisa Econômica Aplicada.
de Souza Noronha, K. V. and Andrade, M. V. (2002) *Social Inequality in the Access to Healthcare Services in Brazil*. Belo Horizonte: UFMG/Cedeplar.
Durand, J. and Massey, D. S. (2010) New world orders: Continuities and changes in Latin American migration. *The Annals of the American Academy of Political and Social Science*, 630 (1), 20.
Estache, A. (2001) Privatization and regulation of transport infrastructure in the 1990s. *The World Bank Research Observer*, 16 (1), 85–107.
Fajans, J. (2006). Regional food and the tourist imagination in Brazil. *Appetite*, 47 (3), 389–98.
Fennell, D. A. (2008) *Ecotourism*, New York: Taylor and Francis.
FIPE (2007) *Caracterização e Dimensionamento do Turismo Doméstico no Brasil 2002 e 2006*. São Paulo: Fundação Instituto de Pesquisas Econômicas.
Forbes (2011) Behind Brazil's billionaire Available at: boom. Available at: www.forbes.com.
Gaffney, C. (2010) Mega-events and socio-spatial dynamics in Rio de Janeiro, 1919–2016. *Journal of Latin American Geography*, 9 (1), 1–29.
Gomes, G. M. (2002) *Regional Development Strategies in Brazil*. Fortaleza: OECD.
Gorney, C. (2011) Machisma. *National Geographic*. 220, 96–121. Washington, DC: National Geographic Society.
Greenpeace (2011) Life in the Amazon. www.greenpeace.org.
IBGE (2010) *Dados do Censo 2010 publicados no Diário Oficial da União do dia 04/11/2010*. Brasília: Instituto Brasileiro de Geografia e Estatística.
IBGE (2011) 2010 Census results.
Maluf, R. S. and Burlandy, L. (2007) *Poverty, Inequality and Social Policies in Brazil*. Rio de Janeiro: ActionAid International Middle Income Countries Initiative.
Ministério do Turismo (2011) *Anuário Estatístico de Turismo 2011*. Brasília: Ministério do Turismo.
Modelli, M. E. d. S., Pratesi, R. and Tauil, P. L. (2008) Alcoolemia em vítimas fatais de acidentes de trânsito no Distrito Federal, Brasil. *Revista de Saúde Pública*, 42 350–2.
Neto, A. L. (2001) *Lessons from Brazil's Regional Development Programs*. Xian: OECD.
Portal Brasil (2010a) Ethnic Groups. Available at: www.brasil.gov.br.
Portal Brasil (2010b) PAC2. Available at: www.brasil.gov.br.
Power, T. J. (1998) Brazilian politicians and neoliberalism: Mapping support for the Cardoso reforms, 1995–1997. *Journal of Interamerican Studies and World Affairs*, 40 (4), 51–72.
Schwab, K. (2010) *The Global Competitiveness Report 2010–2011*. Geneva: World Economic Forum.
Seatrade (2011) *The Importance of Cruising Comes Home to South America*. São Paulo: South America Cruise Convention.
Souza, C. (2002) *Brazil's System of Local Government, Local Finance and Intergovernmental Relations*. Birmingham: University of Birmingham.
Un-habitat (2010) *São Paulo: a tale of two cities*. São Paulo, Un-habitat.
US Department of State (2011) *Background Note*: Brazil.

Wagner, J. E. (1997) Estimating the economic impacts of tourism. *Annals of Tourism Research*, 24 (1), 78–89.
World Bank (2005) *Infrastructure in Latin America: Recent Evolution and Key Challenges*. Washington: World Bank.
World Bank (2011) *Brazil Country Brief*. New York: World Bank.
World Economic Forum (2011a) *The Global Competitiveness Report 2011–2012*. Geneva: World Economic Forum.
World Economic Forum (2011b) *The Travel and Tourism Competitiveness Report*. Geneva: World Economic Forum.

2 Tourism development, policy and planning in Brazil

Lindemberg Medeiros de Araujo and Dianne Dredge

Introduction

This chapter reviews the evolution of key tourism policies in Brazil commencing from the 1990s when Brazil began to engage more actively in tourism development, policy and planning, and links these developments to broad paradigm shifts occurring in the tourism development and planning literature. Until the late 1980s, most tourism development in Brazil took place in a fragmented way with little planning (Yázigi 1999). This situation hindered the exploitation of tourism's full potential as a social and economic development tool. At that time Brazil's basic infrastructure, including roads, airports and communication facilities, was also of a relatively poor standard, which created serious drawbacks in attempts to attract industry investment and promote visitation. By the 1990s this situation had begun to change and government started to target and implement tourism policies aimed at developing the tourism industry in Brazil.

The creation of the Brazilian Ministry of Tourism (MTur) in 2003 provided the first clear evidence that the federal government had identified tourism as a major development sector. This initiative of creating a specific ministry had also been adopted by a range of other developing countries in an effort to stimulate tourism and give it national profile (Tosun and Jenkins 1996; Lea 1988). The MTur's mission was to develop tourism as a sustainable economic activity, focused on job creation, the generation of foreign exchange earnings and the promotion of social inclusion. Brazil was also characterized by very uneven socioeconomic regional development (Lira 2005) so, from 2005 onwards, tourism was also used by the federal government as a regional economic development tool in an attempt to alleviate poverty in the most deprived regions of the country (Cruz 2006).

In discussing tourism development, policy and planning in Brazil, this chapter reviews the evolution of key tourism policies from the 1990s onwards and links these shifts to paradigmatic change discussed in the tourism literature. By way of a case study, this chapter discusses the northeast region, one of the least developed areas of the country, but which also has a number of potentially important natural tourism attractions. The development of these attractions and associated tourism potential was undertaken as part of the pioneering work of the Programme for Tourism Development (PRODETUR). This programme was later implemented in the remaining Brazilian macro regions. In terms of its theoretical foundations, this chapter draws upon a study by Beni (2006), the aim of which was to evaluate the performance of Brazil's tourism system. The chapter also draws from a study by Costa (2001) in which the author developed a comparative analysis between town and tourism planning and identified an 'emerging tourism planning paradigm'. Finally, the study also draws from a study by Cruz (2006) in which the author identifies paradigm shifts occurring in tourism public policies in Brazil. In this study Cruz identifies a number of changes taking place from the early 1990s onwards that have influenced tourism development, policy and planning.

Background

In a study undertaken in the late 1980s and published in 2006, Beni evaluated Brazil's tourism system in order to understand the reasons for the country's perceived poor performance in tourism. The study identified three main issues that affected performance:

1. The lack of a clearly articulated national tourism policy, a situation that did not allow clarity around institutional arrangements, roles and responsibilities to emerge, nor the establishment of management system to support tourism development.
2. The lack of skilled labour and the resultant negative impacts on service quality.
3. The lack of integration and co-ordination among official tourism organizations.

In a large developing country like Brazil, such structural and institutional deficiencies worked against the development of an efficient and competitive industry, with state governments and municipalities working independently and often competing against each other.

However, from the early 1990s onwards the federal government began to address these issues in an attempt to exploit tourism's full development potential. At an international level, there was growing awareness that developing tourism plant alone was insufficient in stimulating the industry; there was a need to better align tourism supply and demand and grow these in tandem. At the same time, markets were expanding and diversifying. Massive growth in ecotourism in the early 1990s is a case in point: traditional ideas about supply-led tourism planning (i.e. the 'build it and they will come' approach) gave way to an increased focus on nurturing tourism markets and increased alignment between tourism products and the needs and expectations of emerging market segments. Tourism planning as a public policy activity began to focus attention on other aspects of the tourism product that affected the tourist experience including environmental quality, capacity limits and conservation (Gunn 1994; Ritchie

2000). In Brazil this prompted the federal government to make provisions for the environmental management of tourism (Oliveira 2003). This shift in approach effectively brought tourism and environmental policy closer together, because until that point, the environment had been seen as a resource to be consumed in the development of tourism. The importance of managing environmental impacts in order to sustain tourism over the long term had not been explicitly acknowledged until this point (Costa 2001; Butler 2006).

At the time Brazil was also undergoing significant social, political and economic change. As discussed in Chapter 1, by the late 1980s Brazil was emerging from a long period of authoritarian rule; the country was undergoing process of re-democratization and at the same time was opening its doors to economic neoliberalization and globalization. These changes brought various challenges for Brazil's political leadership and the institutional structures and processes which needed to be repositioned in an effort to become more accessible and globally competitive. Under these conditions, and where tourism had been recognized as a tool for economic development, new tourism policies began to emerge at national, state and local levels. It was a time of rapid policy activity.

Shifting approaches to tourism planning and policy

At a global level, a number of paradigmatic shifts have been identified in the evolution of tourism planning and policy practice which reflect broader shifts occurring in the social sciences (e.g. see Costa 2001, Dredge and Jenkins 2007). These shifts in tourism policy formulation and tourism planning are also evident in Brazil. Drawing inspiration from the evolution of ideologies and practices in town planning, Costa (2001) argues that tourism planning has evolved through three main paradigm shifts, namely:

- a 'classical planning' phase driven by heavy-handed bureaucratic involvement, supply-led planning and 'blueprint' plans;
- a 'rational planning' phase characterized by the identification of issues, analysis, the development of alternative scenarios and the identification of an overarching tourism strategy to be implemented by government (this assumes government has full control and power to implement the initiatives within the plan);
- a 'post-1980s paradigm' characterized by processes of consultation and participatory plan making, an increased focus on sustainability and the facilitation of private sector investment and industry-led development (as opposed to government-led development).

These paradigmatic shifts go hand-in-hand with profound changes that characterize the rise of neoliberalism and globalization in the latter part of the twentieth century. Globalization, neoliberalism and new public management practices (i.e. an emphasis on cost efficiencies, outsourcing, adoption of market mechanisms to achieve policy goals, etc.) and processes of re-democratization and political modernization (e.g. increased public participation, social inclusion, public–private partnerships, etc.) brought much change in the way governments undertook their roles and responsibilities both in Brazil and across the world (e.g. see Araujo 2009; Beni 2006; Bramwell and Lane 2000; Dredge and Jenkins 2007).

Cruz (2006) captures the changes that took place in Brazil in Table 2.1. This table illustrates the major shifts taking place in approaches to infrastructure provision, economic development, destination management and approaches to markets, nature and space/territory. According to Cruz, the major changes in tourism policy formulation and implementation can be summarized as a shift away from central government control towards a focus on enabling infrastructure (e.g. airports) and initiatives to facilitate tourism investment and industry development.

The broader ideological shifts identified earlier by Costa (2001) are reinforced and given meaning in the shifts identified by Cruz (2006). On the one hand, Costa (2001) explains paradigmatic changes that took place at the global scale, while Cruz (2006) identifies what these shifts meant in the Brazilian context. In Brazil, the changes in government approaches had implications for tourism planning and policy-making practice at all levels. Governments were adopting more comprehensive and integrated planning approaches, evidenced by increased concern for the protection of the natural and cultural heritage of destinations, with the development of participatory planning approaches and partnerships

Table 2.1 Public policies of tourism in Brazil – old and new paradigms

Dominant paradigm	*Past – until the end of the 1980s*	*Present*
Infrastructure	Fostering the development of tourist infrastructure (e.g. road-building)	Creation/improvement of basic infrastructure and transportation facilities (emphasis on airports
Economic development	Creation of wealth (economic development at any cost)	Creation of jobs and income/focus on sustainable development
Destination management	Centralization	Decentralization/ participative management
Geographic scale	National ↔ regional	Regional ↔ local
Markets	State: regulator/intervener	Liberalization/lack of state regulation
Nature	Object of attraction	Object of attraction and protection
Space/territory	Stage for free action	Stage for planned action

Source: Adapted from Cruz (2006)

with community and increased concern for sustainability (Araujo and Bramwell 2002; Castro and Midlej 2011; Bramwell and Lane 2000; Oliveira 2003). Costa (2001) heralds the emergence of this as a 'new' direction in the field of tourism planning. More than a decade later, this shift is now established and is well discussed in the literature (e.g. Dredge and Jenkins 2007).

Federal tourism policies in Brazil

In the last two decades, significant federal government tourism policy development has taken place, leading to a new wave of innovative tourism planning and to significant growth in tourism plant (e.g. attractions, facilities and services), in the range of visitor experiences available and in market development. Table 2.2 identifies key policies that have had a significant impact on tourism development and planning in Brazil during this period (Beni 2006; Cruz 2006). One of the main impediments to tourism development in Brazil before the 1990s was poor infrastructure, a problem that, to some extent, still persists today. To address this issue, in 1992 the federal government created the Programme for Tourism Development of the Northeast (PRODETUR/NE). The PRODETUR/NE was aimed at strengthening tourism in the northeast politico-administrative region (see Chapter 1) through direct and indirect provision of basic infrastructure. This was achieved by stimulating private-sector investment and encouraging co-ordination among national, state, and municipal organizations (Araujo and Bramwell 2002), which were problems identified in the late 1980s as hindering tourism development (Beni 2006). The PRODETUR/NE also helped create very important institutional and organizational structures and processes that were leveraged to promote tourism development and planning in the region. Later, as a result of its success, the PRODETUR was extended to all other Brazilian politico-administrative regions: north, centre-west, southeast and south.

Table 2.2 Key federal public tourism policies in Brazil, 1990–2010

Time	*Policies*
1992	Creation of the PRODETUR/NE (Programme for Tourism Development of the Northeast Region)
1993	Implementation of the PRODETUR/NE
1994	Creation of the PNMT (National Programme for the Municipalization of Tourism)
1996	National Tourism Policy
2003	Launch of the National Tourism Plan (2003–2007)
2004	Creation and implementation of the National Program for the Regionalization of Tourism
2007	Creation of the National Tourism Plan (2007–2010)

Source: Adapted from Beni (2006) and Cruz (2006)

The PRODETUR/NE is a credit-granting scheme the main aim of which is to assist state and municipal governments to build basic tourism infrastructure as a means of attracting further private-sector investment in tourism plant, attractions, services and facilities (Cruz 2000). The programme is financed by the Inter American Development Bank (IDB) with resources being channelled to the states through the Banco do Nordeste (BN), a regional state development bank (Oliveira 2003). Evaluation of the performance of the first phase of the programme (PRODETUR I) identified that poor institutional arrangements for tourism, and related to this, the limited management capacities of tourism organizations, were barriers to achieving the programme's aims and objectives. As a result, in the second phase of the programme (PRODETUR II) provisions were made to strengthen such organizations in order for them to respond more effectively.

As part of the emerging tourism policies, in 1994 the federal government created Brazil's National Programme for the Municipalization of Tourism (PNMT – 1994-2001). That programme was one of the first attempts to decentralize tourism planning and to support state and local governments through the provision of consultants and other types of expert personnel. The idea underpinning this programme was that, with the support of federal tourism organizations, state and local governments would create a local tourism development agenda designed around a participatory planning process. The idea underpinning this approach was that it would help focus tourism planning on the interests and concerns of the local population, and as such, reflects the emerging tourism planning paradigm identified by Costa (2001) and discussed earlier.

In 1996 the federal government introduced the National Tourism Policy (PNT), to be implemented over the period 1996–99. Being the overarching national tourism policy framework, the PNT remained the main policy platform guiding the organization and development of tourism in Brazil until 2002 (Sancho and Irving 2010). The PNT brought about very important changes to how tourism was planned, including the introduction of decentralized destination planning and management, liberalization of the economy and a focus on regional and local development, with the state and municipal governments being responsible for most activities associated with tourism planning and management (Araujo 2000).

Another important tourism policy initiative regarding tourism development and planning in Brazil was the creation of the National Programme for the Regionalization of Tourism, which was launched in 2004. This development was a logical progression from previous policies and addressed the issue of the federal government being so distant from the state and local governments (Araujo 2000; Tosun and Jenkins 1996). The focus of this programme was on facilitating regional growth and was more conducive to exploring and developing tourism products and experiences associated with Brazil's diverse regional natural and cultural heritage.

In addition to these initiatives, the federal government also launched two important National Tourism Plans (PNTs) for the periods 2003–07 and

2007–10. In the 2003–07 plan, tourism acquired priority status because it was aligned with the country's macro-strategies for socioeconomic development and social inclusion (Sancho and Irving 2010). In the 2007–10 plan, the government aimed to increase domestic travel, expand job-creation opportunities, improve destination planning and development, and improve foreign exchange earnings. This plan also aimed at encouraging domestic travel and promoted investment in professional qualification frameworks to support product and service quality.

These initiatives were significant in the evolution of Brazilian tourism policy and planning. Together, these policies invigorated tourism investment and development and have enhanced and clarified institutional arrangements for tourism. Tourism has been established as an important policy sphere, and a federal institutional base has been established which has in turn strengthened the state and municipal involvement in the sector. Nevertheless, some problems remain, particularly regarding the institutional and organizational capacities of municipalities to be involved in tourism and to implement change.

Advances and drawbacks in tourism development and planning

Recent tourism development and planning initiatives in Brazil have benefitted enormously from the combination of the PRODETUR and the regionalization programmes. Due to the time that has elapsed, results are more noticeable with regard to the pioneering PRODETUR/NE created in 1992 in comparison with the more recent PRODETURs of other regions. As a consequence of that pioneering programme, the northeast region has been a focal point of large-scale infrastructure building, investment in tourism products and experience and in the development of tourism institutional structures and processes.

The approach underpinning the PRODETUR and the regionalization programme incorporates the concept of tourism development poles. This approach is based on the concept of the growth pole (originally introduced by François Perroux in 1949 but variously discussed and described since that time), and more recently theories of clusters (Porter 1998) and industrial districts (Novelli, Schmitz and Spencer 2006). Growth pole theory suggests that governments can promote economic growth by investing in and supporting the clustering of industries and that the agglomeration of similar industries will attract further free-market investment. In a similar vein, a cluster has been defined as a 'geographically bounded concentration of interdependent businesses with active channels for business transactions, dialogue, and communications, and that collectively shares common opportunities and threats' (Rosenfeld in Novelli, Schmitz and Spencer 2006: 1142). The initial focus of cluster theory was on the benefits obtained in primary and secondary industry sectors. However, Jackson and Murphy (2006:1019) point out that 'with the rise of the tertiary sector there has been growing interest in the potential of service industries, including information technology development, low cost call centers, retirement and tourism'. In the case of Brazil, the growth pole/cluster approach that has been adopted by the PRODETUR/regionalization programmes has focused on identifying agglomerations of destinations that can be planned together in order for them to take advantage of common resources, unique selling points and geographical assets.

In the remit of the regionalization programme and related tourism development poles, financial grants were only approved if the pole had a Sustainable and Integrated Tourism Development Plan (PDITS). Only if the council of each respective tourism pole approves the PDITS will it proceed to a higher level of business and investment attraction planning by the Bank of the Northeast (BN) and the Inter American Development Bank (IDB). This requirement has contributed to a more comprehensive and consultative tourism planning approach. Prior to the implementation of this programme, tourism development plans in Brazil were desktop exercises, prepared by consultants in a top-down manner, and with the states and municipalities having little participation in such processes. However, in addition to adopting consultative and participatory approaches to develop tourism plans, the councils associated with each tourism pole are comprised of government, business and civil society representatives, and this governance arrangement serves as a check against top-down authoritative implementation. Gaventa (2004) argues that because of the constitutional reforms, social movements and political innovations that have taken place in Brazil since 2000s, the country is one of the most important laboratories in the world to understand the meaning of democracy in the formulation, implementation and monitoring of public policies. Tourism policy developed within this socio-political milieu is therefore innovative not only in Brazil, but on a global scale.

Discussion

The developments and initiatives discussed in this chapter illustrate that Brazil has undergone considerable paradigmatic change in the way it has addressed tourism planning and public policy development since the 1990s. The shift can be characterized as having moved from a centralized national-level approach to a decentralized, participatory and regional/local approach. Over a decade ago, Costa (2001) identified an 'emerging tourism planning paradigm' which in addition to focusing on the technical and rational aspects of planning also paid attention to local-level interests, sustainability and participatory planning processes. It appears that this paradigm is now well established in Brazil.

Paradigmatic change generally occurs quite slowly. In Brazil, change started in the early 1990s but did not lead to immediate growth in either tourist numbers or product development. It took considerable time for results to emerge. The new rationale and focus underpinning tourism planning and policy sought to address three main criticisms of previous policy: the lack of a clearly articulated national tourism policy; the lack of skilled labour and the resultant negative impacts on service quality; and the lack of integration and co-ordination among official tourism organizations. The new approach, which sought to develop a more nuanced participatory and regional approach, was well articulated and embedded in written documents. However, it took time to establish the shift in organizational cultures and at different levels of government. New practices of communication, collaboration and co-operation also had to be learned. With the creation of the MTur and the adoption of the National Tourism Plan (2003–07), the federal government gave tourism full priority status as part of the country's economic development strategy (Sancho and Irving 2010). Within this context, the importance of the federal leadership should not be underestimated.

As the implementation of the new policy paradigm progressed, different types of partnerships were created involving representatives of the MTur, state and municipal tourism secretaries, state planning secretaries and the Brazilian Service for the Support of Small Businesses (SEBRAE), among others. In fact, the federal government encouraged stakeholder participation and partnership development in the implementation of all plans and policy development (Araujo 2000). That approach created innovative development plans (PDITS) whose design was the result of participative, consensus-building planning approaches. Innovation in this case has to do mainly with moving from technical and rational tourism planning approaches prepared by consultants to participative approaches including a broad array of regional and local level stakeholders.

An interesting example of the partnerships that were created include the Local Productive Arrangements (APLs). The APLs are a type of tourism planning and development cluster that is chaired by a partnership between SEBRAE and the states' planning secretaries. The APLs bring together government, business and civil society stakeholders to develop and implement tourism development agendas in collaboration with the regional planning process. For example, the northeast region alone currently has 14 tourism development poles involving 207 municipalities. In addition to developing their respective PDITS, in the remit of these poles there are numerous tourism APLs that have already been implemented and others that are being formed.

Certainly, such large-scale tourism development has only been possible because of the change in the way the federal government dealt with tourism from the late 1980s and early 1990s (Cruz 2006). The development and implementation of the tourism policies that were identified in this chapter have led to the development of new institutional, strategic and operational frameworks for the planning, management and development of tourism in Brazil. The significant tourism development and growth in international and domestic tourism demand described in Chapter 1 should be understood within this context of change and particularly the removal of institutional impediments and investment barriers. For example, with considerable infrastructure investment on the ground (e.g. airports, roads, and to a lesser extent, sewerage and water supply networks), and with the institutional base for tourism planning and management established, the coastal zone of the northeast region has attracted extensive investment in tourism products and services. For example, with 11 of the 14 above-mentioned tourism poles located in the coastal zone, and with the building and/or expansion of resorts underway, the region now plays an important role in the country's tourism activity. Resort development in the northeast region is located mainly in five states: Bahia, Alagoas, Pernambuco, Rio Grande do Norte and Ceará. An interesting point is that the northeast region of Brazil is strategically closer to international tourist markets in Europe and North America when compared with the country's more developed southeast and southern states. These strategic and locational advantages, together with its natural beauty and favourable climate, have led Brazil's northeast region to become a very competitive destination region.

In addition to the tourism supply along the coastal zone of the northeast region, there has also been rapid growth in demand for tourism in rural areas, mainly ecotourism, adventure tourism and rural tourism, in the Amazonian and centre-west regions, as well as in the nine states of the southeast and southern regions. In the Amazon and the Pantanal areas, ecotourism has become an important tool for economic development, generating jobs in local communities (Wallace and Pierce 1996). In the southeast and southern regions, rural tourism, ecotourism and other types of nature-based tourism have contributed to the economic diversification of farms, bringing positive benefits for the sustainability of many small businesses.

However, despite the benefits of the PRODETUR/NE for the participating states and municipalities, that programme did not achieve all of its objectives. In particular, local governments still lack the required institutional apparatus and expertise to join the programme as a major actor, and many were not interested in establishing local tourism organizations. This problem still continues in the majority of municipalities despite the efforts of the federal government. Another problem is that politically less powerful municipalities have not been able to fully exploit the benefits of tourism nor have they benefited fully from the infrastructure that was built by their respective state governments. This is because many municipalities neither have an integrated tourism policy nor do they have the capacity or interest in encouraging participatory tourism planning (Silva and Andrade 2008). The difficulty of some municipalities to respond to federal-level policies has worked as a barrier in achieving the social inclusion and sustainable development objectives that are embedded in Brazil's tourism policies (Sancho and Irving 2010; Cruz 2006). For example, in addition to the above-mentioned problems, lack of tourism planning expertise was also a key problem facing the municipalization programme (PNMT). While some municipalities were capable of taking advantage of the PNMT, the vast majority were not. As a result, the federal government has incorporated the objectives of the PNMT into the regionalization programme in an attempt to overcome such problems.

Further, the significant growth in tourism development, investment and institutional support in Brazil in recent years has been underpinned by very important progress in tourism planning and policy formulation. However, there has not been a parallel emphasis on policy implementation. For example, a study that was conducted by Costa, Sawyer and Nascimento (2009) analysed ten tourism APLs, involving the states of Mato Grosso do Sul (central-west region), Rio Grande do Sul and Santa Catarina (south region), and Alagoas (northeast region) comprising 99 municipalities. The objective of the study was to evaluate the extent to which these APLs were capable of achieving the objectives of sustainable development (economic, social and environmental) that are identified in all federal tourism policies. The study concluded that the projects were insufficient in the way they responded to sustainability, with the focus of most projects on economic aspects of development. That is, there was the prevalence of short-term economic gain to the detriment of medium and long-term benefits of sustainable development.

Conclusions

This chapter reviewed the evolution of key tourism policies in Brazil from the 1990s, when Brazil began to engage more actively in tourism development, policy and planning, and it linked these developments with broad paradigms shifts occurring in the tourism planning and policy literature. A discussion of the way that tourism has developed in the northeast region illustrated the implications of these paradigmatic shifts and policy changes. These policies represent important ideological changes in the way that the country has dealt with tourism. Traditionally, tourism was dealt with in an *ad hoc* top-down manner but, as this chapter demonstrates, there has been a substantial shift towards a 'bottom-up' regional/local focus in which participation and sustainability have become key concerns. Moreover, these changes are similar to international experiences and reflect changes occurring elsewhere (Costa 2001).

In conclusion, Brazil has made significant progress in tourism policy formulation and planning since the 1990s, particularly in relation to the development of federal, state and municipal institutional structures and processes. A major factor in achievements to date is the creation of a federal Ministry of Tourism and the leadership, profile, focus and resourcing that goes along with this. This development signalled tourism as a priority policy sector, and has delivered large-scale infrastructure investment, fostered institutional and organizational development at the federal, state and municipal levels, and addressed drawbacks such as lack of a clear national tourism policy, lack of integration and co-ordination among official tourism organizations, and lack of an inter-sectoral policy for tourism development. However, despite this progress, Brazil still faces regional and local challenges.

Considerable challenges regarding the implementation of tourism plans and projects, and in achieving the development objectives established by the federal government. A key problem is that despite all the efforts of the federal government to strengthen municipal institutions and to establish tourism organizations, these efforts have not strengthened the capacity of many municipalities to facilitate and encourage tourism development. For significant progress to be made into the future, municipal governments need to be made effective partners contributing to social, economic and environmental development.

Finally, the formulation of the tourism policies discussed in this chapter and the exploration of their impact on tourism planning and development in Brazil highlight the opportunities and constraints associated with using tourism as a development tool in large-scale developing countries like Brazil. For example, it has become clear that investing in basic infrastructure has led to a significant expansion of the tourism industry, with the 14 tourism development poles in the northeast region being the most visible outcome of such expansion. Recognition that tourism can destroy the natural assets on which tourism is based has also opened up opportunities for incorporating sustainable development into tourism policies and development plans such as the PDITS. The creation of tourism organizations at federal, state and municipal levels, a trend in Brazil's recent history, may be paving the way for improvements in regional and local control over how tourism is planned and implemented. This development may well represent a positive change towards a more democratic tourism planning and management approach in Brazil. However, further research is needed to assess the positive and negative effects of these changes over the long term.

References

Araujo, L. M. (2000) Stakeholder participation in regional tourism planning: Brazil's Costa Dourada project. PhD thesis, Sheffield Hallam University.

Araujo, L. M. (2009) *Planejamento Turístico Regional: Participação, Parcerias e Sustentabilidade*. Maceió: Edufal.

Araujo, L. M. and Bramwell, B. (2002) Partnership and regional development in Brazil. *Annals of Tourism Research*, 29: 1138–64.

Beni, M. C. (2006) *Política e Planejamento de Turismo no Brasil*. São Paulo: Aleph.

Bramwell, B. and Lane, B. (eds) (2000) *Tourism Collaboration and Partnerships. Politics, Practice and Sustainability*. Clevedon: Channel View.

Butler, R. W. (2006) The concept of a tourist area cycle of evolution: implications for management of resources, in R. W. Butler (ed.) *The Tourism Area Life Cycle vol. 1: Applications and Modifications*. Clevedon: Channel View, pp. 3–12.

Castro, F. M. M. and Midlej, M. M. C. (2011) Planejamento turístico: análise da proposta no município de Valença (BA) no âmbito das recomendações das políticas públicas do turismo no país. *Caderno Virtual de Turismo*, 11(1): 18–35.

Costa H. A., Sawyer, D. R. and Nascimento, E. P. (2009) Monitoramento de APL de turismo no Brasil: o (não) lugar das dimensões da sustentabilidade. *Revista Brasileira de Pesquisa em Turismo*, 3: 57–79.

Costa, C. (2001) An emerging tourism planning paradigm? A comparative analysis between town and tourism planning. *International Journal of Tourism Research*, 3(6): 425–41.

Cruz, R. C. A. (2000) *Política de Turismo e Território*. São Paulo: Contexto.

Cruz, R. C. A. (2006) Planejamento governamental do turismo: convergências e contradições na produção do espaço, in A. I. G. Lemos, M. Arroyo and M. L. Silveira (eds) *América Latina: cidade, campo e turismo*. São Paulo: Clacso/Departamento de Geografia da Universidade de São Paulo, pp. 337–50.

Dredge, D. and Jenkins, J. (2007) *Tourism Policy and Planning*. Milton Keynes: Wiley & Sons.

Embratur/Ministério do Turismo (2005) *Anuário Estatístico Embratur*, Brasília; www.dadosefatos.turismo.gov.br (accessed 9 April 2001).

Jackson, J. and Murphy, P. (2006) Clusters in regional tourism: an Australian case. *Annals of Tourism Research*, 33 (4): 1018–35.

Gaventa, J. (2004) Prefácio, in V. S. P. Coelho and M. Nobre (eds) *Participação e Democracia: Teoria Democrática e Experiências Institucionais no Brasil Contemporâneo*. São Paulo: Editora 34, pp. 7–9.

Gunn, C. A. (1994) *Tourism Planning. Basics, Concepts, Cases*, 3rd edn. Washington DC: Taylor and Francis.

Lea, J. (1988) *Tourism and Development in the Third World*, London and New York: Routledge.

Lira, F. J. (2005) *Corrupção e Pobreza no Brazil*, Maceió: Edufal.

Novelli, M., Schmitz, B. and Spencer, T. (2006) Networks, clusters and innovation in tourism: a UK experience. *Tourism Management*, 27: 1141–52.

Oliveira, J. A. P. (2003) Governmental responses to tourism development: three Brazilian case studies. *Tourism Management*, 24: 97–110.

Porter, M. E. (1998) Clusters and the new economics of competition. *Harvard Business Review*, 76: 77–90.

Ritchie, J. R. B. (2000) Interested based formulation of tourism policy for environmentally sensitive destinations, in B. Bramwell and B. Lane (eds) *Tourism Collaboration and Partnerships. Politics, Practice and Sustainability*. Clevedon: Channel View, pp. 44–77.

Sancho, A. and Irving, M. A. (2010) Interpretanto o Plano Nacional de Turismo sob a ótica da inclusão social. *Caderno Virtual de Turismo*, 10 (3): 103–20.

Silva, L. R. M. and Andrade, J. R. L. (2008) Programa de Regionalização do Turismo e sua aplicação em comunidades autóctones: o caso de Poço Redondo e Canindé do São Francisco. *Caderno Virtual de Turismo*, 8 (2): 15–22.

Tosun, C. and Jenkins, C. L. (1996) Regional planning approaches to tourism development. *Tourism Management*, 17: 519–31.

Yázigi, E. (1999) *Turismo: Uma Esperança Condicional*, São Paulo: Global.

Wallace, G. N. and Pierce, S. M. (1996) An evaluation of ecotourism in Amazonas, Brazil. *Annals of Tourism Research*, 23 (4): 843–73.

3 Community-based tourism

Sustainability as a matter of results management

Eduardo Jorge Costa Mielke

Introduction

Interest in tourism as a tool for sustainability and poverty reduction grew significantly in the 1980s. Two movements were launched almost simultaneously: ecotourism and community-based tourism (CBT) (SNV and UH-University of Hawaii 2007; UNWTO 2004, 2006. The ideas associated with both ecotourism and CBT have often been associated with the promotion of tourism to benefit the communities that reside in or near conservation areas. In Brazil, many organizations, such as the WWF, SOS Mata Atlântica and the Sociedade de Pesquisa em Vida Silvestre e Educação Ambiental (SPVS), have consistently promoted the sustainable development of community-based tourism. In the 1990s and 2000s, several projects were undertaken in Latin America, many of which were established in biomes across Brazil.

In Brazil and across South America, most CBT projects face similar challenges. Researchers have divided these challenges into three groups to describe the processes that can cause a CBT project to fail: market access (Mitchell and Muckosy 2008); internal governance (Goodwin and Santinni 2009); and the management of strategic partnerships (Mielke 2010). The ineffective management of one or more of these processes causes most CBT projects to lose long-term viability. Most CBT projects also require constant external assistance from non-governmental organizations (NGOs) and/or local governments. In addition there is a general lack of co-operation and dialogue among the elements of the local tourism chain. Successful outcomes, however, rely on the development of positive relationships between the key stakeholders (donors and funders, funding agencies, the public sector, NGOs, consultants, local tourism companies and tour agents) and the community (Mielke 2010).

Fortunately, there are also excellent examples in Brazil such as the tourism co-operative and association model described later in this chapter. As a large and diverse country, the major challenge for Brazil is to create local tourism development programmes that address local challenges and not just national objectives. Such an approach makes it easier to encourage communities and agents to develop sustainable and equitable projects.

The aim of this chapter is to discuss CBT in Brazil and to identify the primary reasons for the success or failure of these projects. The chapter also presents four successful CBT projects launched since 2004, each demonstrating that it is possible to overcome the challenges arising from co-operation, management and strategic partnerships between communities and stakeholders. The chapter is divided into four sections. First, we discuss the influences upon CBT projects, relating these influences to the tourism supply chain. Second, the research approach and methods used in the analysis of CBT projects is presented. This includes an analysis of 36 CBT projects out of the 50 projects funded by the Brazilian Ministry of Tourism. Three criteria were used to analyse these projects: management characteristics; processes of co-operation; and the partnerships made with important stakeholders such as tourism intermediaries and local governments. Third, issues such as market access, internal governance arrangements and the management of strategic partnerships are discussed. The chapter describes how these matters were addressed in four successful CBT projects, two involving tourism associations and two involving co-operatives. Fourth, issues around the monitoring and assessment of CBT projects are identified and discussed. Monitoring and assessment are potentially useful stages in a total planning cycle, and can improve understandings about the projects and how communities, NGOs and donors or funders can operate more effectively. However, monitoring and assessment have not been effectively used. Typically, community leaders do not clearly understand how tourism will help their people and what is required to implement a successful project. Finally, the conclusion summarizes the findings, presenting several suggested improvements to help evaluate and monitor CBT initiatives. These approaches are based on case study examples in which co-operation, community autonomy and leadership legitimacy produced results.

The unsustainability of CBT projects

Several authors have reported on the failure of CBT projects around the globe (Spenceley 2008; Dixey 2008). Mitchell and Muckosy (2008: 2) 'reported research by the Rainforest Alliance and Conservation International which reviewed 200 CBT projects across the Americas and which showed that many accommodation providers had only five per cent occupancy'. Goodwin and Santilli (2009:6) state that 'the most likely outcome for an initiative in CBT is the project to be unsustainable after the funding period.' An unsustainable project can cause financial problems that can have flow-on effects for the economic health of small local tourism businesses. Interestingly, the results of these studies have been used as key arguments for generating support and attracting more government funding. However, it remains unclear why most projects fail after producing few tangible results and, most importantly, why success is still rare.

A CBT initiative should be treated like any other business. It is therefore essential to emphasize that tourism projects involving the local community should focus on the fundamental principle of improving local living conditions of residents, especially those who live in regions where they are typically excluded from the formal economy. In these regions, local governments offer little assistance and the only way to increase incomes and generate employment is through tourism-related initiatives. This is probably why such projects begin with high expectations of success.

It is imperative that CBT projects be undertaken with an understanding of the principles of economic development. From a theoretical point of view, this involves a deep understanding of bottom-up development (endogenous development) and a familiarity with agglomeration processes, such as clusters, local networks, production systems and supply chains. In addition to this knowledge, the success of every CBT initiative depends on building and facilitating human relationships. The tourism industry includes different types of companies with different interests and cost structures, and these issues need to be carefully discussed and mutual benefits identified before improved tourism flows and expenditures can be achieved. In other words, where mutual goals and advantages can be identified, the CBT project should aim to facilitate co-operation. This is a learning process through which stakeholders come to understand how to work together and achieve results.

The CBT sector is complex and dynamic. It involves a series of local actors (e.g. communities, tourism and non-tourism businesses, governmental organizations and NGOs) and non-local actors such as tourist intermediaries (Mielke and Pereira 2006). CBT is characterized by a supply chain that requires a high degree of co-operation to achieve common goals. From a business perspective, CBT does not differ markedly from any other commercial relationship: there are buyers and sellers. The exchanges that take place should be made responsibly, they must generate profits for individual businesses and offer balanced growth for all actors directly involved. Further, the benefits of CBT projects also need to be recognized by community members who are indirectly participating in their development.

Because CBT necessitates working with a group of stakeholders, it is important that CBT initiatives be planned far in advance. It is impossible to co-ordinate one or more communities and help them adapt to a new situation in less than 18–24 months. Co-operation requires that the individuals involved be able to trust, communicate and rely on one another. That said, there are factors that affect the capacity to co-operate. For example, access to markets can become a problem when relationships are poorly established and blockages occur within distribution channels. Typically, negotiations between suppliers and one or more tourism operators require a lengthy process of communication and negotiation before a collective agreement can be reached. This is usually because inexperienced communities are not properly prepared for negotiations that require specific skills and an understanding of the tourism industry as a whole. This is especially the case when the negotiations involve tour operators or travel agencies, the interests of which can be quite different to that of local communities. Therefore, the skills necessary to develop and maintain such relationships must be taught to community members. Lack of leadership in this area is a common problem. Unconsolidated leadership usually stems from poor internal governance wherein the democratic flow of information and dialogue is not well developed, which can, in turn, compromise the effectiveness and timeliness of decision-making processes. The most important task then is to identify and address these issues strategically (Mielke 2010).

Although successful CBT initiatives require a long period of investment and training, community members often require and expect short-term results. Therefore, CBT projects must be designed and implemented to include those directly involved with a project and to determine the benefits that will accrue to these groups over both short and long terms. For instance, the collective purchase of common supply items and trade products, such as handcrafts, can bring cost benefits, economies of scale and other efficiencies and can bring increased sales if well managed. Whether these are short-term or long-term benefits needs to be clarified. The business and social management of such actions is crucial. Without good management communities can lose trust in the process, which in turn can compromise the political and economic sustainability of the CBT project.

Furthermore, the lack of clear processes and policies can have a negative effect on the development of CBT. CBT works best in an environment that promotes co-operation, collaboration and constructive relationships between the community, tourism providers, intermediaries, government and the broader public interest. In a competitive market in which the number and diversity of destinations grows every day, it is crucial to make sure that customers are satisfied. For CBT project managers, it is difficult, especially in the early stages of a project, to know how to locate companies (such as tour operators, service providers and intermediaries) that can assist in attracting tourists and growing tourism markets that correspond with the interests of the community. This is an important step in a responsible development process that seeks to minimize the negative impacts of tourism.

Research approach and methods

Between 2008 and 2011, the Brazilian Ministry of Tourism (MTur) invested US$4 million in the development of 50 CBT projects. Priority was given to initiatives for which action had already been taken or those projects that had already begun or were in progress. However, MTur did not specify the level of management or the degree of development these projects should have. The funding of all of these CBT initiatives by the same sponsor, and where each was subject to the same macroeconomic context, presented an ideal setting for this research. Of these projects, 26 participated in this research, with four of them later selected for in-depth case study research. Table 3.1 lists the main tourist activities for each of these 26 projects and their regional location. Some communities did not give permission for their projects to be identified so all projects were allocated a project code to avoid possible identification.

The research reported in this chapter focuses on four key issues: the circumstances of a CBT project before and after the funds were disbursed; the management of the project itself; co-operation and decision-making processes;

Table 3.1 Main tourist activities and macro regions of the CBT projects

Region	*Project number*	*Main tourist activities*
North	Project 1	accommodation and handcraft production
	Project 2	handcraft production and gastronomy
	Project 3	training of local guides
	Project 4	training of local guides
	Project 5	handcraft production
	Project 6	accommodation, handcraft production and gastronomy
Northeast	Project 7	handcraft production
	Project 8	gastronomy
	Project 9	training of local guides
	Project 10	handcraft production
	Project 11	training of local guides and gastronomy
Central West	Project 12	training of local guides
	Project 13	training of local guides and handcraft production
	Project 14	accommodation and handcraft production
	Project 15	handcraft production
	Project 16	training of local guides, gastronomy
	Project 17	gastronomy
Southeast	Project 18	accommodation and handcraft production
	Project 19	training of local guides
	Project 20	handcraft production and gastronomy
	Project 21	handcraft production
	Project 22	handcraft production
	Project 23	training of local guides and gastronomy
South	Project 24	accommodation, handcraft production
	Project 25	training of local guides and handcraft production
	Project 26	handcraft production, training of local guides and gastronomy

and the community's relationship with key stakeholders. To address these issues, a review of the existing academic literature and empirical observations with respect to the preparations for and management of CBT projects in Brazil were undertaken. It is also worth noting that the literature on Brazilian tourism is extremely limited, resulting in a research approach which is exploratory in nature. Of particular importance, the research sought to better understand processes of planning, management and investment in CBT projects.

A three-stage research process took place between July and November 2010. In the first stage, information was gathered on each of the 50 CBT projects via a desktop research process. Most of the information was obtained from original proposals submitted to MTur and was available through the National Bureau for Tourism Development Programmes. In the second stage, previous studies assessing the monitoring and implementation of regional economic development projects were analysed and the results of different projects were compared and contrasted. This assessment revealed that, based on their practical experience with implementing CBT projects, stakeholders highlighted two key issues in the failure of CBT initiatives: project governance and access to markets. Survey participants were encouraged to reflect on these two issues in the following stage of the research process.

In the third stage of the research process, from the 50 projects originally supported by MTur, only 42 received funding. Out of this group, 36 were invited to participate in this research and 26 responded to the questionnaire. This process helped to build an overall understanding from which four case studies were chosen to explore particular issues. The key elements or attributes of the four successful projects (e.g., Cooptur – Cooperativa Paranaense de Turismo; Coopererguaraá-Ecotur – Cooperativa de Ecoturismo de Guaraqueçaba; Associação Acolhida da Colônia and Rede TUCUM) were explored in further detail. An important characteristic of these projects is the way in which co-operation influenced the quality of management, commitment to the project and business planning.

Key sustainability issues

Access to markets

Limited access to markets is one of the central reasons why most CBT initiatives are not successful or sustainable over the long term. This is either because the communities offer low-quality products or because they do not establish trade relationships with intermediaries quickly enough. In many cases, communities feel a certain aversion to working with intermediaries and generally perceive the act of negotiating with agencies and tour operators negatively. Until they understand the importance of working with these intermediaries, communities regularly feel uncomfortable and exploited by them. These feelings and perceptions are often the key challenge in establishing the required access to markets in a project's development (Mielke 2010).

The role that these intermediaries play in CBT development is crucial and must be established when CBT initiatives are initially designed. Representatives from intermediaries are knowledgeable, are able to assist in the effective promotion of tourism products within the community, and can have these products made to high-quality standards. These intermediaries adopt wide-ranging practices; some follow socio-environmentally responsible policies and practices when they bring tourists into communities, and others are not even aware of such issues. In the development of CBT projects, the values and practices of the intermediaries need to be fully considered and aligned with the needs and expectations of the community. Attempting to define these practices at the end of a project is futile and presents a lost opportunity for improving CBT project design.

In terms of establishing some sort of agreement with tourism intermediaries, only one of the 26 CBT projects analysed in this research had a formal agreement (i.e. a juridical contract signed between the CBT entity and tourism organizations). However, many had informal relationships where no formal agreement was established under a contract. Nineteen projects used local community members to promote the community's tourism products and services externally. Ten projects used websites to promote their products, but none of these web pages allowed customers to purchase products online.

When asked about the contributions that these agents make to the CBT projects, 20 communities responded that they perceived their relationships had an imbalance in power relations. The communities believed that this was because the type of product or service they offered would not fit the profiles suggested by tour agencies and operators or that their products did not meet quality standards. The survey also found that 15 projects did not have a good understanding of the tourism market, its key elements or how to promote and market their products and services. Sixteen communities believed they took a passive stance when negotiating the sale of their products and were not developing the necessary skills to negotiate prices and volumes with local hotels, restaurants and so on.

Management of strategic partnerships of interest

There are two types of strategic approaches to develop CBT projects: (1) that the community engages directly with tourists and; (2) the community becomes part of the tourism value chain. In general, it is easier for communities to develop indirect approaches because they lack the skills and knowledge necessary to engage directly with tourists. Agricultural production is the traditional activity most communities engage in an indirect strategic partnership. Hence, linking the community's food production activities into local supply chains for consumption by tourists is an important strategy for communities located near tourist destinations. With effective communication around the importance and benefits of local food supply chains, it would be possible to reorganize both production and marketing strategies and incorporate local produce into hotels' supply chains. In addition, the development and promotion of CBT can generate jobs and improve the quality of life in rural areas. In the State of Bahia, developers working with *Quilombolas*[1] found that it was possible to organize the production of chicken and vegetables and sell these products directly to different regional hotels. This approach offered tourists the opportunity to eat organic food and buy products at lower prices than goods imported into the region.

In other cases, there is a combination of possible strategies for tapping into the tourism market. For instance, local tourism accommodation providers often use suppliers from the local community. This strategy is already being implemented in the case studies previously mentioned in this chapter. Tourism co-operatives and associations in rural areas are organizational models that link local tourist attractions, tourism companies and small farms to optimize co-operative processes. For instance, the village of Castrolanda in the state of Paraná (in the south of Brazil) has an orchid farm. Visitors can take tours of the farm or buy flowers at the reception desk of many small local hotels. This mix of direct and indirect strategies is a collaborative process that produces benefits by allowing farmers to diversify their sales channels through local tourism partners, including restaurants, hotels and even sales of flowers as souvenirs.

One of the case studies for this research, Cooperativa Paranaense de Turismo (Cooptur), located in the region of Ponta Grossa (120 kilometres from Curitiba), was the first Brazilian tourism co-operative. Formed by entrepreneurs from seven different cities, its members are committed to quality tourism products and experiences. They offer tourism packages that involve adventure products and services. They have also sought out strategic partnerships with the private sector, offering their hotels, lodges, restaurants and guides to companies that wish to develop training programmes for their employees. Since the company was launched in 2004, the success of this corporation has relied on effective strategic partnerships and sustainable financial management. Long-term contracts have been used since the beginning of the co-operative's business planning. Effective communication with tourism intermediaries has also led the co-operative's members to constantly look for ways to improve their tourism products and services.

Based on the same principles identified in the above example, the Cooperguará-Ecotur (located on the coast of Paraná) was formed in 2006. This co-operative has been interested in addressing several local problems, including low family incomes resulting from seasonal effects. Their tourism products, which include primarily wilderness experiences and trekking excursions in the forest, are sold by several ecotourism operators, indicating the success of their strategy. In this case, a strong business plan was developed with the complete participation of the community, including direct engagement with tourists through the management of the local restaurant, accommodation and guiding activities, as well indirect engagement through the production of local food sold to the other community businesses. Hence, it was possible to identify and act on impediments (e.g. the community did not have access to mobile phones) and make effective collective decisions about how they would sell their tourism products. Both the Cooperativa Paranaense de Turismo (Cooptur) and the Cooperguará-Ecotur have discovered the basis for empowerment and an approach to building solid relationships within the community and with other stakeholders.

An understanding of the process and strategy of negotiation flows from the assumption that a community group has a 'voice' and the power to exercise it. This 'voice' is usually a person who represents and is recognized by the community and by other stakeholders including tourism intermediaries. The development of tourist products requires the participation of a number of key stakeholders, including transportation and accommodation businesses, guides, restaurants, bars and regional tourist attractions. Each of these companies sets different prices and has different sources of revenue. Their owners therefore have different interests in and visions for the tourist industry in that locality. Sometimes, increasing the price of accommodation will reduce the flow of tourists, which will indirectly impact upon transport companies' cash flow. Mediating this diversity of interests and motivations into a model of collective management (co-operatives or tourism associations) is a challenge. Rising to such challenges allows for both collective and individual profit, which is the principal reason for the formation of such groups. Therefore, contracts among community members and between them and other stakeholders must be formalized (Mielke 2010).

Internal governance

Rules and agreements form part of the management process, and for the majority of the projects analysed in this study, they were still in their early stages. However, communities were aware of the importance of rules and agreements in shaping stakeholder relations in the proper functioning of the projects. In 21 projects, the community needed training to learn about the management process. The survey also revealed that 25 projects did not have internal regulations and rules in place to organize tourism activities and ensure compliance with current legislative frameworks. It is extremely difficult to ensure quality, efficiency and consistency without formal regulations and rules. When asked why they had not established internal rules, 22 respondents argued that they had only realized the importance of such rules after the project was almost complete and did not have sufficient funds to take this action. Interestingly, a small number of respondents stated that the community was too immature, and there were difficulties in identifying who the community was. This is an important issue because community identity is directly associated with the community's culture, sense of connection and self-esteem, which in turn impacts upon how tourism products are developed and how they are sold.

One project that has successfully built its community identity, organization and leadership is the tourism association Acolhida da Colônia. Created in 1998, it encourages farmers to host tourists, thereby providing opportunities for cultural exchange and economic diversification. Under their internal rules and agreements, this association has established a reservation and information centre. The model they employ, adapted and applied to the circumstances in the Brazilian state of Santa Catarina, enables small local farmers to maintain their rural lifestyle while participating in tourism activities. It has created extra income and generated employment in that region by implementing a community-based concept in which each member has duties and responsibilities towards the group.

In the north of Brazil, more than five thousand kilometres from Santa Catarina, the state of Ceará has a community network called TUCUM. Unlike the previous examples in which each entity set its own rules, this organization links 12 communities. Since 1993, the Terra Mar Institute has filled this role with the goal of developing collaborative processes designed to balance the relationship between tourism and community. The institute is responsible for making agreements and partnerships with other institutions in addition to managing tourism initiatives in that region.

Generally speaking, the entire process of establishing and consolidating internal governance or group management passes through a process of community institutionalization to make and record decisions. Because tourism activities require high-quality standards, establishing both a set of collective rules and a commitment to those rules is crucial. Co-operative processes include education and information sharing and these should be undertaken with increasing frequency as a CBT project progresses.

Internal governance is evaluated by setting clear, tangible and measurable goals related to establishing access to markets that are interested in the services offered by the communities. As background to the setting up of internal governance arrangements and setting goals and targets, the pros and cons of the CBT project must be understood by community members, and their doubts and questions about how tourism will impact their lives must be openly discussed. Moreover, structured planning and appropriate strategic partnerships with government and non-government organizations should be developed with the aim of maximizing the benefits of the CBT project. The same is true with regard to intermediaries, with a need to establish more formal agreements with intermediaries that will promote and sell the CBT projects to a broader market.

In general the research results found that as the communities matured, they eventually developed their own methods to decide whether to participate in another project and to continue learning about the tourism industry and its benefits. However, when those participating in the CBT projects were asked whether their communities would be able to 'stand on their own' without any external financial assistance, only three out of 26 answered in the affirmative.

These results suggest the importance of monitoring and evaluation processes in the implementation of CBT projects to ensure they deliver the benefits initially identified. However, setting goals and targets must be done carefully as outcomes are often hard to measure accurately. In the research conducted and reported on in the chapter, few CBT projects had planned to write a business plan or any equivalent document or to establish agreements within the community and with stakeholders. As a result, goals and targets, which would normally be part of this process, are not established early. The challenge of writing a clear business plan, and setting strategic goals and targets were well understood by the respondents in this research, but concrete actions to address these issues were difficult.

CBT project monitoring and assessment

Employing evaluation programmes to monitor the process and results of CBT projects is not simple (Dixey 2008; Goodwin and Santilli 2009). In monitoring, two problems are generally encountered. The first problem is with the criteria or indicators used. As a rule, the organizations that provide resources for a particular project have their own criteria for evaluating projects. The second problem is that evaluations conducted for these organizations, using these predetermined criteria, are often underpinned by self-interest and can violate the principle of impartiality. In other words, following the new paradigm suggested by Ashley and Mitchell (2008) and in the interests of responsibility and accountability in the tourism industry, donors should have more of a presence throughout the monitoring process.

Monitoring programmes are a crucial part of the implementation and policy evaluation process (Reidar 2004). Furthermore, providing funds to an organization with no monitoring in place is a blind investment: it can result in unfulfilled expectations and outcomes, and damage the esteem of people who often already live in marginalized communities. According to the study developed by researchers from SNV and University of Hawaii (2007: 8), 'monitoring is the measurement process usually done through indicators, in order to provide a better understanding of the current situation, as well as some idea of the trends of performance'.

Currently, there is no consensus regarding the criteria to monitor CBT projects (Amorim, Dias and Mielke 2008). However, establishing specific indicators to be used in all cases is problematic and not advisable. Regional communities have their own behaviours and values, and it is therefore important to consider local conditions when conducting programme monitoring and evaluation. In Brazil, due to historical processes of colonization and development, CBT projects in the north and northeast regions are completely different from those in the south or southeast regions. Therefore, the impact of the changes introduced by these projects on local governments differs dramatically between regions (Almeida 2007).

Brooks World Poverty Institute has argued that relatively little attention has been given to the methodologies employed to analyse monitoring and assessment programmes because 'monitoring brings real-time information about the progress of the project as a whole' (BWPI 2009: 5). Mielke and Sperandio (2009) have argued that many of the indicators used in these processes are based on quantitative criteria and unrealistic scenarios. Maris and Schipani (2001) and World Bank (2006) have instead underscored the importance of using qualitative criteria.

The vast majority of the literature on CBT monitoring programmes suggest and discuss quantitative indicators rather than qualitative ones (Reidar, 2004). However, a combination of data is recommended because this allows a series of interactions to take place in which researchers and consultants can collect, analyse and understand both qualitative and quantitative information. This combination also promotes continuous feedback onto the project's scorecard and whether objectives are being met (Jha, Rao and Woolcock 2007, 2008; Morra and Rist 2009). When monitoring, it is also important to consider a group's level of commitment to participation (Sebola and Fourie 2006), the power dynamics in the community organization (Maclellan *et al.* 2007) and leadership and decision-making practices (Ife 2002; Kirk and Kraft 2004). In the research presented in this chapter, these aspects are not often considered when establishing evaluation and monitoring processes; almost all of the CBT projects were developed without establishing any formal criteria.

When asked to explain what type of monitoring programme they had planned for the period after funding had stopped, only 19 of the 26 projects had established a post-funding monitoring framework. Additionally, within this group of 19 projects, 14 mentioned that their processes for monitoring were not yet finalised. Of the seven projects that responded negatively to this question, five stated that the funding organizations should be responsible for this task. For the remaining two projects, the subject of evaluation had not yet been discussed with the community.

From this research it seems that establishing monitoring programmes is not a primary concern in CBT management. This suggests that those involved in CBT management do not understand nor are they aware of the benefits of monitoring their management practices. Nevertheless, the reasons for the failure of most CBT projects are well known in the academic literature. Paradoxically, if there is a consensus about the challenges involved in implementing CBT initiatives within their community, there is a need to establish indicators to properly measure the success of these projects and foster the optimization of resources invested.

Conclusion

The research presented in this chapter has produced two main findings. First, the international literature reviewed for this chapter has suggested two reasons for the failure of most CBT projects: poor governance and weak access to markets. Almost all of the CBT projects analysed in this study were affected by both these issues. It seems that, regardless of the local economic context, these problems are present across Brazil. Second, it was possible to identify why and how each of the reasons can and should be resolved. The four practical examples of tourism associations and co-operatives presented have shown these social organizations can be used as a tool to deal for instance with governance problems.

Optimizing access to markets results from a long-term process of co-operation. The development of local tourism through the organization of a group of people requires mutual trust, which is usually reinforced when good outcomes are achieved. Organizations with limited or no institutional structures and processes impede performance. Rules and agreements must be discussed and agreed upon among the community members and between community members and other stakeholders. Tourism is a dynamic activity, and communities are sometimes unable to change as fast as the market does. This is why monitoring programmes must be undertaken at the beginning of a project and be based on reliable criteria that can be applied regardless of the social context. CBT projects with weak or poor relationships with tourism intermediaries will probably struggle to achieve tangible outcomes. There seems to be an enormous distance between tour operators (even those who have responsible policies) and communities. The longer this condition persists, the further communities will be from accessing appropriate tourism markets.

Poor governance is also a challenging problem. In the four examples included in this chapter, governance is crucial. Good governance means that communities have autonomy and independence and have some control over their mode of operation, how they collaborate with other stakeholders and ultimately, the outcomes achieved. For instance, communities must conduct their businesses in awareness of tourism markets; they should be able to sell their products and services; and they should know how to interact with stakeholders. Moreover, the co-operative relationship is, and always will be, the basis of any sustainable process that seeks to involve local tourism enterprises, multiple independent workers from the community and other stakeholders, such as local governments, other NGOs and the private sector.

Although there are many CBT initiatives whose processes need to be improved and reviewed, there are good examples to be followed. Apparently many communities that have addressed the challenges described herein have succeeded in terms of economic sustainability. Although the product or service that each co-operative or association sells is different, the structural elements of their organization and their tourism management practices are very similar.

Finally, it is clear that more research is needed before these issues and processes are fully understood. In Brazil, and throughout Latin America, there are few successful cases. However, how can these projects describe themselves as successful and according to which criteria? What determines what is success and what is not? If the response to these questions comes from the community itself, the answers will surely be based on the benefits of tourism seen by the community, and benefits will be measured by tangible results.

References

Almeida, A. C. (2007) *A Cabeça do Brasileiro*. Rio de Janeiro: Record.

Amorim, B., Dias, A., and Mielke, E. J. C. Análise de oito metodologias de Indicadores de sustentabilidade para projetos de desenvolvimento turístico, paper presented at *X SIT – Seminário Internacional de Turismo*, Curitiba, September 2008.

Ashley, C. and Mitchell, J. (2008) *Doing the Right Thing Approximately not the Wrong Thing Precisely: Challenges of Monitoring Impacts of Pro-poor Interventions in Tourism Value Chains*. London: Overseas Development Institute. Working paper 291. Available at: www.odi.org.uk/resources/download/1590.pdf (accessed 18 February 2011).

Boesche, L. (2005) *Fidelidade Cooperativa: Uma Abordagem Prática*. Curitiba: Sescoop-PR.

Brooks World Poverty Institute – BWPI (2009) *Using Mixed Methods in Monitoring and Evaluation: Experiences from International Development*. Manchester: BWPI Working Paper 107.

Dixey, L. (2008) The unsustainability of community tourism donors projects: Lessons from Zambia, in A. Spenceley (ed.) *Responsible Tourism: Critical issues for Conservation and Development*. London: Earthscan, 323–42.

Goodwin, H. and Santilli, R. (2009) Community-based tourism: a success? ICRT Occasional Paper 11. Available at www.icrtourism.org/documents/OP11merged.pdf (accessed 24 February 2011).

Ife, J. (2002) *Community Development: Community-based Alternatives in an Age of Globalisation*. Frenchs Forest: Pearson Education Australia.

Jha, S., Rao, V. and Woolcock, M. (2007) Governance in the gullies: democratic responsiveness and community leadership, *World Development*, 35: 230–46.

Kirk, P. and Kraft, M. K. (2004) Community leadership development. *Community Development Journal*, 39: 234–51.

Maclellan-Wright, F., Anderson, D., Barber, S., Smith, N., Cantin, B. and Felix, R. (2007) The development of measures of community capacity for community-based funding programs in Canada. *Health Promotion International*, 22: 299–306.

Maris, G. and Schipani, S. (2001) Monitoring community based ecotourism in the Lao PDR: the UNESCO-NTA Lao Nam Ha ecotourism project monitoring protocol. UNESCO-National Tourism Authority of Lao PDR Nam Ha Ecotourism Project.

Mielke, E. J. C. (2010) *Desenvolvimento Turístico de Base Comunitária*. Campinas: Átomo & Alínea.

Mielke, E. J. C. and Sperandio, D. (2001) Desarollo turístico regional: El diagnóstico estratégico participativo ponderado – DEPP, aplicaciones y retos a la planificación turística. In VI Seminário da Associação de Pesquisa e Pós-Graduação em Turismo.

Mielke, E. J. C. and Pereira. A. (2006) 'Desenvolvimento econômico e social através do turismo: interações entre atores locais, paper presented at V Seminário de Pesquisa em Turismo do Mercosul/III Seminário da ANPTUR – Associação Nacional de Pesquisa e Pós-Graduação em Turismo, Caxias do Sul, Julho 2006.

Mitchell J. and Muckosy P. (2008) *A Misguided Quest: Community-based Tourism in Latin America*, ODI Opinion 102.

Morra, L. and Rist, R. (2009) *The Road to Results: Designing and Conducting Effective Development Evaluations*. Washington, DC: World Bank.

Reidar, D. (2004) Evaluating *Development Programmes and Projects*. New Delhi: Sage Publications.

Sebola, M. and Fourie, L. (2006) Community participation in ecotourism destinations: Maleboho Nature Reserve. *Transactions on ecology and the environment*, 197.

SNV and UH-University of Hawaii (2007) A toolkit for monitoring and managing community-based tourism. Available at: www.snvworld.org/en/Pages/Publications.aspx (accessed 02 March 2011)

Spenceley, A. (2008) *Responsible Tourism: Critical Issues for Conservation and Development*. London: Earthscan.

UNWTO (2004) *Signposts for Sustainable Tourism: A Guidebook for The Development and Use of Indicators for The Development of Tourism Destinations*. Madrid: United Nations World Tourism Organization.

UNWTO (2006) *Poverty Alleviation Through Tourism – A Compilation of Good Practices*. Madrid: United Nations World Tourism Organization.

World Bank (2006) Understanding and setting up a monitoring and evaluation system. Available at: www.worldbank.org/WBSITE/EXTERNAL/TOPICS/EXTPOVERTY/EXTISPMA/0,,menuPK:384336~pagePK:149018~piPK:149093~theSitePK:384329,00.html (accessed 12 February 2011).

Endnote

1 *Quilombolas* are the residents of quilombos. These are poor rural hinterland settlements which are generally founded and inhabited by people of African origin. They represent some of the poorest and most marginalized groups in the country.

4 Tourism transport issues in Brazil

Gui Lohmann and Jakob Trischler

Introduction

Brazil has significant challenges in tourism transport that are derived not only from the sheer size of the country, but also the regimes of investment and distribution of government roles and responsibilities for transport. In exploring these issues, this chapter has two main aims. First, it provides comprehensive insights into Brazil's transport governance and infrastructure and examines specific issues relating to different modes of passenger transport. Second, the chapter presents a case study on river tourism in the Amazon and the challenges of enhancing local, regional and interstate transport in this remote region. Although the findings of this case study are specific to river tourism, a mode of transport rarely considered in the academic literature (Prideaux and Cooper 2009), the discussion of Belém in many ways resembles the challenges faced at the national level, although the remoteness of the region magnifies these issues. In order to better understand tourism transport issues associated with river tourism in the Amazon, this section also provides a description of tourism in Belém, Marajó Island, Santarém and Manaus.

Tourism transport in Brazil

Governance

To prevent further downward pressure on the country's economic performance during the fiscal crisis in the early 1990s, the Brazilian government initiated reforms in the energy, transport and telecommunication sectors (Estache *et al.* 2001). The main goal of transportation reforms was to transfer the operations of railways, roads and ports to privately owned firms because the majority of infrastructure was owned and operated by public monopolies or central government entities (Estache 2001). The reforms were expected to combat the fiscal crisis by reducing public debt. Further advantages included increased investment, stimulating competition, improvement in transport services, and the strengthening of the stock market through widespread participation in the purchase of shares in transport-related entities (Estache, Goldstein and Pittman 2001).

Due to the increased involvement of the private sector in transport operations, the Ministry of Transport predominantly took a regulatory role including the development of policies and strategies. The Ministry also took a support role, initiating socially valuable projects that were unattractive or uncompetitive for private investment (Estache 2001). Since 2001, two regulatory agencies have represented the Ministry of Transport: the National Terrestrial Transport Agency (Agência Nacional de Transportes Terrestres, ANTT), which is responsible for road and railway transport, and the National Aquatic Transport Agency (Agência Nacional de Transportes Aquaviários, ANTAQ), which is in charge of ports and waterways (De Paula and Avellar 2008). The National Department of Transport Infrastructure (Departamento Nacional de Infraestrutura de Transportes, DNIT) supports these agencies by executing public-sector programmes in road, waterway, port and rail projects (World Bank 2005). For most of its existence, the DNIT has been associated with high levels of corruption and inefficiency, leading to a ministerial crisis in the middle of 2011 in which the minister and a number of senior public servants were removed from office for their involvement in corruption (Mello 2011).

Contributing further to the fragmentation of the transport sector, a separate agency manages air transport. Brazil's aviation sector is co-ordinated by the Ministry of Defence. Similar to ANTT and ANTAQ at the Ministry of Transport, the National Civil Aviation Agency (Agência Nacional de Aviação Civil – ANAC) is in charge of civil aviation, with Infraero (Empresa Brasileira de Infraestrutura Aeroportuária) operating major airports and aviation infrastructure (ANAC 2011). Established in March 2006, ANAC took over the structure and function of the former Civil Aviation Department (Departamento de Aviação Civil – DAC) and is responsible for the regulation and safety oversight of Brazil's civil aviation. Infraero, also part of the Ministry of Defence, manages 67 of Brazil's main airports, which represent over 97 per cent of Brazil's air transport traffic (ANAC 2011). Hence, like the former DAC, ANAC and Infraero are centralized federal government-owned entities that do not foster competition within the airport sector and are not connected to the Ministry of Transport. The major reason for the strong monopoly position of Infraero is the current legislation that does not permit private airport operators to offer public services and commercial operations (Prazeres, Esteves and Filho 2011).

Infrastructure

The introduction of a new national constitution in 1988 (see Chapter 1) had a lasting influence on infrastructure investments in Brazil (Souza 2002; World Bank 2005). First, fiscal resources were decentralized from the states to municipalities. Second, the federal government reduced its participation in state and local matters. Third, specific taxes that were tied to infrastructure investments and included state taxes on consumption were abolished. Consequently, public investments in infrastructure dropped sharply, particularly in the transport sector. Ferreira and Araújo (2006) highlight the significant impact of the steady decline in public investment in infrastructure over the 1985–2005 period. For example, direct investment in roads during 2000–5 was only one-fifth of the investment for the 1970–75 period. Further, in 2005, total public investment in the transport sector was less than 0.5 per cent of the GDP of Brazil, whereas the investments of the Ministry of Transport were even lower at only 0.1 per cent of the GDP (Ferreira and Araújo 2006).

Of particular concern is the poor condition of the road network, which affects the efficiency, reliability and cost of road transport services and leads to chaotic traffic conditions in many Brazilian metropolitan areas. The rate of deaths per 10,000 vehicles in 2001 was 6.8, which was three times higher than in the US (1.93) and four times higher than in Germany (1.46) (Ribeiro and Goes 2005). After homicides, traffic accidents are the second leading cause of 'unnatural death' in Brazil (Lohmann, Santos and Allis 2010). Furthermore, passenger transport is dominated by private vehicles and coaches, accounting for nearly 95 per cent of total passengers (World Bank 2005). Only a few of the major highways in the country were privatized during the 1990s and provide reasonable road conditions and services, particularly in the wealthiest Southeast and Southern regions. Attempts at privatization programmes and infrastructure development packages in the 2000s were suspended due to cartel practices and consumer pricing abuses by private operators, which forced the government to suspend its programmes (The Economist 2007b).

Similar to road transport infrastructure, the Brazilian railway system is deficient, evidenced by decreasing freight movements over the 2000s. Private investment peaked in 1994 due to privatization programmes, but investment dropped dramatically in the following years (from US $700 million private and almost US $100 million public investment in 1994 to less than US $40 million private and US $20 million public investment in 1998) (World Bank 2005). Hence, numerous bottlenecks in railway connectivity remain, such as metropolitan train services and accessibility to ports (Estache, Goldstein and Pittman 2001). Long-distance passenger transport in Brazil is almost nonexistent, with priority given to freight transport. The exceptions are three routes operated by Vale do Rio Doce, the largest mining company in the country, and some scenic and heritage short railways.

Since the 1990s, port infrastructure has become a critical factor due to the increasing significance of shipping in Brazil's offshore trading, with an average annual cargo of over 500 million tons, and growing demand for cruise tourism, with over 800,000 passengers in the 2010–11 season (Seatrade 2011). Changes in cabotage laws in 1995 created attractive opportunities for cruise tourism along Brazil's large coastline (Costa, Lohmann and Oliveira 2010). The most frequented ports for cruise ships are Santos and Rio de Janeiro and the coastal destinations of the northeast region. Despite the numerous rivers and waterways in Brazil, they are less well developed. The exception is the Amazon region, where river routes are usually the only means of transport and access (see also Chapter 9 and Figure 9.3). Later in this chapter, the case study of river transport in the Amazon explores some of these issues.

The aviation sector has been characterized by a centralized approach by government. During the military dictatorship (1964–85), developing high standard nationwide airport infrastructure was a priority. However, this approach also led to inefficient and non-competitive practices. One example is the case of São Paulo Guarulhos International, the country's largest gateway for international flights. Guarulhos has reached capacity. However, the need to maintain low-traffic (and often unprofitable) airports has resulted in funds being diverted from Guarulhos International, and it has not received sufficient investment to build a third terminal (The Economist 2007b; World Bank 2005). Further, inappropriate investments in other airports, such as Rio de Janeiro Galeão, have led to overcapacity, but passenger traffic growth has not improved due to Infraero's regulatory framework, which does not foster competition among airports. The removal of regulatory barriers and liberalization of the Brazilian airline industry from 1992 has seen passenger numbers grow faster than airport infrastructure, with airports in São Paulo and Brasília facing capacity issues on both airside and landside areas of their terminals (Oliveira 2008).

The concentration of traffic in a few airports, lack of resources and infrastructure and poorly trained air traffic controllers led to a crisis in 2006 and 2007 (Costa, Lohmann and Oliveira 2010). This crisis began with the collision of a Gol Boeing 737 with an Embraer Legacy 600 executive jet on 29 September 2006, which resulted in the loss of 154 lives (The Economist 2007b). Between December 2006 and the beginning of 2007, flights were cancelled or delayed due to air traffic controller strikes and equipment failures, such as radar outages. The crisis peaked on 17 July 2007, when a TAM Airlines Airbus A320 went off the runway at São Paulo Congonhas Airport due to the combination of rain, poor runway conditions and mechanical problems with the airplane's thrust reversers. The airplane crashed into a warehouse, exploded, and 200 people died (The Economist 2007a).

Modes of tourism transport in Brazil

Air transport

The Brazilian airline industry was dominated by the 'Big Four' (Varig, VASP, TAM, and Transbrasil) until 2001, when Gol Linhas Aéreas (Gol) introduced its operation as the first low-cost carrier in the country (Oliveira 2008). The ensuing years were characterized by strong growth as well as increased competition in the aviation industry, which in turn led to the bankruptcy of inefficient airlines such as Transbrasil and VASP in 2001 and 2002, respectively (Huse and Oliveira 2012). In March 2007, Gol purchased Varig. Since then, Gol and TAM account for over 90 per cent of the domestic market (IATA 2009).

In 2003, due to an excess in capacity and predatory competition, the DAC (now ANAC) partially re-regulated the aviation market by banning new aircraft imports, controlling price competition and disallowing strategic movements by airlines to increase market concentration (Bettini and Oliveira 2008; Oliveira

2006). Nevertheless, air traffic on trunk routes linking the countries' major cities increased rapidly in the following years. In 2009, Brazil's airports handled over 110 million passengers, with São Paulo Guarulhos International airport, the busiest airport, handling almost 20 million passengers and 210,000 aircraft movements (IATA 2009). Similarly, São Paulo's second largest airport, Congonhas, had over 11 million passengers and 190,000 aircraft movements in the same year, as Brazil's most important domestic airport. As explained by Costa, Lohmann and Oliveira (2010), air transport in Brazil is concentrated in only a few airports: Guarulhos International and Congonhas, both in São Paulo; Galeão International, in Rio de Janeiro; and Brasília International, based in the nation's capital city. These four airports account for more than half of Brazil's domestic air traffic. At one time, Congonhas Airport, where the TAM accident occurred in 2007, was handling up to 34 aircraft movements per hour in peak periods despite a maximum capacity of 24 aircraft movements per hour (Nes 2010). It should be noted, however, that Brazilian airports handle fewer passengers than the busiest airports in the world, with Heathrow Airport and Dubai International Airport handling, 65.7 and 47.2 million passengers respectively in 2010 (Dubai International Airport 2011; Heathrow Airport 2011).

Although the Brazilian government has emphasized updating and expanding airport infrastructure and safety, a report by McKinsey & Company (2010) concluded that seven of Brazil's 20 principal airports were struggling with overcrowded passenger areas and plane berths, frequently leading to delays or flight cancellations. The same report projected an increase to 146 million passengers by 2014, with the 2014 FIFA World Cup expected to generate six million additional travellers (McKinsey & Company 2010).

Road transport

Road transport is the dominant mode of transport used by domestic tourists in Brazil. In addition to private vehicles, coach and charter buses account for nearly one-third of all domestic trips. Coaches are used on both short and multiday trips across the country. For many decades, the latter option was the only affordable mode of transport for those on lower incomes. While coach companies have always been very lucrative businesses in Brazil, towards the end of the 2000s, coach companies experienced a decrease in passenger numbers for several reasons. First, 'irregular' coach operations offer fares up to half of those charged by the coach sector. Regulated coach services have high costs associated with their operation, including insurance, taxes, regulations requiring a change of drivers after a certain number of hours and a certain level of comfort. 'Irregular' coaches offer low-quality and, in some instances, unsafe travel. They exist because of a lenient and corrupt enforcement authority and as a response to social and political pressures. They provide the very poor with an affordable way to travel across the country. Second, the increase in competition among airlines, particularly due to the introduction of Gol as a low-cost carrier, decreased the cost of airfares, and in some cases these reached a level similar to coach fares. Some domestic road trips require multiple days, with the total cost of travel inflated due to meal expenses during these journeys. Third, internal migratory movements in Brazil have declined as a result of improvements in economic conditions in the poorest regions of the country since the mid-1990s. Consequently, fewer people use coaches, and there has been a reduction in the demand for travel, particularly among travellers visiting friends and relatives. Fourth, socioeconomic improvements in Brazil since the mid-1990s have made private vehicles more affordable, with record production and sales of private vehicles. Furthermore, it is becoming more common for institutions to finance the purchase of private vehicles, with airlines also allowing passengers to finance domestic airfares through monthly payments. Fifth, with a stronger currency, the Brazilian upper class prefers to travel overseas rather than domestically, which has translated in a shift from coach to air travel for their holidays.

Cruise tourism

Cruise tourism in Brazil has evolved substantially since the introduction of new cabotage legislation (Stuber 1998). As a result, cruise lines are increasingly incorporating a Brazilian stopover into their itineraries, particularly during the off-peak season in the northern hemisphere when it is summer in Brazil (Lohmann and Duval 2011). The demand for cruise tourism was also boosted by the aviation crisis in 2006 and 2007. Many tourists decided to use alternative means of transport, particularly road trips and cruise tourism, as substitutes for air travel. In comparison with the summer of 2005–6, cruise tourism registered a growth of 70,000 passengers in the 2006–7 season, with most of the ships departing from the ports of Santos (less than 60 km from the city of São Paulo) and Rio de Janeiro (Costa, Lohmann and Oliveira 2010). These numbers grew to 800,000 passengers in the 2010–11 season, with six cruise lines operating 20 vessels (Seatrade 2011). However, with growing numbers of passengers, cruise lines face increasing challenges, such as high operation and port costs, deficient infrastructure, a poor regulatory framework and a lack of intermodal integration between water and road transport.

The following case study investigates the transport characteristics of river tourism in Brazil during the 2000s. River transport is a mode of transport that, despite its potential, is not well developed in the Amazon and other remote areas of Brazil. The study's geographical focus is on the city of Belém, the state capital of Pará, its surrounding regional areas and part of Pará's Amazon.

River tourism transport in the Amazon

This case study draws upon an exploratory field trip during which interviews were conducted to examine the challenges to river tourism accessibility from the city of Belém on different route scales. One field trip to the Amazon was conducted in June 2007, with one of the authors spending four days in Belém visiting sites, undertaking three different boat trips and conducting six non-structured interviews with key tourism and transport stakeholders. Among the interviewees were managers of Paratur (the destination management organization of the State of Pará), river transport providers and representatives from the state branch of the Brazilian National Hotel Association. Paratur sponsored part of the field trip and organized contact with the remaining interviewees. In addition to the interviews and personal impressions recorded by one of the authors, secondary data were also used to illustrate the challenges and issues associated with river tourism transport in Belém and part of the Amazon region. These results complement a previous publication on river tourism in the Amazon (Prideaux and Lohmann 2009).

When the interviews were transcribed, certain topics and themes emerged which were then grouped as shown in Figure 4.1. NVivo9 software was used to organize and catalogue information according to the four major nodes: tourism development and products, river routes, stakeholders and transport issues (see Figure 4.1).

Tourism development and products

Tourism in Belém

As the capital of the state of Pará and one of the largest cities of the Amazon, Belém has over 2.2 million inhabitants. The city's development has been heavily influenced by its European history. In 1612, the Portuguese captain Francisco de Castelo Branco led the defence against British, French and Dutch colonization attempts. To successfully defend the region, Castelo Branco chose a riverbank to construct his fort. This riverbank location is known today as Belém, which forms the southern boundary of a significant waterfront heritage precinct

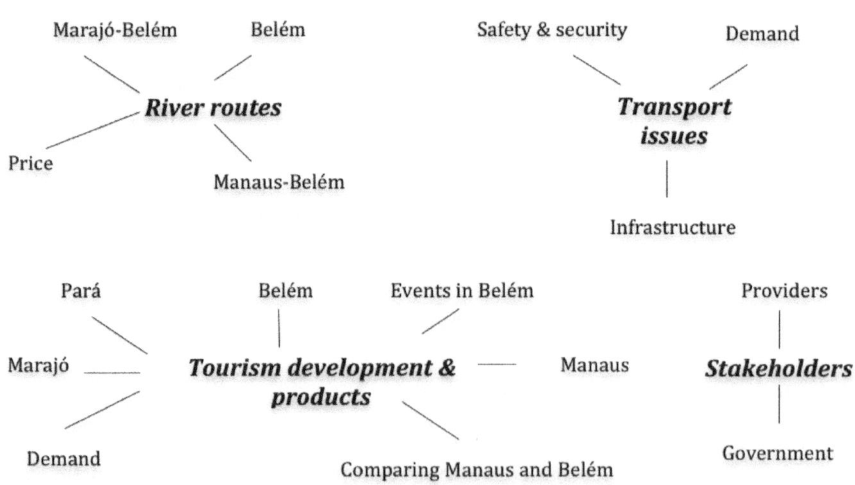

Figure 4.1 Four nodes identified throughout the interviews, with their respective topics and themes

developed by the city administration in association with the State of Pará (see Figure 4.2). Belém is an emerging destination and has set itself some ambitious goals regarding future tourism development. Located on the Pará River, a major river that flows into the delta region at the mouth of the Amazon, the city and Pará state authorities have recently embarked on a strategy to develop Belém as a major hub for Amazonian tourism.

Tourism attractions in Belém are usually linked to either the exuberant nature that surrounds the city in the form of the river and the native forest or the heritage culture (e.g. Presépio Fort, Sacred Art Museum, the Peace Theatre, Ver-o-Peso Market, the House of Eleven Windows) from the nineteenth century, when Belém was a prosperous interport for the export of rubber. Following international trends in waterfront tourism precints, the city has recently begun a beautification process, involving the development of its riverbanks with tourist areas. Among these facilities are the Estação das Docas, three former warehouses that were converted into multipurpose commercial areas with upscale restaurants, a microbrewery, shops and a convention centre with a cinema and art exhibits. Another attraction, located by the Guamá River, is the Mangal das Garças

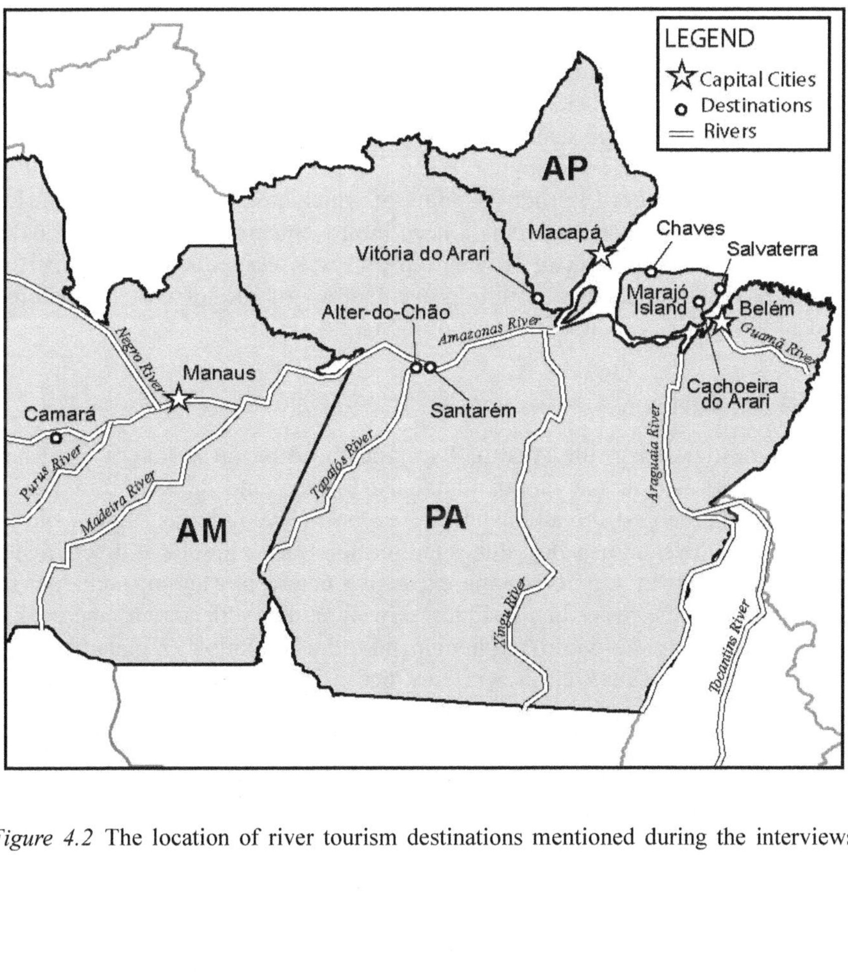

Figure 4.2 The location of river tourism destinations mentioned during the interviews

(Mangrove of the Egrets), an environmental conservation project that includes an aviary, a tower view, ponds with aquatic plants and a navigation museum.

In terms of its major markets, in 2006, Belém received over half of its domestic tourists from only three Brazilian states: São Paulo (22.5 per cent), Pará (20.8 per cent) and Amapá (9.1 per cent). In terms of international demand, in the same year, the top markets were France (16.3 per cent), the US (14.3 per cent), Italy (7.8 per cent), Germany (7.4 per cent) and Japan (6.3 per cent) (Paratur 2007). In particular, the proximity of French Guiana to Pará and the long-term cultural and business ties between the Amazon region and France explain why France is the most important international market.

Based on the field trip and the data gathered during the interviews, it was evident that accommodation facilities in Belém need to be revamped. Even with the presence of well-established international chains such as Hilton and Crowne hotels, accommodation standards are not as high as in other destinations in Brazil. Average occupation rates were approximately 52 per cent in 2005 and 2006 (Paratur 2007), with one interviewee suggesting that nearly 90 per cent of guests were on a business or event trip.

While Belém hosts one of the largest religious events in the world, the Círio de Nazaré procession that attracts over two million people to the streets of Belém, in addition to the hundreds of boats that follow the river, those interviewed considered business events to be the major product in Belém's tourism future. With the recently established convention centre, which can accommodate up to 3,000 people, Belém will consolidate its position as the major event destination in the Amazon. However, to support event and convention related tourism, there is a need for a number of products, some of which are already well established (such as gastronomy) and others that need improvement, particularly the quality of the accommodation sector. River transport services, infrastructure and the regulatory environment also need improvement in order to increase accessibility to local destinations such as the island of Marajó.

Marajó and the Amazon region

A major destination in the state of Pará and the Amazon region is the island of Marajó, located at the mouth of the Pará River and 80 km from Belém. Considered the largest fluvial island in the world (50,000 km^2 of land), Marajó has placid white sand beaches, dunes and buffalo farms that have diversified to cater for tourists. In addition to the expansive nature in Marajó, including the rich fauna of birds, fishes and buffalos as well as the wetlands and the bush, a major attraction is the pororoca phenomenon, the formation of gigantic waves when the river's waters clash with the ocean. Currently, the major tourism segments in Marajó include ecotourism, rural tourism and fishing tourism. The major tour operators in Brazil, such as CVC, MGM, New Line and Freeway, offer packages to Marajó combined with a visit to Belém, making the river a scenic link between the two destinations.

The interviews suggested that despite the quality of the natural environment and its tourism potential, Marajó requires better planning to make its tourism sustainable. For example, food consumed by tourists could be produced on the island, but it is imported from other places. As is the case for most destinations in Brazil, there is an overriding expectation that having a magnificent product is enough to attract tourists and there is little realization of the need for proactive tourism and transport strategies. Apart from Marajó, a number of other destinations along the Amazon region are dependent on the Amazon River as a means of tourism transport. The major destination is Manaus, the capital of Amazonas, which has always been Belém's principal competitor in becoming the main international gateway to the Amazon region. Manaus, located about 1,450 km upriver from the Atlantic Ocean, has emerged as the best-known Amazonian destination and has a developing reputation as a nature-based destination (Prideaux and Lohmann 2009).

Manaus is one of the largest cities of the north region, with over 2 million inhabitants. Located at the confluence of the two Amazonian rivers Negro and Solimões, Manaus, like Belém, was strongly influenced by European colonization movements. Initially famous for its rubber boom during the nineteenth and twentieth centuries, Manaus developed into a popular tourist destination due to its cruise trips into the surrounding jungles and the nearby beaches in Ponta Negra. Ponta Negra beach is particularly well known for its scenic beaches, luxury resorts, nightlife and numerous events held in its large amphitheatre.

According to one of the interviewees, the international image that Manaus promotes is stronger than Belém in terms of its association with the Amazon region. This is due, in part, to the resort investment made in Manaus by Varig, the major domestic and international Brazilian airline from the 1970s until the late 1990s. However, according to the owner of Atakan Amazon, which is responsible for organizing luxurious boat trips between Belém and Manaus, the choice to establish his business in Belém was due to the fact that 'Belém is the entrance for the fluvial system in the Amazon and the fact that there are several medium and large ships based there'. Although there are differences in the tourism segments targeted by both destinations (with Manaus having a strong focus on the resort and lodge accommodation market as well as fishing tourism), the locations share many similarities, dating to when they were the two major Brazilian rubber export centres in the nineteenth century.

In addition to Belém and Manaus, Santarém is emerging as a third tourism destination. Also known as the 'Pearl of the Tapajós River', Santarém is the largest city in the western part of the state Pará, with over 275,000 inhabitants. The city is situated where the Tapajós River joins the Amazon River. Also surrounded by forests, Santarém offers pristine nature, such as the flooded forest areas called igapós, river lagoons (igarapés) and numerous river beaches during the low water season (Prideaux and Lohmann 2009). Santarém is also characterized by a rich history and culture from both the indigenous population and the European colonies. One of the most popular attractions of the city is the phenomenon called 'the meeting of the waters', which occurs when the Amazon and Tapajós Rivers run next to each other for several kilometres but do not mix due to their different temperatures. This phenomenon is spectacular as the waters from both rivers have distinct colours (Prideaux and Lohmann 2009).

River routes

Surprisingly, the Amazon rivers have attracted only a few large cruise lines, including CVC, the largest tour operator in Brazil. Commercial passenger boats operate regular services in many areas and between the major cities of the Amazon region, with river tours ranging from half-day local trips out of Belém to several day luxury cruises to Manaus.

Local routes in and around Belém

Due to its geographical location and physical presence, the Pará River shapes the city in many ways, including transport, leisure and urban development. Thousands of boats of different shapes and sizes serve as public transport for the local population and for tourists. Where they exist, roads generally radiate inland from river ports rather than following the river and are continually subject to maintenance problems, particularly during the rainy season. There is a large number of transport operators that provide transport for tourists, ranging from a couple of hours' sightseeing along the major tourist attractions of Belém to a one-day tour to nearby destinations, particularly the popular Mosqueiro Island (60 km from Belém).

During the field trip for this research, one of the authors participated in two commercial river tours. The first one was a typical tourist experience, with dance and music provided onboard while the boat undertook circular trips, passing by Belém's riverfront and some of the attractions previously described. The second trip, a half-day excursion, provided a more authentic experience that explored the channels and tributaries into the middle of the forest. The walk was professionally organized, with a well-informed tour guide who spoke several foreign languages. This experience contrasted with the general comments made during the interviews regarding human resource training. The restaurant at which lunch was served was a precarious wooden construction located by the river that had delicious fish dishes, but the conditions of the toilets were quite unsanitary. The scene was a very common one in most isolated parts of Brazil, where expensive food is served in buildings that lack the most basic level of hygiene (see overall contrasts in Brazil presented in Chapter 1).

Regional routes to Marajó, the rest of Pará and Manaus

Pará River is the most accessible way to reach Marajó from Belém. The river provides not only a means of transport but is also an attraction in itself, as travellers can observe the phenomenon of the pororoca. Two operators provide regular passenger-only trips between Belém and Marajó. They offer very similar services and timetables, with trips ranging between two and three hours. In addition, one daily ferryboat service is available, with a capacity for 35 vehicles and passengers and the journey lasts approximately four hours.

From the perspective of the interviewees, transport is the major bottleneck for tourism development in Marajó. According to the interviewees, the most challenging aspect of the service provided is that departures from Belém occur only once in the morning, with vessels immediately returning to Belém in the afternoon. This makes day trips to Marajó impossible, creating a major issue when the average stay of tourists in Belém is only 3.5 days. The main reason for having early services departing from Belém with an immediate return is that the crossing can be quite rough, particularly between the months of November and March, when waves can reach up to three metres. Low tides are more common in the mornings than later in the day.

In terms of the level of service, an important consideration is that the majority of demand is from the poor local population, with no specific transport service for tourists. Standard fares are approximately ten American dollars, which is usually affordable for most tourists, but the level of comfort is uncertain. There is an option to travel by cabin, but the price is more expensive, at around US$50. Boats are usually old and operate at very slow speeds. The major challenge in addressing this problem is that the tourist demand is not sufficiently consistent for daily trips. There was once a service designed for this purpose, but the operational costs were very high, and demand was inconsistent. A ship accommodating 150 passengers and travelling 35–45 miles an hour would require an investment of approximately US$15 million, and with high operational costs and low income generation during low season, the business case is weak.

Two of the interviewees involved in the tourism sector blamed the government and the regulatory environment, which reduces the incentive for competition and better service (benefits that would also help the local population). For example, several of the boats in operation are more than 70 years old, with some boats over a hundred years old.

In addition to Marajó, other important river routes along the Pará River and the Amazon River include trips to Santarém, the second most important city in the state of Pará, and to Manaus. The route between Belém and Manaus is probably the oldest in the Amazon, served by very slow ships on trips that last five days. In the 1960s and 1970s, the service was operated by a state-owned company called ENASA, with subsidies provided to facilitate movement of the local population between the two cities. ENASA was subsequently liquidated, and this route was taken over by the private sector. However, considering low demand and the long trips, attempts to implement faster services were unsuccessful. Currently, wealthy tourists have the option of travelling between Belém and Manaus as well as other places in the Amazon with companies such as the Atakan Amazon. Atakan offers two itineraries: a five-day trip between Belém and Macapá and a ten-day trip between Belém and Manaus. Atakan has three modern boats with capacities of 8 (Atakan I), 13 (Atakan II) and 22 (Atakan III) passengers, with three, five and eight cabins, respectively. These all-inclusive trips cost approximately US$800 per person per day, depending on the type of cabin.

There are also large, international cruise lines operating along the Negro and Amazon Rivers. The Iberostar Grand Amazon, for example, offers luxury cruises starting from the city of Manaus and stopping at several points along the Amazon jungle, from where it undertakes excursions into the jungle with smaller boats (Iberostar 2011). The *Iberostar* contains 73 cabins, two suites, two pools, two restaurants and one conference room. The rates range from US$350 to US$680 per day and per person (Iberostar 2011). Furthermore, a number of international cruise lines offer cruise vacations that include the Amazon River as part of their multi-country itineraries (Amazon River Cruises 2011). The regularly frequented ports are Belém, Manaus, Santarém and Boca da Valeria. These international cruise operators include global players such as P&O Cruises, Crystal Cruise Line and Regent Cruise Line, and they are recognized as important enhancements to the international tourism industry in the Amazon.

Stakeholder interests

Given the previous discussion it is apparent that further development in river transport accessibility is dependent on supply-side improvements, supported by marketing, to stimulate demand. A favourable policy environment that provides incentives to expand supply and generate demand is also necessary. The challenge in the poorer states of Brazil is that investment in social programmes is perceived as a priority. In some instances, interviewees mentioned that investments made in tourism are considered by the local population as only benefiting tourists and are less important than priority policy areas such as health, housing and education. In terms of transport, politicians are highly involved with transport providers who make high profits in a non-competitive market, paying back providing major financial support of their political campaigns (when corruption is not involved, as discussed earlier in this chapter).

At the national level, government roles and responsibilities for state-level river transport are fragmented in Pará. In addition to SETRAN/PA (Secretaria Executiva de Transportes do Pará, the State Department of Transport), the Capitania dos Portos, a department within the Brazilian Navy, is responsible for river transport safety for both ships and passengers and is also responsible for pollution caused by ships. However, the Capitania dos Portos is not responsible for the quality of service provided by transport providers.

Transport issues

In addition to the issues previously discussed, two other major tourism transport challenges were identified during the interviews: issues pertaining to demand and security and safety (see Figure 4.1).

First, tourism and transport development in Belém and the Amazon region is subject to a number of issues. The local population is socioeconomically disadvantaged, with transport services either of low quality (particularly public transport) or exclusively for the use of tourists, as in the case of local routes out of Belém. Challenges in the Belém–Marajó route include the lack of targeting of appropriate demand, as daily trips out of Belém to Marajó are not viable. Marajó needs to be promoted as a destination itself rather than a sub-destination while on a short stay in Belém. As one interviewee stated, while independent travellers to the Amazon, particularly backpackers, are willing to experience an authentic transport journey without necessarily using a segregated service exclusively for tourists, these travellers expect a level of safety and security that is currently unavailable.

Second, safety and security are major issues throughout Brazil due to a combination of negligence, awareness of the need for and proper use of safety equipment, inadequate government control and regulation, corruption and crime. Security and safety issues related to transport are responsible for a high proportion of deaths in the country. In the Amazon, these matters become even more complicated due to the extent of the forests, with most of the region isolated from major centres. In terms of river transport, some of the issues that affect tourist safety include the operation of very old ships that are only required to be inspected every five years, and the problem of scalping, in which travellers with long hair, usually women, are injured when their hair becomes stuck in the ship's propeller. Security issues involve the existence of pirates who take advantage of the slow speeds of old ships and speed restrictions (eight knots to avoid washes produced by larger ships and which impact upon the navigability of smaller ships and canoes) to rob passengers on board the ships.

Conclusions

This chapter has dealt with tourism transport, a key component for tourism development in any destination, particularly in a continental country as Brazil.

In this chapter show that in spite of the transformations that have taken place, notably the privatization of highways, ports and railways and the creation of agencies to deal with regulatory and policy matters for the various modes of transport, Brazil still has many transport challenges to address.

At the federal level, transport policy planning and implementation is carried without a cohesive multimodal governmental structure, with the Ministry of Defence controlling the air transport system, and the Ministry of Transport and a number of independent agencies overseeing water, road and rail passenger transport individually. In addition, during the 1990s and 2000s the Ministry of Transport and later the National Department of Transport Infrastructure (DNIT) were constantly under investigation due to corruption (Marques and Caitano 2011). In the case of air transport, the National Civil Aviation Agency and Infraero were both accused of negligence in the case of the TAM accident that took place in São Paulo in 2007.

On a local and regional scale these matters are aggravated as state governments and city councils have less financial resources to deal with tourism transport issues. In the case of the Amazon, remoteness also makes tourism more challenging, as transport accessibility is scarce to and within Amazonian destinations. In addition, the north region of Brazil is one of the poorest in the country (see Chapter 1), with transport services lacking quality of service and proper law enforcement. The case study provided in this chapter examined river trips generated out of Belém. Belém has not only a geographical location that favours river transport, but also due to the efforts undertaken by its tourism marketing organization and some innovative management approaches that allowed for the establishment of new tourism attractions, the city has become a magnet for tourism activities. During the field trip and the interviews it was possible to identify three different river tourism routes out of Belém, which vary from two extremes between luxurious trips across the Amazon region and low-quality cheaper options that mainly target the local population. The interviewees identified conflicts between transport and tourism providers, low tourism demand and conflict of interests between politicians and transport providers as the major inhibitors of river tourism development out of Belém.

Acknowledgements

Gui Lohmann would like to acknowledge the financial support provided by Paratur, the tourism marketing department of the State of Pará, and the Federal University of Pará (UFPA), which sponsored the fieldwork conducted by the authors. The authors would also like to thank the owner of Atakan Amazon for his kind support in this project. Prof. Bruce Prideaux was involved during the field research, and his support is very much appreciated. Mariana Aldrigui's role in contacting Paratur and UFPA was crucial for the field research. The authors are also grateful to Anna Masella for transcribing the interviews.

References

Amazon River Cruises (2011) Oceangoing Cruise Lines.

ANAC (2011) *About ANAC*. Brasília: Agência Nacional de Aviação Civil.

Bettini, H. F. A. J. and Oliveira, A. V. M. (2008) Airline capacity setting after re-regulation: The Brazilian case in the early 2000s. *Journal of Air Transport Management*, 14: 289–92.

Costa, T. F., Lohmann, G. and Oliveira, A. V. (2010) A model to identify airport hubs and their importance to tourism in Brazil. *Research in Transportation Economics*, 26: 3–11.

De Paula, G. M. and Avellar, A. P. (2008) Reforms and infrastructure regulation in Brazil: The experience of ANTT and ANTAQ. *The Quarterly Review of Economics and Finance*, 48: 237–51.

Dubai International Airport (2011) *Fact Sheets, Reports and Statistics*. Dubai: Dubai International Airport.

Estache, A. (2001) Privatization and regulation of transport infrastructure in the 1990s. *The World Bank Research Observer*, 16: 85–107.

Estache, A., Goldstein, A. and Pittman, R. (2001) Privatization and regulatory reform in Brazil: The case of freight railways. *Journal of Industry, Competition and Trade*, 1: 203–35.

Ferreira, P. C. and Araújo, A. H. (2006) *On the Economic and Fiscal Effects of Infrastructure Investment in Brazil*. Rio de Janeiro: Fundação Getúlio Vargas.

Heathrow Airport (2011) *Heathrow at a Glance*. London: Heathrow Airport.

Huse, C. and Oliveira, A. V. (2012) Does product differentiation soften price reactions to entry? Evidence from the airline industry. *Journal of Transport Economics and Policy*, 46: 189–204.

IATA (2009) *The impact of international air service liberalisation on Brazil*. Montreal: IATA.

Iberostar (2011) *Iberostar Amazon riverboat*. Madrid: Iberostar.

Lohmann, G. and Duval, D. T. (2011) Critical aspects of the tourism-transport relationship, in C. Cooper (ed.) *Contemporary Tourism Review*. Oxford: Goodfellow Publishers.

Lohmann, G., Santos, G. and Allis, T. (2010) 'Los hermanos' visiting the south region of Brazil: a comparison between drive tourists and coach tourists from Argentina, Paraguay and Uruguay, in B. Prideaux and D. Carson (eds) *Drive Tourism – Trends and Emerging Markets*. Oxford: Routledge.

Marques, L. and Caitano, A. (2011) *Alfredo Nascimento deixa Ministério dos Transportes*. São Paulo: Editora Abril.

McKinsey & Company (2010) *Study of the Air Transport Sector in Brazil*. Rio de Janeiro: Mckinsey & Company.

Nes, E.F. (2010) *A Snapshot of Brazilian Airport Infrastructure*. São Paulo: The Brazil Business.

Oliveira, A. V. M. (2006) Patterns of Low Cost Carrier Entry: Evidence from Brazil, in D. Lee (ed.) *Competition Policy and Antitrust*. Oxford: Elsevier.

Oliveira, A. V. M. (2008) An empirical model of low-cost carrier entry. *Transportation Research Part A: Policy and Practice*, 42: 673–95.

Paratur (2007) *Dados Estatísticos de Turismo*. Belém: Paratur.

Prazeres, D. L., Esteves, L. L. and Filho, R. P. (2011) Diagnosis of the Brazilian airport system and the alternatives for its privatization. *Revista de Literatura dos Transportes*, 5: 229–44.

Prideaux, B. and Cooper, M. (2009) (eds) *River tourism*. Wallingford: CABI Publishing.

Prideaux, B. and Lohmann, G. (2009) The Amazon: A river tourism frontier, in B. Prideaux and M. Cooper (eds) *River Tourism*, Cambridge: CABI Publishing.

Mello, F. (2011) Anatomia de corrupção, *Revista Veja*. São Paulo: Editora Abril, 8 June 2011: 120–8.

Ribeiro, S. F. and Goes, J. R. (2005) Road accidents in Brazil. *IATSS Research*, 29: 68–70.

Seatrade (2011) *The Importance of Cruising Comes Home to South America*. São Paulo: S.A.C. Convention.

Souza, C. (2002) *Brazil's System of Local Government, Local Finance and Intergovernmental Relations*. Birmingham: University of Birmingham.

Stuber, W. D. (1998) *Project Finance in Brazil*. São Paulo: C.F.I.L. Studies.

The Economist (2007a) An accident waiting to happen? *The Economist*, London: The Economist.

The Economist (2007b) From crisis to crisis in Brazil. *The Economist*, London: The Economist.

World Bank (2005) *Infrastructure in Latin America: Recent Evolution and Key Challenges*. Washington: World Bank.

5 Sustainability dilemmas for Brazil in hosting mega-sport events

Arianne Carvalhedo Reis and
Lamartine Pereira DaCosta

Introduction

The impacts of major sport events on host communities have received significant attention from scholars of various disciplines (Cashman and Hughes 1998; Lenskyj 2007; Waitt 2003). Of particular interest have been the direct and indirect economic impacts of such events on the local, regional and national communities (Preuss 2000), and, more recently, the environmental impacts that mega-events may have on their hosts' communities (Collins, Jones and Munday 2009). These impact studies have been important in developing an understanding of the sustainable management of the event and sport tourism industries. However, despite the growing inclusion of sustainability initiatives in the bidding for and awarding of mega-events, there are still frequent protests and legal actions against host cities/nations and/or organizing committees that stem from a breach of community expectations of sustainability and/or breaches in statutory obligations concerning environmental protection in the development and staging of mega-sport events (Chappelet 2003; Dredge *et al*. 2010; Lowes 2004). Therefore, there is still a significant gap between the written commitment of host governments and organizing committees, and the actual implementation of environmentally responsible events.

The difficulties involved in hosting a sustainable event are amplified for developing nations, as sustainability initiatives of any kind are generally marginalized in the pursuit of economic growth. Brazil is now faced with this challenge on a scale never before seen. Within a two-year time frame, the country will host the two biggest sport events in the world: the 2014 FIFA World Cup and the 2016 Summer Olympic Games. Such complex tasks, to be implemented in a developing country that possesses a well-known history of corruption (Geddes and Ribeiro Neto 1992; Habib and Zurawicki 2006), need to be closely inspected and analysed if positive outcomes are to be achieved. This chapter investigates the main pressures and challenges faced by Brazil as a host nation in the planning of a sustainable event management during the 2014 FIFA World Cup and the 2016 Rio de Janeiro Summer Olympic Games. The main arguments of this chapter are the following: governance issues in relation to accountability underpin the implementation of other sustainability principles, particularly in the context of developing countries; governing sporting bodies and the government of Brazil focus excessively on matters of infrastructure for the event at the expense of greater economic, social and environmental issues; and the track record of Brazil and its hosting of large sporting events leads to a conclusion that there are significant lessons still to be learned if, indeed, the events are to live up to their green promises.

Sustainability and mega-sport events

The environmental impacts of mega-sport events are one of the newest concerns of event organizers, sponsors, environmentalists and citizens. The Olympic Games were one of the first events to be significantly scrutinized with respect to their environmental impacts, and the International Olympic Committee (IOC) was one of the first major sport organizations to include in their mission statement, the Olympic Charter, a commitment to environmental sustainability (IOC 2007). Such a move did not happen by chance, however. Global awareness of the impacts of development on non-renewable resources, and the consequent pressures from the wider community, gained momentum in the 1970s and governments worldwide started to officially discuss environmental sustainability. It was, however, the highly controversial operations of the 1992 Albertville Winter Olympic Games that triggered the changes in the IOC's official position with respect to the environment (Cantelon and Letters 2010) and, more broadly, in the practices utilized by the sport events industry. The 1992 Winter Games were considered an environmental disaster (Cantelon and Letters 2010), and the negative publicity generated by the environmental mismanagement of the event, together with the staging of the Rio de Janeiro Earth Summit in the same year, were significant catalysts for the substantial reform of IOC's policies. However, following the Albertville disaster, the IOC, one of the most influential transnational organizations in the sport events industry, chose to adopt a vision of sustainability that is limited to environmental protection. This narrow association is explicit in the Olympic Charter, where there is only one mention of sustainable development: 'the IOC's role is: ... to encourage and support a responsible concern for environmental issues, to promote sustainable development in sport and to require that the Olympic Games are held accordingly' (IOC 2007: 15). By adopting such a position, the IOC limited the capacity of the Olympic Games to promote a more holistic approach to sustainability. In following the Olympic Charter, Organizing Committees for the Olympic Games (OCOGs) may restrict their actions to the management of natural assets and overlook other important aspects in the development of sustainable events and, consequently, in the development of societies and human lives.

Within this context, there has been increased criticism within the academic and non-academic literature regarding the real sustainability of mega-events, particularly due to this narrow understanding of the concept of sustainability (Smith 2009). Critics have raised concerns over community displacement (Hall and Hodges 1996; Porter *et al.* 2009), the financial burdens being transferred to tax payers (Hall and Wilson 2011; Lee and Taylor 2006), the discontinuation of social projects (Lenskyj 2007), the uneven distribution of benefits within host communities (Gaffney 2010) and the use of facilities after the event (Hall and Wilson 2011; Hiller 2006). In this chapter, a broader framing of sustainability and environmental impacts is adopted. With the understanding that humans are a fundamental part of the natural environment, notions of sustainability and environmental impacts must necessarily address issues of social justice (The Earth Charter 2001). According to the UN document *Our Common Future* (Brundtland 1987: 3), it is 'futile to attempt to deal with environmental problems without a broader perspective that encompasses the factors underlying world poverty and international inequality'.

This understanding of sustainability and environmental impacts as inseparable from social and environmental justice and from the democratic access to goods and services leads to another important position adopted in this paper: that the notion of sustainability is not a universal concept and it cannot be exported from one place to another without localized interpretation. Strategies and approaches must be adapted to each locality to achieve sustainable outcomes (Dredge and Jamal 2011). There is a need, therefore, to question practices and solutions that are imported from the global north to the developing south, where a high proportion of the population is poor and live under different cultural systems. As Jamal, Everett and Dann (2003: 144) suggest, we must ask, 'what is being sustained, by whom and for whom? Who decides what sustainability means and entails, and who dictates how it should be achieved and evaluated?'

One last clarification must be made with respect to our understanding of sustainability. As will become clear later in the chapter, democracy and governance accountability underpins sustainability, particularly in developing countries. This is because, without political will and interconnected actions between different governmental agencies and departments, there can be no structured, unified strategy to achieve the common goal of sustainability (Brundtland 1987). If independent government actions are driven by an instrumental approach to sustainability, then social and environmental justice are at risk of not being prioritized, and the well-being of natural and human communities may be jeopardized (Jamal, Everett and Dann 2003). To this end, this chapter highlights some issues that Brazil faces in regards to its approach to sustainability in the hosting of the two aforementioned mega-sport events.

Research approach

This chapter works under the rationale that to develop a thorough critique of initiatives and management actions, it is useful that an *ex-ante* study be conducted to provide the basis for analysis (Schulenkorf 2009). Furthermore, following Getz's (2005) recommendation, if problems are identified early in the planning stages, intervention can be recommended and implemented, thus achieving the desirable link between research and practice. With this in mind, a case study approach was adopted to gain a deeper understanding of the problems and challenges Brazil is currently facing in planning and hosting sustainable mega-events.

According to Yin (1981: 59), the case study method is suitable when the investigator's main aim is to examine '(a) a contemporary phenomenon in its real-life context, especially when (b) the boundaries between phenomenon and context are not clearly evident'. Case studies are useful as a means to learn from particular experiences, and although context and contingencies will vary widely between cases, there are patterns of social behaviour that can be identified and used to inform the analysis of other cases (Flyvbjerg 2006). As Gerring (2007: 1) points out, 'sometimes, in-depth knowledge of an individual example is more helpful than fleeting knowledge about a larger number of examples. We gain better understanding of the whole by focusing on a key part.'

The two above-mentioned events are particularly interesting as both are major events of similar proportions, though significantly different in their breadth and underlining policy frameworks. The Summer Olympic Games are hosted by one city only, although sometimes including nearby towns or villages, and are held under the auspices of the IOC, an entity that has shown increasing commitment to sustainable practices but is still heavily criticized in terms of their implementation (Lenskyj 1998a, 1998b, 2008). The Football World Cup is usually hosted by one country with several cities serving as hosts of the tournament's games. The Fédération Internationale de Football Association (FIFA), the governing body of the Cup games, so far has not demonstrated a great commitment to environmental sustainability measures and their guidelines seem to be focused primarily on the technical capabilities of the Cup's hosts (see material provided in their official website: www.fifa.com). The following sections analyse some of the strategies and discourses used by the organising committees of these two events, as well as other governing bodies, as they relate to sustainability issues and the environment, in particular.

When exploring the possibilities of case study research, Yin (1981: 58) notes that case studies commonly use evidence from 'fieldwork, archival records, verbal reports, observations, or any combination of these'. Here, it is the combination of secondary data, reports, personal experiences and observations that form the material presented in this chapter. The analysis compared and contrasted the two events with reference to previous cases in Brazil's recent history of hosting mega-events, as well as national and international literature on the topic.

Publicly available bidding, budget and planning documents formed a significant part of the secondary data used here. These were sourced from the organizing committees' websites, from FIFA's and IOC's web pages, and/or from the websites of various Brazilian ministries and departments. Most of these documents are presented in English, as they are the official submissions to the international sport organizations. However, some other documents that are more specific and detailed, such as current budget plans and planning documents, were found only in Portuguese.

Also of significant value were government audits and minutes of official meetings. These data were collected using online searches in the archives and general areas of government websites, webpages of NGOs directly or indirectly involved with the events, and regulatory and fiscal agencies' websites in Brazil. Brazilian media releases and newspaper articles were also included in the analysis, thereby taking into consideration discussions that are current and in the public domain.

To build on previous examples of mega-events hosted in Brazil and to make the case study discussed in this chapter more relevant through the means of comparison, we will draw upon the experiences of the Pan American Games in Rio de Janeiro in 2007, particularly when discussing the 2016 Summer Olympic Games. It seems appropriate to highlight some of the problems faced by the prior host of this event to provide a thorough discussion of event sustainability.

The rest of this chapter explores the sustainability issues experienced by Rio de Janeiro as a host of a mega-sport event, the 2007 Pan American Games, and highlights through comparison some of the challenges the city is now facing to improve the socio-environmental outcomes of the 2016 Summer Olympic Games. Without attempting to present a full analysis of the impacts of the 2007 Pan American Games on Rio de Janeiro, this chapter draws upon significant research presented after the event that discusses some of the major issues that emerged in 2007 and contrasts these results with the documents presented by the bidding committee for the Olympic Games. It is important to note that the membership of the committees involved with the organization of the Rio de Janeiro 2007 Pan American Games and the Rio de Janeiro 2016 Summer Olympic Games is, unsurprisingly, similar, despite several allegations over corruption and the misuse of public money on that occasion.[1]

In the last section, the discussion about the 2014 FIFA World Cup presents the main pressures and challenges in staging mega-events in Brazil. This analysis leads to a greater understanding of the complexities involved in the development of strategies for the sustainability of large-scale events in nations that struggle with social (in)justice that, consequently, tend not to prioritize socio-environmental policy and practices.

The 2007 Rio de Janeiro Pan American Games and the 2016 Rio de Janeiro Olympic Games – lessons to be learned

Although unfamiliar to most countries outside of the Americas, the PanAmerican Games may be considered the major multi-sporting event on the American continent, attracting a significant number of tourists to the host country (Ministério do Turismo 2007). In 2007, over 5,500 athletes participated in the event in Rio de Janeiro, representing 42 of the continent's 59 nations and participating in more than 300 competitive events. The Pan American Games in Rio de Janeiro aimed to test and showcase Rio's ability to host a mega-sport event with a format similar to that of the Olympic Games to present a stronger case to the IOC and to the Brazilian community during the bidding process for the 2016 Summer Olympic Games. The event did indeed pave the way for Rio de Janeiro, and in October 2009, the city was selected to host the XXXI Olympic Summer Games.

The initial promises and legacy discourses of the Pan American Games in Rio de Janeiro failed to translate into sustainable practices both during and after the event and, therefore, into tangible sustainable legacies. Araújo, Rezende and Leitão (2008) focus their analysis on the transportation legacies of the event and conclude that major infrastructure developments promised by event organizers, such as the construction of new subway stations to link different areas of the city as well as major road plans to improve transportation linkages and infrastructure, were not delivered and were, after the event was finished, automatically transferred to the development plans for the 2016 Olympic Games (Rio2016 2009). The traffic congestion and chaos experienced during and after the Pan American Games were due to unfinished infrastructure works, and the promised positive environmental impacts associated with a cleaner and more efficient transportation system were not delivered (Rezende and Leitão 2006; Araújo, Rezende and Leitão 2008). This has become a significant negative environmental legacy from these 2007 Games.

Another important issue raised by Araújo, Rezende and Leitão (2008), Gaffney (2010) and Sánchez and Bienenstein (2009) involves the geographical distribution of benefits to the host population through the development of new infrastructure and facilities. From the information provided by the organizing committee in the bid book (Rio2016 2009), it appears that Rio de Janeiro is prepared to follow the same strategy of creating what Gaffney (2010) labelled 'sportive constellations', or pockets of sport activity, dispersed across the city. As can be seen in the two official maps (provided in the official bid books: Rio2016 2009; Rio2007 2007), the competitions for the 2016 Summer Olympic Games will be held in the same four areas of the city as the 2007 Pan American Games. Unless there is improvement in the transportation links between these locations, the potential benefits created by the Olympic Games will be as disappointing as they were for the 2007 Pan American Games (Araújo, Rezende and Leitão 2008; Gaffney 2010). Facilitating the efficient movement of people during and after the event is vitally important in addressing a range of sustainability issues, including energy consumption and carbon emissions, which will, in turn, improve the Game's environmental scorecard. At present, construction is under way to improve Rio's subway system and implement a system of rapid buses (Bus Rapid Transit lines) to tackle this issue, but there is, as of yet, no official guarantee of their likely completion for the 2016 Olympic Games.

More significantly, for the 2016 Olympic Games, the rationale behind the locations for the venues and competitions was significantly dictated by the availability of pleasant natural surroundings in an attempt to showcase the best of Rio and, consequently, attract tourists and international media interest (Rio2016 2009). The potential for place promotion is a recognized benefit of hosting major events and is driven by neoliberal ideologies that suggest cities need to compete on the world stage for brand/place recognition to benefit from ongoing post-event business (Dredge *et al.* 2010; Hall and Wilson 2011). On another occasion, we have argued that these decisions were camouflaged as Rio de Janeiro's sustainability strategy in the bidding documents, as if being physically close to beautiful beaches and forests meant more environment-friendly practices in event planning and management (Reis and DaCosta 2011). The major problem, however, is that the sustainability talk in official documents both of the organizing committee for the 2016 Games and the IOC is elusive and unclear, leaving a considerable margin for interpretation and manoeuvrability (Holden, MacKenzie and VanWynsberghe 2008). The sustainability section of the contract involving the two organizations is a good example of such elusiveness:

> The City, the NOC[2] and the OCOG undertake to carry out their obligations and activities under this Contract in a manner which embraces the concept of sustainable development, and which serves to promote the protection of the environment. In particular, the concept of sustainable development shall address the legacy of the Games, including the concerns for post-Olympic use of venues and other facilities and infrastructures.
>
> (IOC 2009:19)

Clearly, the inclusion of such a clause in the contract between the IOC and the Organizing Committee is a step forward, particularly when compared with arrangements between FIFA and the host cities of the 2014 World Cup. Nevertheless, it is still a weakly worded requirement that does not place clear and decisive responsibility on the host cities to act firmly and consistently towards defined measures of sustainability in the planning, management and execution of the event. The contract is binding, but because the requirements are not clearly defined in the document, or elsewhere, it is up to the host country to define the measures and strategies to be adopted and to determine to what extent they will be carried forward in the planning and staging of the Games. It is not the responsibility or the domain of the IOC, although some authors have argued that these transnational organizations have a global environmental responsibility to provide stewardship and, therefore, demand action from event organizers (Lenskyj 1998b). To this end, recent legislation has been approved in Brazil giving ample power to the IOC and to FIFA to influence and demand changes in the construction works related to their respective events, and these demands will be treated confidentially; that is, no public audits of public infrastructure works, and such works are able to surpass initial budget proposals. Although this is an extremely contentious change in current practices of public money administration, there is a chance for the events' governing bodies to intervene to ensure sustainable practices. However, this scenario is also highly unlikely, as the obvious motivations of these agencies are predominantly to ensure the timely development of facilities and to ensure a profitable event.

In the case of the Pan American Games, even though there were no preconditions similar to the IOC requirements, a number of environmental laws were relaxed to facilitate and enable infrastructure development in certain areas that were of interest to the Games (Behnken and Godoy 2009; Benedicto 2009; Mascarenhas and Borges 2009). The elusive nature of these documents with respect to their sustainability goals may, therefore, allow for the same problems to be repeated in 2016. So far, there is little evidence to suggest that negative sustainability outcomes will not be repeated in Rio.

The 2014 FIFA World Cup and challenges for Brazil

In 2014, Brazil will host the largest single-sport event in the world, the FIFA Football World Cup. Together with the Olympic Games, the FIFA World Cup has been considered the pinnacle of mega-sport events (Florek, Breibarth and Conejo 2008). It is the most important football event worldwide and is hosted by a different country every four years. Brazil hosted the event once in 1950, and it is the country that has won the most cups and has played in more finals than any other country in the event's history.[3] Due to the significance of football to the Brazilian culture (Agostino 2002; Soares 2003), this is certainly the most anticipated sporting event since the Cup's inception in 1930. Its economic significance has been extensively explored (Baade and Matheson 2004; Horne and Manzenreite 2004), and its estimated economic contribution has been shown to surpass the US$ billion dollar mark. In contrast to other mega-sport events, such as the Olympic Games, where activities and games are mostly concentrated in one city and possibly a few satellite locations within the same region, the Football World Cup is hosted by a nation, and therefore, games take place and athletes' venues are located in several different cities within the country. In fact, previous events have also been co-hosted among neighbouring countries.

In the case of Brazil, due to recent changes in FIFA rules, 12 cities, instead of the usual 8 to 10, will host the games of the 2014 Cup over a period of four weeks during the Brazilian winter season. The elected cities are widely dispersed across the country, a situation that heightens the complexities of organizing procedures and policies that are to be applied and adopted by all localities. The matter becomes even more complex when the number of different government bodies is taken into account. The list comprises 12 local governments, 12 state governments (each host city is located in a different state), the national government and the committees created within different ministries to oversee certain aspects of the event. There are other important stakeholders involved in the decision-making processes, particularly the Local Organizing Committee (COL) and FIFA itself. Within this context, it is important to note that in Brazil, a democratic country, there are 27 different political parties, and unlike other presidential systems, most political parties do have seats/representatives in the different levels of government. Therefore, local and state governments are often administered by different political groups and are governed by often disparate political ideals and agendas. How to align these differences into one integrated environmental strategy is obviously a complex task for the agencies involved in the hosting of the event. This must be kept in mind when discussing the intricacies involved in the implementation of sustainable practices for the event.

The next section discusses three themes that are crucial in the analysis of the official discourse and the current practices in the planning for the 2014 FIFA

World Cup: governance issues and the prioritization of (economic) development as part of sport and mega-events, the role of natural settings and nature-based tourism in the sustainability strategy of events, and the relationship between infrastructure development and social sustainability.

The official discourse and current practices in planning for 2014

In June 2010, four years before the event, the Ministry of the Environment created a working group to 'propose and coordinate actions for the environmental sustainability of the 2014 FIFA World Cup' (Diário Oficial da União, n.223, 15/06/2010). However, this group has an advisory responsibility only and does not have the power to legislate or demand actions from the organizing committee or other government bodies involved in hosting the games. The working group has the task to develop a working plan that includes a summary of previous environmental strategies used by host countries to inform practices to be used in Brazil; a list of protected areas (regional and national parks/reserves) within close access to the host cities to be prioritized in terms of their potential to attract tourists/visitors during the event period; and a list of projects that must be scrutinized with respect to environmental assessments. This plan has not been released to the public at the time of writing. Furthermore, the internal deliberations and the outcomes of the working group illustrate the lack of transparency that characterizes this process.

Following the establishment of the working group, in July 2010, the Tourism and Sports Commission within the House of Representatives held a public meeting to discuss the Green Cup, the term currently used to highlight the efforts being made to produce an environmentally sustainable FIFA World Cup. During the proceedings, the president of the commission stated that, according to the Ministry of Sport, the federal government's position with respect to a Green Cup refers to stadia having environmental certifications, public transport being prioritized, the use of bio fuel, the availability of products with the organic label, and the promotion of ecotourism. It is significant that the social pillar of sustainability is completely absent from the discussions, and therefore, important socio-environmental questions, such as the relocation of entire communities to provide the necessary space for the construction of facilities and venues and the impact of these constructions on the social, cultural and physical environments of the region, are ignored (Porter *et al.* 2009).

More alarming is the statement by the president of the Commission that 'the 2014 FIFA World Cup does not have the duty to solve the tourism, the social inclusion or the sustainability problems of the country. The World Cup's mission in Brazil is to put on football games and, if possible, have Brazil be the winner'[4] (Câmara dos Deputados 2010: 1). Indeed, it is unrealistic to expect that any event, be it a mega-sport event or any other, has the power to solve the problems of an entire country. However, media coverage of the bidding process and general advocates for Brazil's candidature to host the 2014 FIFA World Cup have repeatedly argued how this event can be a major catalyst for significant changes in the country. Comments in the media such as, 'This golden opportunity for the development of the country comes 64 years after Brazil hosted its first and only FIFA World Cup' (O Globo, 24/10/2008) and the government's official statement below highlight the recurrent emphasis on a vast legacy that will reach the entire population.

> More than a big party, the World Cup in Brazil will bring important benefits to the population [...] not only through the football stadia, which will become modern, comfortable and safer, but also in airports, ports, hotel industry and public transport, that will be all enhanced to operate with more efficiency and speed.
>
> (Ministério do Esporte 2011a)

The president's statement oversimplifies the matter and seems to ignore the prevalent governmental and media discourse around the legacies of mega-sport events:

> Mega sport events are regarded as a catalyst for implementing investment plans that have the aim to improve infrastructure and the living conditions of a society. The FIFA World Cup is, therefore, more than organising football games. The country embraced this task understanding its strategic character to consolidate a long-term economic growth perspective, having as the starting point the good economic position enjoyed by the country at present.
>
> (Ministério do Esporte 2011b)

The Tourism and Sports Commission's president's message that the main aim and responsibility of the organizing committee and other major players is to put on a great show and to make the population happy by having their country win the sought-after Cup contradicts the legacy discourse present in most official documents, as obvious in the quote above. Her statement aligns well, however, with the political perspective of '*panis et circenses*' (bread and circus). Such a perspective uses the euphoria of entertainment provided to the masses by a popular event to mask social injustices, inequalities and other social urban problems (Waitt 2008). In Brazil, football games, in particular, have been repeatedly associated with the 'bread and circus' political agenda (Pecenin 2008; Soares Filho 2010).

Another aspect of the involvement of the Ministry of the Environment with the 2014 FIFA World Cup is the concentrated effort in promoting the national parks and conservation areas as destinations for the sport tourists visiting the country and travelling around the different regions to watch the games. The initiatives align well with the government's proposition that ecotourism is one of the main pillars for a 'Green Cup'. Investments in recreation facilities and basic management infrastructure in national parks is not only necessary but long-awaited by outdoor recreation participants and general visitors to conservation areas in the country (Lima, Ribeiro and Gonçalves 2005). However, it seems naive and inefficient to build a strategy of sustainability around promoting visitation to national parks only. Even though showcasing the natural wonders of the country might stimulate more environmentally friendly behaviours from tourists and from the local population or stimulate conscientious nature-based tourism development in the country (Ceballos-Lascuráin 1996), a strategy that relies on ecotourism promotion as one of the main drivers for sustainability seems superficial and not focused on the broader concept of hosting sustainable events. Such a position from the Ministry of Tourism confirms those findings from research in other parts of the world that indicate government organizations emphasize economic development, particularly during large-scale events, at the expense of social and environmental sustainability imperatives (Dredge *et al.* 2010).

Furthermore, environmentalists are concerned that great amounts of public money will be spent on facilities that over-commercialize the conservation areas and transform public open spaces into enclaves built for a minority who can afford to pay for access to public conservation land and enjoy commercial services during their visit (Curi, Knijnik and Mascarenhas 2011; Mascarenhas and Borges 2009). Rather than promoting positive environmental behaviour, these issues, in effect, pose more problems for the environment as traditional users are displaced due to a political agenda that prioritizes economic development and image-building over social and ecological justice (Brechin *et al.* 2003; Callicot 2008; Geisler 2003). The Brazilian and the international literature on this topic has repeatedly emphasized the negative consequences of the displacement of traditional owners/users and the over-commercialization of natural resources to the natural environment (Diegues 1998, 2001; Jamal, Everett and Dann 2003; Krueger 2009; Spinola 2006). This political agenda is evident also in other significant environmental issues in Brazil. For example, the international media have criticized Brazil because it has relaxed laws on deforestation and provided amnesties for previous environmental crimes (The Independent, 26 May 2011), an action that symbolizes the lack of political commitment toward addressing environmental issues in Brazil in recent times.

Another important point that must be addressed with respect to Brazil's strategy for a 'Green Cup' is the stadia infrastructure. Brazil is constructing six new world-class stadia for the 2014 FIFA World Cup, and six of the remaining stadia will be, or are already, in the process of being completely renovated to meet FIFA requirements. FIFA requirements are based on a standard that fits developed countries and Western cultures, but they are not necessarily ideal for economies of developing nations where poverty rates are high and consumer power is reduced (Curi, Knijnik and Mascarenhas 2011). Bale argues that the construction of stadia under these international requirements fits a conformist model that is characterized by five attributes:

> (a) the standardized values inherent in internationalized, globally televized, synthetic entertainment; (b) the gigantism reflected in the formlessness and lack of human scale [. . .] of proposed mega stadia; (c) uniformity of design in international styles of stadium architecture; (d) the stadium as part of an entertainment district, resulting from its purpose of attracting outsiders ('other-directedness'); and (e) the tendency towards both futurism in some cases and museumization in others.
>
> (Bale 1993: 41, as cited in Curi, Knijnik and Mascarenhas 2011:146)

The construction of these sites of luxury that fit the conformist model proposed by Bale exacerbate the social gap existent in developing nations such as Brazil and, literally, exclude the masses from enjoying the event from within. In research conducted during the Pan American Games in Rio de Janeiro in 2007, Curi, Knijnik and Mascarenhas (2011) highlighted the contradictions posed by this sort of approach to developing stadia for world-class mega-sports events in developing countries. The authors revealed that the demands posed by FIFA, the IOC and the Pan American Sport Organization to extend VIP and press areas in the stadia were implemented at the expense of general spectator seating. This privileges the elite and the outside consumer (through television broadcasting) over the local populace who could not afford to pay the high ticket prices associated with attendance and, therefore, do not fit in in the luxurious environment created inside the stadium.

The consequence of creating elite sporting and entertainment spaces in countries where a significant proportion of the population is poor is that this infrastructure will become either a collection of white elephants, empty and under-utilized (Mangan 2008), or they will quickly be degraded to fit the norm of the local society who will eventually need to pay for and make use of the facilities. In fact, apart from one of the four big stadia constructed for the 2007 Rio de Janeiro Pan American Games, all of the other stadia are currently being under-utilized or have been degraded. The promises made by the Pan American Games Organizing Committee, the Brazilian Olympic Committee and the local and state governments during the bidding process to make these facilities, centres for sport practice and developments for marginalized communities are yet to be fulfilled (Araújo, Rezende and Leitão 2008; Mascarenhas and Borges 2009; TCMRJ 2009).

Conclusions

The aim of this chapter was to reflect on the issues, pressures and challenges faced by Brazil in hosting green and sustainable events for the 2014 FIFA World Cup and the 2016 Rio de Janeiro Summer Olympic Games. The rationale behind this review was to provide an *ex-ante* critical discussion of the issues associated with the planning and staging of these two mega-events and determine whether they provide their host cities, and Brazil as a whole, with positive sustainable legacies. Significantly, our approach to environmentally sound events incorporates the notion of social justice and contends that environmental issues are also social and that the only possible way of achieving true sustainability is through practices that benefit the community at large, particularly the economically and socially marginalized.

Legacies from mega-sport events have been defined as 'planned and unplanned, positive and negative, intangible and tangible structures created through a sport event that remain after the event' (Gratton and Preuss, 2008: 1924). However, the interpretation of what these structures are and how they can be created to produce sustainable legacies varies enormously between events and organizers. For FIFA, the main legacy derived from the 2014 World Cup in Brazil will relate to the construction of state-of-the-art football stadia and to investment in transport and accommodation, as is stated in the legacy session of their inspection report (FIFA 2007). Not surprisingly, the Brazilian authorities have not yet demonstrated a firm commitment to delivering an event that embraces the three pillars of sustainability by focusing not only on developing infrastructure, as highlighted by FIFA, but also on environmentally sound, socially appropriate and economically viable practices.

It is apparent that event-governing bodies, such as FIFA, the IOC and governments, be they local or national, that bid for and support the hosting of mega-events are guided by a Western economic development philosophy that uses these events as neoliberal tools for growth (Hall and Wilson 2011). As a consequence, priorities are subverted and instead of public money being spent in education, health and environmental conservation, it is spent in stadia construction and other arguably superfluous investments that will benefit mostly the upper classes. The perspective of legacy underlying FIFA's and IOC's statements is Eurocentric and overlooks pressing social matters present in developing nations, such as the need for social and environmental justice (Ngonyama 2010). Without a firm focus on social matters, mega-events held in countries such as Brazil will fail to properly address environmental issues in a sustainable way.

This chapter has discussed the issues associated with Brazil's sustainability promises. The last example of a mega-event hosted in the country, the 2007 Pan American Games in Rio de Janeiro, highlights how environmental commitments were forgotten and not implemented. Within this context and based on the actions observed thus far to promote the sustainability of the two mega-events, it is crucial that the local communities, and Brazilian society in general, are properly informed and, consequently, able to actively engage in decision-making to induce sustainable development and create a positive legacy for the whole population.

References

Agostino, G. (2002) *Vencer ou Morrer: Futebol, Geopolítica e Identidade Nacional*. Rio de Janeiro: Mauad.

Araújo, S. D., Rezende, V. F. and Leitão, G. (2008) Impactos dos XV Jogos Pan-Americanos de 2007 na Barra da Tijuca e Baixada de Jacarepaguá, cidade do Rio de

Janeiro. *Proceedings of Nutau 2008. Espaço Sustentável: Inovações em edifícios e cidades*. São Paulo: Nutau/USP.

Baade, R. A. and Matheson, V. A. (2004) The quest for the Cup: Assessing the economic impact of the World Cup. *Regional Studies*, 38: 343–54.

Behnken, L. M. and Godoy, A. (2009) O relacionamento entre as esferas pública e privada nos Jogos Pan-Americanos de 2007: Os casos da Marina da Glória e do Estádio de Remo da Lagoa. *Esporte e Sociedade*, 4: 1–36.

Benedicto, D. B. D. M. (2009) Desafiando o coro dos contentes: Vozes dissonantes no processo de implementação dos Jogos Pan-Americanos, Rio 2007. *Esporte e Sociedade*, 4: 1–29.

Brechin, S. R., Wilshusen, P. R., Fortwangler, C. L. and West, P. C. (eds) (2003) *Contested Nature*. Albany: State University of New York Press.

Brundtland, G. (1987) *Our Common Future: The World Commission on Environment and Development*. New York: Oxford University Press.

Callicott, J. B. (2008) Contemporary criticism of the received wilderness idea, in M.P. Nelson and J.B. Callicott (eds) The wilderness debate rages on. Athens: The University of Georgia Press.

Câmara dos Deputados, Brasil (2010) *Audiência Pública N. 0961/10: Discussão sobre as providências relativas à organização da Copa do Mundo de 2014 – Copa Verde: o desafio da sustentabilidade*. Comissão de Turismo e Desporto, Câmara dos Deputados. Retrieved from www2.camara.gov.br/atividade-legislativa/comissoes/comissoes-permanentes/ctd/notas-taquigraficas

Cantelon, H. and Letters, M. (2000) The making of the IOC environmental policy as the third dimension of the Olympic Movement. *International Review for the Sociology of Sport*, 35: 294–308.

Cashman, R. and Hughes, A. (eds) (1998) *Staging the Olympics: The event and its impact*. Sydney: University of New South Wales Press.

Ceballos-Lascuráin, H. (1996) *Tourism, Ecotourism and Protected Areas: The State of Nature-based Tourism around the World and Guidelines for its Development*. Cambridge: IUCN.

Chappelet, J.-L. (2003) The legacy of the Olympic Winter Games: An overview, in M. Moragas, C. Kennett and N. Puig (eds) *The Legacy of the Olympic Games: 1984-2000*. Lausanne: International Olympic Committee.

Collins, A., Jones, C. and Munday, M. (2009) Assessing the environmental impacts of mega sporting events: two options?. *Tourism Management*, 30: 828–37.

Curi, M., Knijnik, J. and Mascarenhas, G. (2011) The Pan American Games in Rio de Janeiro 2007: Consequences of a sport mega-event on a BRIC country. *International Review for the Sociology of Sport*, 46: 140–56.

Diegues, A. C. (1998) *O Mito Moderno da Natureza Intocada*. São Paulo: Hucitec.

Diegues, A. C. (2001) As áreas naturais protegidas, o turismo e as populações tradicionais, in C.M.T. Serrano and H. Bruhns (eds) *Viagens à Natureza*. São Paulo: Papirus.

Dredge, D. and Jamal, T. (2011) Editorial: Certification and indicators. *Tourism Recreation Research*, 36 (3): 203–4.

Dredge, D., Ford, E.-J., Lamont, M. J., Phi, G., Whitford, M. and Wynn-Moylan, P. (2010) Event governance: The rhetoric and reality of the World Rally Championship, Northern Rivers, NSW. *CAUTHE 2010: Challenge the Limits*. Hobart, Tasmania: University of Tasmania, February 2010.

The Earth Charter (2001) Earth Charter International Secretariat. Available at www.earthcharter.org.

FIFA (2007) *Brazil Bid: Inspection Report for the 2014 FIFA World Cup*. Zurich: FIFA.

Florek, M., Breitbarth, T. and Conejo, F. (2008) Mega event = mega impact? Travelling fans' experience and perceptions of the 2006 FIFA World Cup host nation. *Journal of Sport and Tourism*, 13: 199–219.

Flyvbjerg, B. (2006) Five misunderstandings about case-study research. *Qualitative Inquiry*, 12: 219–45.

Gaffney, C. (2010) Mega-events and socio-spatial dynamics in Rio de Janeiro, 1919–2016. *Journal of Latin American Geography*, 9: 7–29.

Geddes, B. and Ribeiro Neto, A. (1992) Institutional sources of corruption in Brazil. *Third World Quaterly*, 13: 641–61.

Geisler, C. (2003) A new kind of trouble: Evictions in Eden. *International Social Science Journal*, 55: 69–78.

Gerring, J. (2007) *Case Study Research: Principles and Practices*. Cambridge: Cambridge University Press.

Getz, D. (2005) *Event Management and Event Tourism*, Elmsford: Cognizant Communication Corporation.

Gratton, C. and Preuss, H. (2008) Maximizing Olympic impacts by building up legacies. *International Journal of the History of Sport*, 25: 1922–38.

Habib, M. and Zurawicki, L. (2006) Corruption in large developing economies: the case of Brazil, Russia, India and China, in S.C. Jain (ed.) *Emerging Economies and Transformation in International Business: Brazil, Russia, India and China*. Northampton: Edward Elgar Publishing, pp. 452–77.

Hall, C., and Hodges, J. (1996) The party's great, but what about the hangover? The housing and social impacts of mega-events with special reference to the 2000 Sydney Olympics. *Festival Management and Event Tourism*, 4: 13–20.

Hall, C.M. and Wilson, S. (2011) Neoliberal urban entrepreneurial agendas, Dunedin Stadium and the Rugby World Cup: Or 'If you don't have a stadium, you don't have a future', in D. Dredge and J. Jenkins (eds) *Stories of Practice: Tourism Policy and Planning*. Farnham: Ashgate, pp. 133–52.

Hiller, H. (2006) Post-event outcomes and the post-modern turn: The Olympics and urban transformation. *European Sport Management Quarterly*, 6: 317–32.

Holden, M., MacKenzie, J. and VanWynsberghe, R. (2008) Vancouver's promise of the world's first sustainable Olympic Games. *Environment and Planning C: Government and Policy*, 26: 882–905.

Horne, J. D. and Manzenreite, W. (2004) Accounting for mega-events: Forecast and actual impacts of the 2002 Football World Cup finals on the host countries Japan/Korea. *International Review for the Sociology of Sport*, 39: 187–203.

IOC (2007) *Olympic Charter*. Lausanne: International Olympic Committee.

IOC (2009) *Host City Contract: Games of the XXXI Olympiad in 2016*. Lausanne: International Olympic Committee.

Jamal, T., Everett, J. and Dann, G. M. S. (2003) Ecological rationalization and performative resistance in natural area destinations. *Tourist Studies*, 3: 143–69.

Krueger, L. (2009) Protected areas and human displacement: improving the interface between policy and practice. *Conservation and Society*, 7 (1): 21–5.

Lee, C. and Taylor, T. (2006) Critical reflections on the economic impact assessment of a mega-event: The case of 2002 FIFA World Cup. *Tourism Management*, 26, 595–603.

Lenskyj, H.J. (1998a) *Green Games or Empty Promises? Environmental Issues and Sydney 2000*. London, Ontario: International Centre for Olympic Studies, The University of Western Ontario, pp. 173–180.

Lenskyj, H. J. (1998b) Sport and corporate environmentalism. *International Review for the Sociology of Sport*, 33: 341–54.

Lenskyj, H. J. (2007) *The best Olympics ever?: Social impacts of Sydney 2000*. Albany: State University of New York Press.

Lenskyj, H. J. (2008) *Olympic Industry Resistance: Challenging Olympic Power and Propaganda*. Albany: State University of New York Press.

Lima, G. S., Ribeiro, G. A. and Gonçalves, W. (2005) Avaliação da efetividade de manejo das unidades de conservação de proteção integral em Minas Gerais. *Revista Árvore*, 29: 647–53.

Lowes, M. (2004) Neoliberal power politics and the controversial siting of the Australian Grand Prix Motorsport event in an urban park. *Society and Leisure*, 27: 69–88.

Mangan, J. A. (2008) Prologue: Guarantees of global goodwill: Post-Olympic Legacies – Too many limping white elephants?. *International Journal of the History of Sport*, 25: 1869–83.

Mascarenhas, G. and Borges, F. C. D. S. (2009) Entre o empreendedorismo urbano e a gestão democrática da cidade: Dilemas e impactos do Pan-2007 na Marina da Glória. *Esporte e Sociedade*, 4:1–26.

Ministério do Esporte (2011a) Copa 2014. www.esporte.gov.br/assessoriaEspecialFutebol/copa2014/default.jsp

Ministério do Esporte (2011b) Primeiro balanço da Copa 2014 – Janeiro 2011. Available at: www.esporte.gov.br/arquivos/assessoriaEspecialFutebol/copa2014/balancoCopa2014.pdf

Ministério do Turismo (2007) *Movimentação Econômica dos Jogos Pan-Americanos*. www.turismo.gov.br/dadosefatos

Ngonyama, P. (2010) The 2010 FIFA World Cup: critical voices from below. *Soccer and Society*, 11: 168–80.

Pecenin, M. F. (2008) Discurso, futebol e identidade nacional na Copa de 1998. *Cadernos de Semiótica Aplicada*, 6: 1–19.

Porter, L., Jaconelli, M., Cheyne, J., Eby, D. and Wagenaar, H. (2009) Planning displacement: The real legacy of major sporting events; 'Just a person in a wee flat': Being displaced by the Commonwealth Games in Glasgow's East End; Olympian master planning in London closing ceremonies: How law, policy and the Winter Olympics are displacing an inconveniently located low-income community in Vancouver; Recovering public ethos: Critical analysis for policy and planning. *Planning Theory and Practice*, 10: 395–418.

Preuss, H. (2000) *Economics of the Olympic Games. Hosting the Games 1972–2000*. Sydney: Walla Walla Press.

Reis, A.C. and DaCosta, L. P. (2011) Is the booming sustainability of Olympic and Paralympic Games here to stay? From an environment-based procedure to a dubious overall legacy, in G. Savery and K. Gilbert (eds) *Sustainability and Sport*. Champaign: Common Ground Publishing.

Rezende, V. F. and Leitão, G. A. (2006). Barra da Tijuca e Baixada de Jacarepaguá: razões e impactos das intervenções públicas para a realização dos XV Jogos Pan-Americanos de 2007, na cidade do Rio de Janeiro. *Proceedings of the 52nd Congreso Internacional de Americanistas, Simpósio A Arquitetura da Cidade nas Américas*. Sevilha 2006. Florianópolis, Núcleo de Investigação em Conformação e Morfologia em Arquitetura e Urbanismo. Available at www.pgau-cidade.ufsc.br/ica52/

Rio2007 (2007) *Official Report of the XV Pan American Games and the III Parapan American Games Rio 2007*. Available at www.cob.org.br/sobre_cob/documentos_rio2007.asp.

Rio2016 (2009) *Candidature File for Rio de Janeiro to Host the 2016 Olympic and Paralympic Games*. Available at www.rio2016.org.br/

Sánchez, F. and Bienenstein, G. (2009) Jogos Pan-Americans Rio 2007: um balanço multidimensional. *Proceedings of the XXVIII International Congress of the Latin American Studies Association: Rethinking Inequalities*. Rio de Janeiro: Latin American Studies Association.

Schulenkorf, N. (2009) An ex ante framework for the strategic study of social utility of sport events. *Tourism and Hospitality Research*, 9: 120–31.

Smith, A. (2009) Theorising the relationship between major sports events and social sustainability. *Journal of Sport and Tourism*, 14: 109–20.

Soares, A. J. G. (2003) Futebol brasileiro e sociedade: a interpretação culturalista de Gilberto Freyre, in P. Alabarces (ed.) *Futbologías. Fútbol, identidad y violencia en América Latina*. Buenos Aires: CLACSO, pp. 145–62.

Soares Filho, S. (2010) Brasil, a continuidade da política do pão e circo ou é só impressão?. *Revista Estudos Jurídicos UNESP*, 14: 335–58.

Spinola, C. D. A. (2006) O ecoturismo, o desenvolvimento local e a conservação da natureza em espaços naturais protegidos: Objetivos conflitantes? *Revista de Desenvolvimento Econômico*, 8: 50–59.

TCMRJ – Tribunal de Contas do Município do Rio de Janeiro (2009) *Auditoria Legado dos Jogos Pan-Americanos – Rio 2007*. Rio de Janeiro: Secretaria de Controle Externo, Secretaria Municipal de Fazenda.

Waitt, G. (2003) Social impacts of the Sydney Olympics. *Annals of Tourism Research*, 30: 194–215.

Waitt, G. (2008) Urban festivals: geographies of hype, helplessness and hope. *Geography Compass*, 2: 513–37.

Yin, R. (1981) The case study crisis: Some answers. *Administrative Science Quarterly*, 26: 58–65.

Notes

1 Media articles presenting and discussing some cases of corruption and misuse of public money can be found, for instance, in *O Globo* 14/17/2008, 25/09/2008, 02/06/2011; The *New York Times*, 22/05/2007.

2 National Olympic Committee.

3 Five World Cups and seven World Cup Finals. Germany has also played in seven World Cup finals.

4 It is significant to note that, as mentioned before, football is one of the greatest passions of Brazilians, and it is an important part of Brazil's national identity.

6 Challenges and opportunities for small businesses in and around Brazilian protected areas

Paulo Jordão de O. C. Fortes and José Antonio Puppim de Oliveira

Introduction

This chapter discusses some of the challenges associated with management of small tourism businesses located in proximity to protected areas in Brazil. Improved management could be the key to local sustainability, making businesses viable, generating more jobs and providing better incomes and quality of life to communities. In addition, these communities may then support protected areas, rather than oppose them. This chapter analyses a case study comprising a cluster of small and medium enterprises (SMEs) around the Serra da Capivara National Park in southern Piauí state in the northeast of Brazil. The park was created in 1979 and became a UNESCO World Heritage Site in 1991 due to its unique landscape and the presence of innumerable prehistoric artifacts and paintings. Since the park was established, tourism has become a key source of income for the local population, turning initial community resistance to the creation of the national park into support. The banning of other traditional and culturally embedded resource uses such as hunting and timber gathering has been a source of conflict between the local community and the American Men's Museum Foundation (FUMDHAM), the organization that manages the park. Most of the conflicts were sorted out by the creation of new community ventures such as apiculture, goat and art craft co-operatives directly outside of the park (Silva and Mota 2002). Once business ventures fail to generate income and to provide jobs to the local population, the locals return to exploit the natural resources available in the park, undertaking destructive activities to provide for their livelihoods.

This chapter examines the development of a ceramic art craft co-operative around the Serra da Capivara Park that is represented by Serra da Capivara Ceramic (SCC), a small enterprise located in the municipality of Coronel José Dias, which has 4,506 inhabitants (IBGE 2011). Most of the problems encountered in Serra da Capivara Ceramic are also typical in the other SMEs in the region and other tourism clusters in Brazil. However, SCC overcame many of the obstacles that SMEs suffer and became a successful local enterprise. Thus, the SCC case can provide interesting lessons for other SMEs in similar tourism clusters in Brazil and other countries, particularly those in and around protected areas.

Tourism, protected areas and small enterprises

Tourism has become one of the driving forces in the creation of protected areas in Brazil and in different parts of the world, both to promote tourism and protect the environment from tourism's unmanaged negative impacts (Ceballos-Lascurain 1996; Puppim de Oliveira 2005a, 2008a). Tourism management within and around protected areas must maintain a balance between the environmental resources, which attract tourists and economic activities. One of the main challenges in creating and enforcing regulations on protected areas, particularly in developing countries such as Brazil, is obtaining support from local communities and authorities (Puppim de Oliveira 2005b). Many communities often develop economic activities that rely on the environmental resources within the protected area, such as the collection of plants, hunting, mining and agricultural development. Tourism-related activities in and around protected areas can become a new source of sustainable income for the communities. These communities would then be viewed as the guardians of the management of the environmental resources and protected area guidelines rather than environmental offenders. However, there are several obstacles in generating economic opportunities that benefit communities within and around protected areas, particularly when the tourism activity is just beginning. These obstacles range from the low returns from the developing tourism activity to lack of local control and empowerment because outsiders with more capital and skills control tourism businesses (Lerner and Haber 2001; Morrison and Teixeira 2004).

Many of the economic activities for local communities that are generated from tourism in protected areas located in developing countries are led by SMEs, both in the formal and informal sectors, such as guides, small restaurants, shops, art craft production companies and accommodation facilities. On one hand, the small scale of the business poses less threat to the environment (large-scale projects and business can overshoot the carrying capacity of the area). SMEs are easily developed by local communities, as they require less capital to begin. On the other hand, small firms pose a management challenge, as small local entrepreneurs in developing countries often lack familiarity with the tourism activities and the skills to manage businesses effectively and efficiently so as to generate economic and social benefits. Poor infrastructure and low education of the tourism workforce affect service quality, which also contributes to the challenges.

Case study background

The Serra da Capivara National Park guards one of the largest concentrations of archaeological sites in the Americas (Arruda 1993). It encompasses over 400 sites and more than 130,000 paintings, making the park a valuable historical resource (Guidon 1997). Nevertheless, it officially receives fewer tourists than Sete Cidades National Park, which is also located in Piauí state and is ranked as Brazil's smallest national park with fewer attractions but better connected by different kinds of transportation (Table 6.1).

Table 6.1 Annual tourist visitation in Serra de Capivara and Sete Cidades National Parks, 2000–2005

	2000	*2001*	*2002*	*2003*	*2004*	*2005*
Serra da Capivara National Park	n/a	5,274	3,014	3,908	7,107	6,938
Sete Cidades National Park	17,641	16,930	21,566	21,212	17,951	17,062

Source: Logbooks from both parks

Table 6.1 shows that the Serra da Capivara Park receives between 3,000 and 7,000 tourists per year, supporting a tourism cluster of SMEs comprising three hotels, ten hostels, one camping site and 23 restaurants in the São Raimundo Nonato and Coronel José Dias municipalities (Oliveira Filho 2007).

The tourism cluster is subject to considerable infrastructure constraints. It is located between two of the worst highways in Brazil in terms of maintenance (Ribeiro 2009). The only highway to provide accessibility is in poor condition, and does not allow vehicles to go faster than 50 km/h. The São Raimundo Nonato International airport remains incomplete, leaving the tourism services cluster in a difficult situation with regard to efficient and effective access to tourist destinations. The internet is also limited, further limiting business marketing, sales and communication.

Serra da Capivara Ceramic (SCC) was created as an association of small entrepreneurs. Today, it has five different businesses run by private management, a restaurant, a hostel, a T-shirt factory, a ceramic factory and a store. The last two are integrated into one business, which is the focus of this chapter. The SCC was created with the intention of targeting tourism as its primary source of income. However, even with poor internet services, poor roads and limited air freight service, the SCC could upgrade through product innovation, quality improvement and market diversification from direct sales to tourists to bulk sales at trade fairs or to wholesalers. It operates with 19 employees and has annual sales estimated around US$200,000.00 to US$500,000.00.[1] It offers over 162 ceramic products. SCC uses diverse strategies to obtain sales such as fairs and web sales.[2]

The history of the development of Serra da Capivara Ceramic

The Serra da Capivara Ceramic Association was created in 1985 by the FUMDHAM – Fundação Museu do Homem Americano (American Men's Museum Foundation), a non-profit organization created by Brazilian and French researchers, which is funded by both public and private sectors to support the park management and to promote research and cultural activities. The association has the following two aims: to generate for the local community a new income source from tourism and to incorporate technical classes for art and craft-making into the school programme; and conserving the environment on which the tourism activity is based. After the creation of the local association, FUMDHAM hired a ceramic specialist from Japan in 1987. This specialist selected the best clay mixture using 84 different clay samples present in and around Serra da Capivara national park. He also provided the initial technical instructions on how to produce high-quality ceramic products from the raw materials available.

It took eight years of continuous investment before the association was ready for production. In 1993, the association added value to the ceramic production by incorporating into the designs the drawings found in the Serra da Capivara archaeological sites. In 1994, FUMDHAM began a training programme in the elementary schools in the communities that surround the park for ceramic, candle and recycled paper, plastic arts, clothing and honey production. FUMDHAM's investment in local schools aimed at changing the community's perception of how to live by exploring income-generating opportunities in the National Park of Serra da Capivara without harming the environment. Unfortunately, the association did not have total control over some aspects of their production, illustrated when the local government privatized the school and removed the technical programme in 2004. These actions hindered the continued development of technical skills within the local population. An extra group of ceramicists was hired, resulting in a new varnishing technique in 1999, the introduction of the liquid clay technique in 2000, and the addition of a local sales representative, in 2001.

Recognizing the lack of co-ordination between production and sales, FUMDHAM hired a professional manager from a multinational company in 2001 to manage the association. After hiring the new manager, FUMDHAM outsourced the management of the association to a private company. The requirements imposed by FUMDHAM were that the private company would proportionally share profits with the employees, would not make employees redundant due to business downturns and would oblige every employee to sign an agreement to abandon any practices that harm the local environment such as hunting, limestone (calcium carbonate, $CaCO_3$) mining and timber collecting.

In 2003, the ceramic factory started new ceramic and drawing courses for factory employees. From 2004 to 2007, the private company invested approximately R$200,000 (US$120,000) in the construction of five new ovens, reaching a total of seven ovens. In 2004, the company was only able to sell to wholesalers. However, in 2005, exporting began. By 2007, it had its first direct sale in a fair located nearly 1,700 km from its production site. The company by then had three small shops; one near the factory for direct sales to tourists, one store in São Raimundo Nonato and a third inside the park.

During the creation of SCC, FUMDHAM intended to target high-income foreign tourists. The SCC did not predict that due to poor road infrastructure, the tourist profile was primarily comprised of domestic tourists (95 per cent), of whom 51 per cent live within 500 km of the national park. Further, 59 per cent of tourists visit as part of school/college field trips; these tourists spend little time at the park or in the cities and they tend to not have high spending patterns (Oliveira Filho and Monteiro 2007, 2009).

Research rationale and methodology

One of the main challenges to small business in the tourism sector is the difficulty of providing continuous upgrades in product, process, functions and markets in order to generate income and jobs. Many small businesses do not succeed, particularly in the initial years of operation, because they are unable to upgrade their business model and undertake continuous innovation. Therefore, they continue to struggle to offer quality products or to provide sustainable practices to satisfy external demands. This chapter aims to understand the origin and the actors responsible for the upgrades in SCC and its relation to the rest of the tourism cluster. The focus of the research is on the upgrading[3] initiatives needed to innovate and increase aggregated value in small enterprises, both in products and services (Giuliana, Pietrobelli and Rabelloti 2004: 6). In this context, upgrades can be classified follows:

1. *Process upgrading* is related to transforming inputs into outputs more efficiently by reorganizing the production system or introducing superior technology.
2. *Product upgrading* means moving into more sophisticated product lines in terms of increased added value per unit.
3. *Functional upgrading* implies acquiring new, superior functions in the chain, such as design or marketing, or abandoning existing low-value-added functions to focus on high-value-added activities.
4. *Intersectoral upgrading* represents applying the competence acquired in a particular function to enter a new sector.
5. *Social upgrading* aims at the long-term development strategy based on formalized firms paying taxes, following environmental, labour, health and safety regulations and spurring local social development (Puppim de Oliveira 2008b).[4]

SMEs often suffer from lock-in, when a business depends on a small group of much larger corporations to buy their products with the relationship manifesting as quasi-hierarchical (Fortes 2006; Humphrey and Schmitz 2000, 2001, 2002). The large corporations have access to much larger and more sophisticated markets. They can help upgrade the business product and process to reduce costs and to comply with international demands through process and product innovation. However, these relationships prevent functional and intersectoral upgrades (Humphrey 2003), which can cause problems for the enterprise in the future.

Tourism can offer local SMEs the opportunity to access new and sophisticated markets, which can bring income to local communities and facilitate employment, thereby reducing participation in more environmentally destructive activities. Tourism can also help local enterprises develop alternative income streams keeping the business economically viable in the long term. The upgrade of SCC can provide lessons for other small businesses in similar regions in Brazil and other countries where the infrastructure is poor and opportunities from tourism exist but are limited.

For the current study, the Serra da Capivara Ceramic business was visited three times between January of 2009 and July of 2010. During the investigation, one business assistant, one manager and 12 factory employees were interviewed. The research identified a list of upgrades since the association's creation and investigated which agent originated the upgrade (relationship with the value chain, relationship with local aid organizations and relationship with public policy) and the classification of the upgrade (product, process, functional, intersectoral and social).

Findings: the process of upgrading in the SCC

Identifying the upgrades

Although the SCC business has existed for over 25 years, the first sale to a wholesaler was not until 2004. Tourism was essential in maintaining the business, especially in the early years when the small sales were mostly generated in the local shop to tourists who visited the park. In the beginning, the products had low quality because of the lack of quality in the mix of clays for the ceramics and in the production process. However, the SCC was quite innovative over time, especially when local management was replaced by a more professional approach. The upgrades promoted quick growth from 2001 to 2007. Table 6.2 presents the identified upgrades form the ceramic factory, while Table 6.3 summarizes the upgrades and their origin and classification.

The different types of upgrades

Since its creation the SCC was able to promote a series of upgrades with the help of local actors, and later with the new manager that brought the much-needed experience that it was lacking. Most of the upgrades came with improved relations in the value chain, particularly contact with clients that needed certain products with improved quality. In the beginning, FUMDHAM was key to the development of the tourism cluster as a whole, and the ceramic business in particular. It stepped in to help create a profitable business. There were no intersectoral upgrades, but these may be possible in the future. The upgrades can be summarized as follows.

Product upgrades

There were four product upgrades, which accounted for only 17 per cent of the 23 upgrades. The limited number of product upgrades is explained in the small market penetration, which did not demand a large number of alternative products. The company is still experimenting with products in the hope of identifying either niche markets or 'cash cow' products.

Process upgrades

There were nine process upgrades, accounting for 39 per cent of the 23 upgrades. The higher presence of process upgrades is explained by the heavy investment of FUMDHAM in building SCC capabilities to compete in the market. The clay-cooking techniques used by the SCC guarantee product quality.

Functional upgrades

There were four functional upgrades, representing 17 per cent of total 23 upgrades. These upgrades only appeared after the association hired a new manager. The introduction of new commercial knowledge permitted the SCC to expand their business opportunities.

Intersectoral upgrades

There were no intersectoral upgrades. Typically, small businesses in developing countries focus more on product and process upgrades to comply with market demands. Even with the introduction of new management, the SCC does not have sufficient market contacts to be able to expand or change sectors.

Social upgrades

There were five social upgrades, representing 22 per cent of the total 23 upgrades. The SCC was created with the intention of alleviating poverty in the studied region as well as providing the local population with new means for learning a sustainable way of life. The social upgrades were maintained even after the company's management shifted from an association to a private entity.

The main drivers of the upgrades

There are three main divisions of the drivers of the upgrades, as follows:

Relationship with the value chain

There were 13 upgrades originating from improved relationships within the value chain, representing 57 per cent of the total 23 upgrades. Process and functional upgrades were more prevalent due to the high level of investment intended to guarantee a high product quality. These upgrades were apparent especially after 2001, with the replacement of an association leader with a professional manager from a multinational corporation.

Relationship with local aid organizations

There were nine upgrades resulting from the development of a relationship with the local aid organization, particularly FUMDHAM, representing 39 per cent

Table 6.2 Serra da Capivara chronological upgrades

Year	*Upgrade*	*Responsible*	*Origin*	*Type of upgrade*
1979	Establishment of Serra da Capivara National Park	IBDF/MMA (Ministry of Environment)	Public policy	Social
1985	Creation of the local ceramic association	FUMDHAM	Relationship with local aid org.	Social
1985	Beginning of the Serra da Capivara Ceramic Project. Technical visit from a specialist in ceramic and creation of potential products	FUMDHAM/ Japanese expert	Relationship with local aid org.	Product
1987	Modification of clay mixture	FUMDHAM/ Japanese expert	Relationship with local aid org.	Process
1993	Beginning of artisanal ceramic production	Local association	Relationship with the value chain	Process
1993	Usage of local inscriptions found on stone from the national park to aggregate value	Local association	Relationship with the value chain	Product
1994	Ceramic, plastic arts, candle making, recycling paper, honey harvesting, and clothing classes for children that lived around the park to improve the locals' skills	FUMDHAM	Relationship with local aid org.	Social
1999	Improvement of varnishing technique. (Temperature near vitrification makes the usage of painted utensils oven safe)	FUMDHAM/ Japanese expert	Relationship with local aid org.	Product
2000	Insertion of liquid clay technique for better utensils modelling	FUMDHAM/ Italian expert	Relationship with local aid org.	Process
2001	Insertion of ceramic direct sales agent to create a good marketing relationship	FUMDHAM	Relationship with local aid org.	Process
2001	Creation of a store located at the SCC production base, located in Coronel José Dias	Local management/ Professional manager	Relationship with the value chain	Functional
2002	Creation of a concession by FUMDHAM to have a private company to manage the ceramic production base and store in Coronel José Dias	Local management/ Professional manager	Relationship with the value chain	Functional

Year	*Upgrade*	*Responsible*	*Origin*	*Type of upgrade*
2002	Insertion of profit sharing with workers (value not revealed by management, but workers informed that salary ranges from 2 to 3 times the minimal wage salary)	Local management/ Professional manager	Relationship with the value chain	Social
2003	Technical drawing classes for workers	FUMDHAM	Relationship with local aid org.	Process
2003	Technical ceramic production classes for workers	FUMDHAM	Relationship with local aid org.	Process
2003	Creation of social contract with workers that guarantee worker stability regardless of the production and demands workers to avoid activities that harm the environment	Local management/ Professional manager	Relationship with the value chain	Social
2004	First wholesale sale to a large chain	Local management/ Professional manager	Relationship with the value chain	Product
2004	Construction of two new ovens, increasing the number of ovens to four	Local management/ Professional manager	Relationship with the value chain	Process
2005	First direct export	Local management/ Professional manager	Relationship with the value chain	Functional
2006	Construction of one new oven, increasing the number of ovens to five	Local management/ Professional manager	Relationship with the value chain	Process
2007	Construction of three new ovens, increasing the number of ovens to eight	Local management/ Professional manager	Relationship with the value chain	Process
2007	First bulk direct sales in event fairs	Local management/ Professional manager	Relationship with the value chain	Functional
2009	The ceramic business obtained fair-trade label	Local management/ Professional manager	Relationship with the value chain	Functional

Table 6.3 Upgrades and the relationship between origin and classification

Type of upgrade	*Relationship with the value chain*	*Relationship with local aid organizations*	*Relationship with public policy*	*Total*
Process	4	5	–	9
Product	2	2	–	4
Functional	5	–	–	5
Intersectoral	–	–	–	–
Social	2	2	1	5
Total	13	9	1	23

of the total 23 upgrades identified in the study. Process upgrades were heavily represented in this category due to FUMDHAM's investments in new techniques for clay production. These upgrades were particularly evident during the SCC structuring phase.

Relationship with public policy

There was only one upgrade emerging from the relationship with public policy, the creation of the park by law. Even the creation of the park was an isolated action; it consolidated the tourism clusters and allowed the establishment of different businesses in the community.

Lessons

The case of the small business Serra da Capivara Ceramic (SCC) highlights several lessons for the improvement of tourism-related SMEs in Brazil and other developing countries, as many of the challenges faced by this small venture are similar to those faced by small businesses around the developing world. The upgrade process also sheds light on possible paths for SME upgrades in other parts of Brazil and other developing countries where tourism is emerging and the population lacks some of the skills needed to take advantage of the new tourism activity. Lessons drawn from this case study include the following.

Links between the activity and tourism are important for SME upgrades

The links with tourism drove many of the upgrades in the business that is the subject of this case study. The creation of the park and the influx of tourists created a demand for locally based products. The use of prehistoric designs in the pottery created a strong connection with the locality and the community during tourists' visits.

The role of external actors in supporting changes to local economic activities

In developing countries, particularly in areas where access to education is limited, the support from external actors is fundamental in preparing the local community to shift from certain types of economic activities based on the consumption of non-renewable resources, and which are generally environmentally damaging, to sustainable tourism activities. Locals generally lack the capital and expertise to make this transition smoothly. Moreover, initial tourism flows may be small and external actors can support the local community by providing vision, strategic direction and technical support in order to get to a breakeven point so they can continue the activities themselves.

Constant upgrades in small businesses are important to continuing production over the long term

Although some tourists are accustomed to rustic infrastructure and products, there are minimum standards of safety, health, comfort and product quality that must be satisfied to maintain the activities over the long term. Small businesses created by the local community generally do not have these standards in the beginning and need to continuously upgrade to reach appropriate and competitive business standards. Upgrades are also important to avoid takeover by outsiders, who will implement predatory tactics to take over poorly performing businesses.

Business sustainability beyond tourism

Local business should not be completely dependent on tourism for total revenues because tourism is a discretionary activity and can be subject to significant shifts in demand when conditions change. This can place pressure on businesses when minimum operational earnings cannot be achieved. In the case study, the link with wholesalers outside of the tourist area and with other markets, such as corporate souvenirs, helped to upgrade the business by driving new innovations and increasing the sales.

Outside managerial expertise may be important, but governance mechanisms should guarantee benefits to locals

Outside managers can bring much-needed business expertise in order to promote upgrades in local firms, particularly in areas where access to education is limited and educational attainment levels are low. Creating a concession to a private company to run the ceramic business could overcome the challenge of finding managerial capability suitable for the SME. In this case study, the external manager helped to boost sales and upgraded many of the processes to make the business economically independent from FUMDHAM's aid. Prior to the arrival of the external manager, the ceramic association, even with FUMDHAM's support, found it difficult to organize the production base and start a profitable market relationship in the long term. The distribution of benefits to locals even when the business was not succeeding helped to avoid job and income losses and helped to gain the support from the local community for the changes in the management. The ceramic business social upgrade of guaranteeing payments, even when sales decreased, helped the factory maintain its employees. There are some employees who have been with the factory for over 17 years.

Conclusions

Upgrades were of vital importance to making SCC a viable economic opportunity to the local community in the Serra da Capivara National Park. Local tourism and external links led to many upgrades in the SCC. These upgrades, which might be small to any large corporation or multinational, brought local economic benefits to the community and assisted economic diversification and generation of income and jobs in one area where poverty is widespread and opportunities for regular jobs are scarce.

Local organizations helped the cluster (and the SCC in particular) to innovate, improve local skills, to manufacture the product and manage the business. With the introduction of new management, the SCC became more efficient, and upgrades introduced into the value chain emerged at a faster rate. Further, market demand originating from within the value chain was converted into upgrades and were fed by new investment in skills and infrastructure for production.

Converting market demand into real upgrades requires that the SMEs have internal management capabilities. For this reason, the conversion of functional and process upgrades was only present after the insertion of new management. The SCC, even with difficulties in selling its product, could find different ways to use its internal knowledge.

Public policy actions in support of the SCC and the local community were limited. The public policy upgrade in this case study was the creation of the protected area, which made the Serra da Capivara touristic cluster possible. A stronger public policy approach is necessary to create the infrastructure needed for a cluster to prosper. In the current case, a local organization took over this role, which enabled the cluster of SMEs to create tourism jobs to lead the economic activities away from extraction of resources from the park. It is also necessary to note that the second public policy action hindered possible upgrades, as municipal public schools ended social programs intended to transfer new abilities/skills to locals and to increase the younger population's incentive to conserve the environment, especially around the park.

In sum, small tourism businesses around protected areas in Brazil often suffer from poor financial performance, reducing the capacity of SMEs to generate jobs and household income that could assist communities make the transition away from environmentally damaging activities. In this case study, the relationships between the businesses and external actors, such as public organizations, other businesses and tourists, meant that the ceramic business lacked the capacity to undertake various upgrades so that it could remain competitive and sustainable over the long term. This chapter has explored the opportunities and limitations of managing small businesses located in or adjacent to protected areas in Brazil and identified lessons from the upgrades that were introduced. While these findings are specific to the Serra da Capivara locality, and may not be able to be generalized beyond the case at hand, the significance of this research is in the power of example. These findings are valuable to other similar enterprises around protected areas in Brazil and, quite possibly, elsewhere.

References

Arruda M.B. (1993) Ecologia e antropismo na área do Município de São Raimundo Nonato e Parque Nacional da Serra da Capivara (PI). Masters Thesis in Ecology, Brasília: Universidade de Brasília.

Ceballos-Lascurain, H. (1996) *Tourism, Ecotourism and Protected Areas*. Gland, Switzerland: The World Conservation Union (IUCN).

Fortes, P.J.O.C. (2006) *Melhorias em Arranjos Produtivos Locais*. Masters Thesis, Rio de Janeiro: EBAPE/FGV.

Giuliana, E., Pietrobelli, C. and Rabelloti, R. (2004) Upgrading on global value chains: Lessons from Latin American clusters. *Quaderno n. 72, Deparment of Economic Science and Quantitaitve Methods*. University of Oiemonte.

Guidon, N. (1997) Cultural assets and conservation units in Brazil, in *Congresso Brasileiro de Unidades de Conservação*. Anais do Congresso Brasileiro de Unidades de Conservação, 15–23 November 1997, Curitiba.

Humphrey, J. (2003) *Opportunities for SMEs in Developing Countries to Upgrade in a Global Economy: Series on Upgrading in Small Enterprise Clusters and Global Value Chains*. Seed working paper, no. 43, University of Sussex.

Humphrey J. and Schmitz, H. (2000) *Governance and Upgrading: Linking Industrial Clusters and Global Value Chain*. IDS working paper no. 120, University of Sussex.

Humphrey, J. and Schmitz, H. (2001) Governance in global value chains. *IDS Bulletin*, 32, (3): 19–23. University of Sussex.

Humphrey, J. and Schmitz, H. (2002) *How does Insertion in Global Value Chains Affect Upgrading in Industrial Clusters?*, Institute of Development Studies: University of Sussex.

IBGE (2011) *Dados Estatísticos de Cidades – São Raimundo Nonato*. Brazilian Institute of Geography and Statistitcs. Available at: www.ibge.gov.br/cidadesat (accessed 27 April 2011).

Lerner, M. and Haber, S. (2001) Performance factors of small tourism ventures: The interface of tourism, entrepreneurship and the environment. *Journal of Business Venturing*, 16: 77–100.

Morrison, A. and Teixeira R. (2004) Small business performance: a tourism sector focus. *Journal of Small Business and Enterprise Development*, 11: 166–73.

Oliveira Filho, R.C. (2007) *Valoração Econômica da Atividade Turistica na Parque Nacional da Serra da Capivara*. Masters Thesis, TROPEN/PRODEMA, Universidade Federal do Piauí.

Oliveira Filho, R. C. and Monteiro, M. S. L. (2007) Valoração econômica da prática do ecoturismo no semi-árido: O caso do Parque Nacional da Serra da Capivara – Piauí. *VII Encontro da Sociedade Brasileira de Economia Ecológica, Fortaleza.*

Oliveira Filho, R.C. and Monteiro, M. S. L. (2009) Ecoturismo no Parque Nacional Serra da Capivara: trata-se de uma prática sustentável? *Turismo em Análise*, 20 (2), 230–50.

Puppim de Oliveira, J.A. (2005a) Tourism as a force for establishing protected areas: The case of Bahia, Brazil. *Journal of Sustainable Tourism*, 13: 24–49.

Puppim de Oliveira, J. A. (2005b) Enforcing protected area guidelines in Brazil: What explains participation in the implementation process? *Journal of Planning Education and Research*, 24: 420–36.

Puppim de Oliveira (2008a) *Implementation of Environmental Policies in Developing Countries: A Case of Protected Areas and Tourism in Brazil*. Albany. NY: State University of New York – SUNY Press.

Puppim de Oliveira (ed.) (2008b) *Upgrading Clusters and Small Enterprises in Developing Countries: Environmental, Labour, Innovation and Social Issues*. Hampshire: Ashgate Publishing.

Ribeiro, B. (2009) 'Brazil 10's best and worst roads by Guia 4 Rodas'. *Travel and Leisure*. Available at: gobrazil.about.com/b/2009/03/13/brazils-10-best-and-10-worst-roads-by-guia-4-rodas.htm (accessed 2 February 2010).

Silva, N. C. B. and Mota, J. A. (2002) Gestão de parques nacionais: O caso do Parque Nacional da Serra da Capivara, in Encontro da Associacão Nacional de Pós Graduação e Pesquisa em Meio Ambiente, São Paulo: ANPASS.

Notes

1 Total sales were not by the SME due to commercial-in-confidence arrangements provided. The value was estimated by the authors using production data and worst- and best-case scenarios.

2 www.ceramicacapivara.com

3 Upgrading – Making better products, more efficiently, or move to more privilege place on the value chain (Porter 1999; Kaplisky 2000; Giuliana, Pietrobelli and Rabelloti 2004).

4 The inclusion of social upgrades was an adaptation of the methodology of Giuliana, Pietrobelli and Rabellotti (2004). Social upgrades do not have the intention of direct economic gains through improving the product or the production process or the intention of conquering new markets.

7 Tourism development and distribution channels in Brotas

Brazilian adventure capital

Sandro Carnicelli-Filho and Gui Lohmann

Introduction

The term 'adventure capital' has been used by the tourism industry in different geographical locations around the world to market adventure tourism offerings. Queenstown, New Zealand, for example, is the self-proclaimed 'adventure capital of the world'; the Cumbria region is the 'adventure capital of the United Kingdom'; Whistler is the 'adventure capital of Canada'; and the Victoria Falls is considered the 'adventure capital of Africa'. The natural resources of all these places are utilized by the adventure tourism industry to attract tourists interested in activities such as mountaineering, white-water rafting and mountain biking.

Like other adventure resorts around the word, the self-proclaimed 'Brazilian adventure capital' is a small town named Brotas that, in the 2010 census, registered a population of 21,491 inhabitants (IBGE 2010). Located in the 'heart' of the State of São Paulo (242 km from the state capital city of São Paulo), Brotas has become a major destination for tourists searching for adventure sports and eco-activities. Brotas is still a 'new' adventure destination when compared with the aforementioned world-famous adventure resorts. The first adventure tourism operators in Brotas started their business in the late 1990s, exploring the rapids of the Jacaré-Pepira River and the waterfalls and caves of the region. Today, in addition to white-water rafting and kayaking, tourism operators offer activities such as hiking, mountain biking, canyoning, and high-rope circuits.

This chapter aims to investigate two different and complementary issues related to adventure tourism in Brotas: its development and distribution marketing channels. Two separate sets of fieldwork were undertaken by each of the authors over different time periods. The tourism development data were collected in February 2011 with the aim of understanding how the adventure tourism industry in Brotas has developed and the steps that have been taken to market and attract tourists to this adventure tourism resort. The perceptions of 15 local tourism stakeholders regarding the development of tourism in the town and their perspectives for the sector's future were considered. Understanding issues related to development and the perceptions of the tourism industry regarding future issues can contribute to both identifying the needs of the industry in Brotas and to a critical review of the government's tourism plans. Complementing these interviews, tourism distribution channel research was undertaken some years earlier, between June 2006 and April 2007, and was part of a larger study on tourism distribution channels focused on different tourism segments within the State of São Paulo (Lohmann and Nascimento 2007). With data obtained from both sets of fieldwork, it was possible to map tourism distribution channels in Brotas, providing an opportunity for comparison with the study developed by Schott (2007) at another tourism adventure destination, Queenstown, New Zealand. This comparative approach highlights the differences and similarities between a mature destination (Queenstown) and a developing destination (Brotas).

To address the aims of this research, this chapter starts by exploring the development of the adventure tourism industry in general, and adventure tourism in Brazil in particular. These sections are followed by an explanation of the data collection methods and data analysis. Following this, the findings of the empirical research regarding the tourism development and distribution channels in Brotas are presented, from which conclusions are drawn.

Adventure tourism: development and distribution channels

The adventure concept has been well explored in the tourism and leisure literature (Bentley and Page 2008; Cater 2006; Swarbrooke et al. 2003). The idea of adventure as a form of leisure or recreation is presented by Vester (1987) as a multidimensional concept of experience that was extensively discussed in the 1980s (Ewert and Hollenhorst 1989; Martin and Priest 1986). However, adventure as an aspect of tourism attracted little academic attention until the early 1990s, when the first adventure resorts started to emerge in countries such as Canada, New Zealand and Australia (Kane and Tucker 2004).

According to Vester (1987), 'adventure' is the leisure component that helps overcome the mundane social world and its everyday routine because it represents uncertainty and risk. For Holyfield, Jonas and Zajicek (2005) the term 'adventure' includes voluntary engagement in an uncertain and emotionally intense recreational activity that needs to have a balance between risk and safety. Indeed, some tourism destinations, including the town of Waitomo in New Zealand, started to observe the economic potential of incorporating experiences that represent an 'escape from routine' and elements of uncertainty and risk in tourism products: these could attract tourists with an adventurous profile (Pavlovich 2003). Activities involving risk and adventure became known as adventure recreation, and according to Weber (2001), originated from outdoor recreation. However, Ewert and Hollenhorst (1989) believe that adventure recreation differs from outdoor recreation because it involves a deliberate search for risk and uncertainty. To resorts exploring the commercialization of these activities (e.g. Brotas, Queenstown, Waitomo), understanding the origin of adventure and its meaning can be useful in planning activities and in developing marketing strategies.

The commercialization of adventure recreation activities, and even the commodification of the places where these activities occur, has developed into a marketing opportunity for the tourism industry. Varley (2006: 188) develops an 'adventure commodification continuum' of different possible adventure experiences, presenting a relationship between highly controlled, strategically marketed and commodified activities and the 'essential ideal of the original adventure'. In his model, Varley (2006) establishes three different phases of adventure. Phase A is highly saleable as a tourist product. Phase B encompasses the outdoor pursuit market, which involves skills courses, guided and expert-led expeditions. Phase C is not usually a commercial product because it is too close to possible misadventure and includes activities such as solo mountaineering and independent expeditions. According to Varley, the less risky an activity can be, the higher the level of participant comfort and the higher the commercial and marketing appeal to mass markets. Indeed, adventure tourism resorts, including Queenstown and Brotas, usually explore in a commercial sense phases A and B because these activities are saleable to people without or with limited knowledge and skills.

Galloway (2006) asserts that adventure is a relative concept because both 'adventure' and 'risk' are subjectively perceived, defined and valued. Indeed, it is likely that one would find different levels of perceived risk when comparing a tourist with a guide (Morgan 2000). Risk perceptions in adventure tourism are also explored by Cater (2006), who believes there is a movement towards risk-taking behaviour during leisure moments, which counters a trend in the reduction of risk in everyday life. However, the idea of tourists having more accentuated risk-taking behaviour during their holidays is just one possible approach in the understanding of tourist behaviour. In fact, when tourists arrive at their destination, they can also behave in the same way they do at home (Krippendorf 1999), avoiding unnecessary risks and searching for everyday emotional experiences. Tourist behaviours can be induced because the marketing strategies used at the destination can stimulate the interest and imagination of consumers. An example of this effect could be when a place is branded as 'the adventure capital', playing an important role in the decision-making process of tourists in going to the destination. Queenstown, Whistler and Brotas are examples of destinations marketed for their adventure experiences. The first two are well-known international resorts. Brotas, however, is still being developed as a resort and is growing in line with the expansion of the adventure tourism industry in Brazil more generally.

Considering that one of the aims of this chapter is to understand tourism development in an adventure resort, it is also important to understand the characteristics of tourism distribution channels and their implications for the development of adventure tourism. Schott (2007) is one of few researchers to provide some empirically grounded research exploring the distribution channels of 16 adventure tourism operators that provide more than ten different types of adventure activities in Queenstown. He found that while businesses provide a variety of direct and indirect channels, the most effective channels are those provided 'at the destination'. Despite the larger international market of Queenstown in comparison with Brotas, the internet has played a primary role in raising awareness and providing information about adventure activities. Although travellers to New Zealand visit a number of different places while touring around the country, adventure tourism activities are seen as an impulse purchase, with tourists making up their minds about what activities to undertake once they arrive in Queenstown.

Adventure tourism in Brazil

According to Pimentel (2009), the 1960s represented an important period in the development of nature-based activities in Brazil, with 'hippies' and feminists identified as social groups contributing to the re-approximation of how humans relate to the natural environment. Bruhns (2009) notes that during the 1960s and the 1970s, activities such as trekking, canyoning and white-water rafting started to be sold as touristic products. However, it was only in 2009 that the Brazilian Association for Adventure Tourism (ABETA) and the Ministry of Tourism (Ministério do Turismo) published a guidebook where the adventure tourism industry in Brazil and its history were analysed. According to ABETA and the Ministério do Turismo (2009), the first businesses started to offer adventure tourism in Brazil between 1975 and 1986. Nevertheless, the commercial boom did not occur until the 1990s, and it was characterized by a lack of safety rules and standardization of the activities. Additionally, the inexperience of business owners, who were predominantly local adventurers without any knowledge of business management, was a problem for quality product assurance and development. During the mid-1990s, most tourism operators founded by former adventurers were regulated by the Brazilian government and contributed to the professionalization of the adventure tourism industry (ABETA and Ministério do Turismo 2009).

During the same period (1994–98), there was an increase in the number of international visitors in Brazil (see Figure 1.2), including regions previously seen as remote, such as the Amazon Forest in the northern part of the country (see Chapters 4 and 10). Ruschmann (1992), citing a study carried out by the Department of Regional Development and Environment of the Organization of American States (OAS), identified adventure tourism as the second most common type of tourism attracting international visitors to the Brazilian Amazon. Tourists usually associate the Amazon region with adventure; however, many other destinations in Brazil focus specifically on the adventure tourism niche. Other examples of adventure destinations are sand-boarding in Jericoacoara, a famous beach in the northeast region of Brazil, the trekking and mountaineering routes of Chapada dos Veadeiros in the central part of the country, and white-water rafting, canyoning and high-rope circuits in Brotas.

Adventure tourism in Brotas benefits particularly from two main geographical advantages. First, the Jacaré-Pepira River, one of the best rivers in the state of São Paulo for white-water activities, attracts people interested in white-water rafting and kayaking. Second, its geographical location and proximity to the city of São Paulo, one of the largest and wealthiest urban agglomerations in the world, offers an escape from the polluted and overcrowded urban environment. Brotas benefits from its proximity to São Paulo, particularly targeting families and young professionals willing to (re)connect with nature and outdoor activities during weekends and holidays.

Methods

As previously mentioned, the data for this chapter were collected during two separate field trips: fieldwork over a period of nearly ten months between 2006 and 2007, which examined tourism distribution channels in Brotas; and a second more recent field trip in 2011 where past, present and future development issues were explored. Together, these two sets of fieldwork included a combination of semi-structured interviews, participant observations, informal conversations and a survey of 190 visitors and tourists in Brotas. The semi-structured interviews lasted between 50 and 90 minutes and sought to examine the perspectives of different stakeholders. The interviews were conducted and analysed in Portuguese and quotes were translated for the purpose of this chapter.

The 2011 fieldwork involved 15 members of the tourism industry in Brotas to capture the perspectives of different members of the tourism industry regarding the past, present and the future of the adventure resort. The participants included four members of the city council, three owners of adventure tourism operators, three owners of hotels and five adventure guides. Notes taken during the interviews were also analysed, and themes that emerged during the data collection and analysis were clustered and compared using the constant comparison method (Strauss and Corbin 1998). Consequently, questions that arose as a result of the earlier analyses were considered and reflections on previous data were discussed. Through an analysis of past development, perceptions of the present situation and issues and discussions about the future, the following sections explore adventure tourism in Brotas.

The tourism distribution channels fieldwork comprised seven interviews with four accommodation business owners, one tourism local organization manager and two adventure tourism operators. These interviews took place in June 2006. In Brotas, it is common for tourism business operators to provide 'at destination' cross-bookings between their products, one example being an accommodation provider booking an adventure tourism experience for guests. Hence, it is relevant to have the perspectives of other businesses rather than just gathering data from adventure tourism providers, as was the case with Schott's (2007) study on adventure tourism in Queenstown. The two adventure tourism providers interviewed were large, well-established operators. This fieldwork was followed by a survey of 190 domestic visitors and tourists throughout different periods aiming to target long weekends in October and November 2006, as well as Easter 2007, and the high-season summer holiday period in January and February 2007. Considering that Brotas is not a well-known destination for international tourists, only questionnaires in Portuguese were made available to target the domestic market. A total of four trips were made to Brotas to collect visitor data, including socioeconomic and demographic information, trip arrangements and their perceptions and use of distribution channels.

Findings

Tourism development in Brotas

The past

The history of tourism in Brotas began in the early 1990s when the local government decided to install a tannery to deal with the high rates of unemployment in the region (Aguiar 2005). However, environmentalists and the NGO Rio Vivo, concerned with pollution of the Jacaré-Pepira River, organized a petition against the tannery and mounted arguments in favour of tourist activities such as white-water rafting and 'bóia-cross'. According to a member of the Department of Tourism in Brotas, 'the "bóia-cross" is a recreational activity that has been practised by Brotas citizens since the 1960s'. The main intention of Rio Vivo was to offer the local community training courses to transform unemployed locals into adventure guides able to conduct river activities. Barrocas (2005) asserts that it took almost a decade for Brotas to be transformed from an agriculture-based to a tourism-based economy. Environmentalists connected with Rio Vivo organized seminars for the local community in which the potential ecological damage of the tannery was discussed and the benefits of developing tourism were emphasized.

In 1993, members of the Rio Vivo movement decided to establish a tourism operation named Mata Dentro, the first company aimed at promoting ecotourism and adventure activities in Brotas. This company contributed to structuring the white-water rafting activity in Brotas, and it held discussions with farm owners concerning access to the river and the sections of rapids that could be safely used for tourism operations. In addition to white-water rafting, Mata Dentro also commercialized activities such as cascading and trekking. The success of the company and the use of the river for kayak competitions attracted other business operators to Brotas. In 1997, a French mountaineer founded Alaya Expedições to provide activities involving mountaineering techniques and high ropes. A full circuit of high ropes began operation in 2001 under the name Verticália. After Mata Dentro and Alaya Expedições, many other businesses started to operate in Brotas in the early 2000s. According to the Chair of the Department of Tourism in Brotas, 'some of the companies that came in at the end of the 1990s and the early 2000s were still in operation in 2011, but many of the small companies could not compete against those that were already well known in the region. By 2004–2005, there were ten or twelve white-water rafting and adventure tourism operators in Brotas; in 2011, we had just five or six.'

Thus, seven years after the beginning of adventure tourism in Brotas, the town was already offering numerous activities, including cascading, trekking, white-water rafting, kayaking, a high-rope circuit and 'bóia-cross'. However, the wider tourism industry of Brotas was not ready to deal with the increasing number in tourists visiting the town, particularly during weekends and holidays. According to one hotel owner, 'until 1996, there were just two hotels and a few restaurants in Brotas, and the hospitality industry started to grow because businessmen from São Paulo decided to invest in the town, establishing new hotels and developing infrastructure to attend to tourists' needs'. This information is in agreement with data presented by Aguiar (2005) and Vitte and Aguiar (2009), who assert that the main development of the tourism sector in Brotas occurred between 1999 and 2004, with the number of hotels/hostels increasing by 300 per cent, in comparison with 1993–99, when growth was at a 200 per cent rate.

The development of the tourism and hospitality industry in Brotas experienced a boom when, in 1999, Veja, one of the main national magazines in Brazil, published an article about adventure tourism and the increasing commercialization of activities involving risk and the natural environment. The article emphasized not only the charm of the colonial houses in Brotas but also the adventure activities offered in the town and the professionalism of the white-water rafting operators. Since then, the operators have become even more professional and organized in terms of safety issues and marketing strategies.

Current issues

The current adventure tourism scenario in Brotas has evolved compared with the 1990s and early 2000s, as exemplified by the number of accommodation establishments and restaurants currently available that are, according to one hotel owner, 'sufficient, considering the influx of tourists during holidays and high season peaks'. Data presented in a report by Brotas' Department of Tourism indicate that there are 35 establishments offering accommodation services, including camping sites, low-budget and high-quality hotels and 39 food providers such as restaurants and bars. However, in terms of accommodation and food services, a different range of participants, including a member of the Department of Tourism, a hotel owner, and an owner of an adventure tourism operation were unanimous in asserting the necessity of an internationally known hotel brand, citing specifically the French brand Accor, as well as fast-food companies including McDonald's and Burger King. Another need mentioned by some of the participants was the development of a convention centre where conferences, meetings and corporate events could be held. These participants believed that hosting business events could also contribute to increasing the adventure industry in Brotas, as white-water rafting, cascading and high-rope activities are increasingly seen as activities in which corporate values, including co-operation, team working, confidence and courage, are developed.

The adventure activities in Brotas are also currently presented and marketed differently to past efforts. According to one of the participants, a tourism operator, 'today, adventure needs to be marketed to the whole family; our intention is to attract not just the crazy young adventurers but families as well. We are ready to offer enjoyable adventure activities to everyone.' A member of the Department of Tourism corroborates this view, saying, 'we want to transform Brotas into an open and nature-made Disneyland, where people from all ages can visit and do something exciting and different from daily life'. In search of a different profile of clients, operators including Alaya and Ecoação are investing in new activities. While Alaya has created the longest circuit of zipline in Brotas, at 1,240 metres, Ecoação has invested in a low-cost park with lakes, ziplines and a circuit of high ropes for beginners. One of the members of the Department of Tourism asserted that 'nowadays, new, creative and innovative activities and sites are needed to attract tourists. People who work with tourism in Brotas cannot stop and be satisfied with promoting just white-water rafting, canyoning and high ropes circuits; operators need to offer distinct activities to attract different types of tourists.' Indeed, the intention of the operators and the government is to expand their tourism strategies and attract more tourists and new markets to Brotas.

The presence of international tourists is still rare and limited compared with key global adventure resorts such as Queenstown and Whistler, where the number of international tourists during the high peak season can supersede domestic numbers. According to a member of the Department of Tourism, Brotas' main market is domestic tourism, and more specifically, people from the state of São Paulo (see Table 7.1), the most populated in the country and with the largest GDP. To one of the adventure tourism operators, 'international tourists who are visiting Brazil do not associate the country with adventure activities, but rather with beaches, football, the Amazon Forest, and Iguaçu Falls, and these are what they want to see. That is how the country is marketed to overseas visitors and this is why it is so difficult to attract international visitors to Brotas.'

Adventure tourism in Brotas is also characterized by the increasing professionalization of guided activities. There is a movement organized by the Department of Tourism to develop a Guides' Association, which will be a union dedicated to defending the rights of adventure and tourism guides in Brotas. Some of the participants interviewed believe that having a union for guides could facilitate training and address issues such as safety in collaboration with adventure companies and the local council. Indeed, the Chair of the Department of Tourism believes that there is increasing co-operation between the public bodies, the tourism operators and the tourism workers in Brotas, a situation that has changed in recent years as communication has increased. Today, members of the Department of Tourism believe that this dialogue has been facilitated by the government and will start to show results in the short term. The Chair of the

Department of Tourism affirmed that 'in just the eight months that I have been in charge of the Department of Tourism, I have been able to create a deeper relationship amongst the adventure tourism operators, hotels, restaurants and the workers of the tourism industry'.

The future

To achieve the aim of developing adventure tourism in particular, and the industry in general, some suggestions were offered by the participants of this study. Other than implementing a business and convention centre, the owner of one of the hotels in Brotas and one of the rafting guides suggested that the town needs to improve the public signage by providing more information about available tourist attractions. It was also noted that signs in English and Spanish could better orientate international tourists visiting the town, despite the small international market attracted to Brotas. The owner of a hotel and a restaurant also suggested that the town should be modernized and adorned with new gardens and an entrance portal identifying the town as 'the adventure capital of Brazil'. According to a participant who works in the Department of Tourism, the main problem in Brotas is the lack of infrastructure. Participants interviewed also identified that the roads connecting Brotas to large cities such as São Paulo, Campinas, São Carlos, Piracicaba and Jaú should be improved to attract tourists who usually arrive by road transport.

One of the rafting guides interviewed believed that in the near future, the local council should strengthen its policies regarding the conservation of the natural environment to offer even more protection to the Jacaré-Pepira River and the waterfalls near Brotas. According to the same rafting guide, the environment is the best economic resource Brotas has, and it should be conserved with strong legislation. The conservation and development of sustainable tourism should start with an assessment of the environmental impact of activities offered in Brotas. Such an assessment could contribute to the development of a plan for the sustainable management of the river and its surrounding natural landscapes (Barrocas 2005).

An important question raised by the participants in this research was whether there is value in transforming Brotas into an international adventure capital. Several participants asserted that the future of tourism in Brotas will focus on targeting domestic tourists primarily from the state of São Paulo, followed by other states in Brazil. Such a policy is supported by the size of the market in the state of São Paulo, which exceeds 40 million inhabitants. Compared with Queenstown (a town with 20,000 inhabitants in a country of only four million people), it becomes clear how dependent the future of the local adventure tourism industry in Brotas is on its geographical proximity to São Paulo. However, even if there is no intention to market Brotas internationally, something that, according to one adventure operator, is too expensive, there is still an intention to improve the quality of the visitor experience and services to international tourists who, nevertheless, arrive.

Two members of the Department of Tourism share similar points of view when considering the future of Brotas and its tourism industry. According to the Chair of the Department of Tourism, the future of Brotas relies on increasing the quality of the services offered and in dealing with more demanding clients who require excellent customer service and professionalism from all the tourism industry workers. Following this idea, one employee from the Department of Tourism asserts that the bankruptcy of some adventure tourism operators is 'eminent in Brotas, and the companies that will "survive" are the ones that are creating new products to offer and are increasing the quality of their service'. The owner of an adventure operation believes that families will be one of the main markets that will be targetted in Brotas in future years and, considering that 'parents want to offer safety and controlled adventure to their children', the adventure tourism industry will be forced to address safety issues proactively and to invest in technology that will assist with this goal.

Finally, the Chair of the Department of Tourism believes that the tourism and hospitality sectors will continue to increase their economic and social relevance to the town. According to the Chair and to the activities administrator of the department, in a few years, tourism will be as important to Brotas as orange and sugarcane production. Consequently, greater investment in tourism will be made to improve the services offered to tourists. Moreover, the Chair of the Department of Tourism asserts that her dream is to see Brotas as a model of sustainability, with the tourism industry playing a leading role in transforming Brotas into an environmentally friendly town.

Tourism marketing distribution in Brotas

Research on market characteristics and distribution channels can help understand the issues that affect the growth and development of adventure tourism in Brotas. In particular, exploring distribution channels can: highlight the characteristics of demand and the mix of activities undertaken by adventure tourists with a view to providing more targeted information about products to the market, and it can highlight booking patterns which in turn can help in the development of marketing strategies. With this in mind, a survey was conducted of 190 domestic visitors to Brotas.

Pattern of demand

As previously mentioned from the interviews undertaken from other fieldwork, Brotas attracts a high proportion of visitors from the city of São Paulo. The survey identified 43.1 per cent of the respondents as coming from the city of São Paulo and a total of 95.8 per cent coming from the state of São Paulo (Table 7.1). This fact relates to the earlier discussion of targeting future demand from the state of São Paulo rather than overseas. Nearly 97 per cent of visitors come to Brotas for leisure, with 93 per cent travelling by car and nearly all of them (99.4

per cent) staying in hotels. Because Brotas is a small town, VFR is not common there. Approximately 15 per cent of the respondents were visitors, not staying overnight, with the majority of respondents staying either two (29.3 per cent) or three (25.5 per cent) nights, characteristic of the weekend and long weekend, respectively, when the surveys were undertaken. Regarding repeat visitation, 56 per cent of the respondents had not previously been to Brotas. Thus, nearly half of the visitors and tourists had been to Brotas before and were, to some degree, familiar with the destination.

The visitors' profiles presented in Table 7.1 reveal that Brotas is a destination in which travellers accompanied by groups of two (47.0 per cent), three (18.6 per cent) and four (20.8 per cent) are the most common. This result appears to support previous discussions on the future strategy to target families. The typical traveller is male (59.5 per cent), either single (44.7 per cent) or married (47.4 per cent), and is between 25 and 34 years of age (40.9 per cent) or 35 and 44 years of age (28.5 per cent). Household income is particularly high for the standards in Brazil, which reflects professional occupations (18.4 per cent) and employees in the private sector (40.5 per cent). This result is not surprising considering that the state of São Paulo is the wealthiest in the country and that the type of activities offered in Brotas appeal to people with a higher income and a more upscale market.

The survey shows that, in terms of when the decision was made to travel to Brotas, 19 per cent of travellers did so three to six days in advance, nearly a quarter (24.9 per cent) between seven and 14 days in advance and over one-fifth (22.2 per cent) between 15 to 30 days in advance. The survey also shows a high level of planning regarding the booking of accommodation and activities, with 62.4 per cent of travellers planning and booking everything in advance and 18.0 per cent planning and booking most things in advance. Direct purchases were undertaken by 91.4 per cent of the travellers, emphasising a trend found during the interviews with the stakeholders, where travellers are moving away from booking with travel agents, preferring to make their reservations directly with the operator. Travel agents 'at origin' were used to make bookings for accommodation, with most adventure activities booked through intermediaries 'at destination' either through accommodation providers or tour operators (see Table 7.1).

The perspective of suppliers and intermediaries

One of the adventure tourism operators indicated that participation of travel agents in bookings is decreasing, although the commissions paid by adventure tourism operators in Brotas are relatively high. He noted that there is a trend in the market in which direct purchases are perceived as being less expensive, even though the price charged directly or via a travel agent is the same. Moreover, in the past, young coach groups were common, and they relied particularly on travel agents for their reservations. Currently, Brotas has been receiving more

Table 7.1 Visitors' profiles and travel and booking patterns derived from the survey in Brotas, 2006-7

Visitors' profile	*Freq.*	*Travel patterns*	*Freq.*	*Booking patterns*	*Freq.*
Occupation	(n=186)	City of origin (distance to Brotas)	(n=189)	When decision was made to travel?	(n=189)
Professional	18.4%	São Paulo (242 km)	43.1%	Same day	6.3%
Private sector	40.5%	Bauru (105 km)	5.8%	1–2 days in advance	9.5%
Public sector	8.9%	Campinas (140 km)	5.3%	3–6 days in advance	19.0%
Student	10.0%	Ribeirvão Preto (150 km)	4.2%	7–14 days in advance	24.9%
Marital status	*(n=186)*	Jaú (50 km)	3.7%	15–30 days in advance	22.2%
Single	44.7%	São José do Rio Preto (275 km)	3.2%	More than 30 days in advance	18.0%
Married	47.4%	Pirassununga (90 km)	2.1%	*Degree of planning and booking for the trip*	*(n=189)*
Travelling accompanied	*(n=186)*	*State of origin*	*(n=173)*	Everything planned and booked	62.4%
Yes	97.3%	São Paulo	95.8%	Most things planned and booked	18.0%
Size of group	*(n=183)*	*Purpose of Trip*	*(n=189)*		
Two people	47.0%	Leisure	96.8%	Some activities planned and booked	10.6%
Three people	18.6%	Event	2.6%	Almost nothing planned and booked	1.6%
Four people	20.8%			Nothing planned and booked	7.4%
Five or more	13.0%				
		Mode of transport	*(n=189)*	*Use direct bookings (accommodation or another service*	*(n=185)*
		Private car	93.1%	Yes	91.4%

Table 7.1 continued

Visitors' profile	*Freq.*	*Travel patterns*	*Freq.*	*Booking patterns*	*Freq.*
Gender	*(n=185)*	Coach	3.2%	No, via intermediary	8.6%
Male	59.5%	Rental car	1.1%	*Intermediary for the accommodation*	*(n=8)*
Age	*(n=186)*	*Have been to Brotas before*	*(n=189)*	Tour operator 'at destination'	37.5%
15–24	15.1%	No	56.5%	Travel agent 'at origin'	62.5%
25–34	40.9%	One time	15.9%		
35–44	28.5%	Two times	12.2%	*Intermediary for adventure activity*	*(n=11)*
45–54	15.1%	Three times	9.0%	Accommodation 'at destination'	27.3%
55+	0.5%	Four or more times	6.3%	Tour operator 'at destination'	72.7%
Household monthly income	*(n=172)*	*Number of nights in Brotas*	*(n=188)*		
R$700–1,500	2.3%	None	15.4%		
R$1,501–3,000	29.1%	One	17.0%		
R$3,001–5,000	40.1%	Two	29.3%		
R$5,001 and over	28.5%	Three	25.5%		
		Four or more	12.8%		
		Type of accommodation	*(n=162)*		
		Hotel	99.4%		

middle-class families from São Paulo who travel independently by car to Brotas and who prefer to book their tourism products directly. Traditional large package tour intermediaries in Brazil, such as CVC (equivalent in the UK to Thompson Holidays, First Choice and Thomas Cook), have not been successful in offering packages to Brotas. The reason is that, because Brotas is so close to the largest market in Brazil, namely, the city of São Paulo, air travel is not required, which is usually the most lucrative part of the packaged product. TAM Viagens, the package tour provider for TAM, the largest airline in Brazil, offers a package to Brotas, but sales are minimal according to one adventure tourism provider.

Alternative distribution channels present in Brotas include 'at destination' travel agents and accommodation providers. Several reasons explain the use of these distribution channels in Brotas, most of them relating to the way tourism is organized. First, being located in close proximity to its main market, the city of São Paulo, means that many visitors come to Brotas as independent visitors and have unstructured itineraries. Second, the large number of returning visitors, who become familiar with the destination and its products, facilitate direct bookings and purchases (see Table 7.1). Third, as pointed out by the Director of Tourism Brotas, visitors from the city of São Paulo (the 'paulistanos') are used to booking their accommodation first and, only afterwards, deciding on the activities they would like to engage in. This pattern of booking accommodation first comes as a consequence of the experience these travellers usually have when booking vacations at the coastal resorts of São Paulo, where due to high popularity and seasonality over summer, it is important to book accommodation prior to arriving at the destinations. As 'paulistanos' comprise the most important market to Brotas, they bring the same accommodation booking pattern to Brotas, which is reflected in Table 7.1 in terms of the degree of planning and booking for the trip, with nearly 80 per cent of travellers having everything or most things planned and booked in advance. In the case of the use of 'at destination' intermediaries, accommodation providers and tour operators are the preferred channels to book adventure tourism activities for those few travellers without prior booking.

Discussion and conclusion

This chapter addressed two key aims: to investigate tourism development in Brotas and to explore its marketing distribution channels. First, it explored perspectives related to the past, present and future of the tourism industry in Brotas. The main objective of the Brotas' tourism industry is to consolidate the destination's attractiveness within its main market, the state of São Paulo. It seeks to offer a non-urban destination to visitors who want to practise adventure activities or simply be in contact with the natural environment. Therefore, Brotas is primarily competing against other tourist destinations in São Paulo state, including the mountains of Campos do Jordão and the coastal resorts of São Paulo. To attract tourists and to be an 'adventure capital', Brotas is planning to improve road conditions, public signs and tourist accessibility in general terms. The participants in this research also believe that a convention centre would help attract business visitors, who could also become potential consumers of the adventure activities.

According to the interviewees, Brotas has been trying to develop a marketing strategy to attract families, with the concept of 'adventure for all'. Attracting families instead of casual adventurers is the strategy many adventure operators in Brotas are adopting to consolidate the destination's appeal and increase visitor numbers. The family market is larger and is seen as a potentially stronger and more robust market.

Operators in Brotas are also investing in new products and attractions with the aim of reducing their dependence on white-water rafting, canyoning and high-rope circuits. The development and professionalization of adventure guides is also being processed through the creation of a guides' union and the organization of seminars and courses to update and train guides. Countries with established adventure industries, including Australia and New Zealand, have rigorous qualification requirements for adventure guides, including the necessity of formal education and participation in courses and seminars, and adventure operators have systems in place to reduce the risk of injury to clients (Bentley, Page and Walker 2004; Weiler and Davis 1993). Considering the involvement of risk related to adventure activities, it seems that training and safety are of paramount importance also for the continuing success of tourism in Brotas.

The second aim of the chapter was to contribute to better understandings of the distribution channels used by visitors. In comparison with the study developed by Schott (2007), the results presented here focused on Brotas as a destination, with interviews conducted with not only adventure tourism operators but also other relevant stakeholders. A multi-stakeholder approach was also used, with data being collected from travellers. In contrast to the case of Queenstown, where predominantly 'at destination' distribution channels were identified, direct sales 'at origin' is the most common practice in Brotas. Different travel patterns by those visiting Brotas and Queenstown can explain the distribution practices at the two destinations. Queenstown is usually part of a larger circuit trip where tourists, particularly international travellers, visit several destinations while touring around New Zealand (Lohmann and Pearce 2010). Travellers are less likely to have a rigid and structured approach to the booking of activities under those circumstances. Brotas is not part of a travel circuit, with travellers visiting the destination as a short break. Considering the booking behaviour of the market from the city of São Paulo, where travellers tend to book their holidays far in advance because of their experiences when travelling to popular coastal resorts in the state of São Paulo, this same behaviour seems to be replicated in Brotas. It seems that impulse decisions are less frequent in Brotas than in Queenstown.

Acknowledgement

Part of the results presented in this chapter were collected while one of the authors was leading a research grant on tourism distribution channels at the Faculty of Economics, Business Administration and Accounting at Ribeirão Preto (FEA-RP), Universidade de São Paulo (USP), Brazil. This grant was sponsored by FAPESP, the State of São Paulo Research Foundation (Grants # 2005/01483-9 and 2005/03669-2). The author acknowledges the support received by both FAPESP and FEA-RP/USP for this project as well as the data collection process undertaken by Guilherme Miranda, a former undergraduate student from UNAERP.

References

ABETA and Ministério do Turismo (2009) *Diagnóstico do Turismo de Aventura no Brasil*. Belo Horizonte.

Aguiar, P. H. (2005) Representação da natureza, transformações espaciais e turismo em Brotas-SP. *Department of Geography*, Masters in Geography, Campinas: UNICAMP.

Barrocas, R. (2005) A (trans)formação do turismo no Município de Brotas, SP: a relação entre o morador e o turista. *Department of Geography*, PhD, Rio Claro: UNESP.

Bentley, T. A., Page, S. and Walker, L. (2004) The safety experience of New Zealand adventure tourism operators. *Journal of Travel Medicine*, 11: 280–86.

Bentley, T. A. and Page, S. J. (2008) A decade of injury monitoring in the New Zealand adventure tourism sector: A summary risk analysis. *Tourism Management*, 29: 857–69.

Bruhns, H. T. (2009) Ecoturismo e ambientalismo: explorando relações, in A. Marinho and R. Uvinha (eds) *Lazer, Esporte, Turismo e Aventura: a natureza em foco*. São Paulo: Alinea.

Cater, C. I. (2006) Playing with risk? participant perceptions of risk and management implications in adventure tourism. *Tourism Management*, 27: 317–25.

Ewert, A. and Hollenhorst, S. (1989) Testing the adventure model: empirical support for a model of risk recreation participation. *Journal of Leisure Research*, 21: 124–39.

Galloway, S. (2006) Adventure recreation reconceived: Positive forms of deviant leisure. *Leisure/Loisir: Journal of the Canadian Association for Leisure Studies*, 30: 219–31.

Holyfield, L., Jonas, L. and Zajicek, A. (2005) Adventure without risk is like Disneyland, in S. Lyng (ed.) *Edgework: the sociology of risk-taking*. New York: Routledge.

IBGE (2010) Dados do Censo 2010 publicados no Diário Oficial da União do dia 04/11/2010, 2011. Instituto Brasileiro de Geografia e Estatística.

Kane, M. J. and Tucker, H. (2004) Adventure tourism: The freedom to play with reality. *Tourist Studies*, 4: 217–34.

Krippendorf, J. (1999) *The Holiday Makers: Understanding the Impact of Leisure and Travel*. Oxford: Butterworth-Heinemann.

Lohmann, G. and Nascimento, G. M. L. (2007) Mapeando os canais de distribuição do turismo rural na região de ribeirão preto – SP, in B. G. D. Oliveira, E. F. Zardo and R. Michelon (eds) *Turismólogo: Identidade, Oportunidades e Novos Cenários*. São Paulo: Roca.

Lohmann, G. and Pearce, D.G. (2010) Conceptualizing and operationalizing nodal tourism functions. *Journal of Transport Geography*, 18: 266–75.

Martin, P. and Priest, S. (1986) Understanding the adventure experience. *Journal of Adventure Education*, 3: 18–21.

Morgan, D. (2000) Adventure tourism activities in New Zealand: perceptions and management of client risk. *Tourism Recreation Research*, 25: 79–89.

Pavlovich, K. (2003) The evolution and transformation of a tourism destination network: the Waitomo Caves, New Zealand. *Tourism Management*, 24: 203–16.

Pimentel, G. G. A. (2009) Atuação profissional em recreação na natureza, in A. Marinho and R. Uvinha (eds) *Lazer, Esporte, Turismo e Aventura: A Natureza em Foco*. São Paulo: Alinea.

Ruschmann, D. V. D. M. (1992) Ecological tourism in Brazil. *Tourism Management*, 13: 125–28.

Schott, C. (2007) Selling adventure tourism: a distribution channels perspective. *International Journal of Tourism Research*, 9: 257–74.

Strauss, A. L. and Corbin, J. M. (1998) *Basics of Qualitative Research: Techniques and Procedures for Developing Grounded Theory*. London: Sage Publications.

Swarbrooke, J., Beard, C., Leckie, S. and Pomfret, G. (2003) *Adventure Tourism: The New Frontier*. Oxford: Butterworth-Heinemann.

Varley, P. (2006) Confecting adventure and playing with meaning: The adventure commodification continuum. *Journal of Sport and Tourism*, 11: 173–94.

Vester, H. G. (1987) Adventure as a form of leisure. *Leisure Studies*, 6: 237–49.

Vitte, A. C. and Aguiar, P. H. (2009) Da representação ao fetiche da natureza. O exemplo do turismo no município de Brotas (SP), Brasil. *OLAM – Ciência & Tecnologia*, 9: 289–334.

Weber, K. (2001) Outdoor adventure tourism: A review of research approaches. *Annals of Tourism Research*, 28: 360–77.

Weiler, B. and Davis, D. (1993) An exploratory investigation into the roles of the nature-based tour leader. *Tourism Management*, 14: 91–8.

8 Protecting sea turtles via ecotourism

The case of the TAMAR project in Praia do Forte, Bahia

Fernanda de Vasconcellos Pegas

Introduction

The widespread harvesting, habitat loss from coastal development, ocean pollution, and death in fisheries bycatch have led to the severe decline of sea turtle population numbers worldwide (CITES 2011). Of the seven species, three are classified as endangered and three are critically endangered (IUCN 2011). Different conservation approaches have been implemented in efforts to control these activities and minimize their impacts on sea turtle survival (Spotila 2004). One such strategy is to provide communities with economic alternatives to sea turtle consumption.

Since the signing of the United Nations' Brundtland Report in 1987 (Brundtland 1987) and the initiation of socially 'sustainable' approaches to conservation, conservation strategies are increasingly taking into greater consideration the socioeconomic needs of local communities in addition to the needs of nature (Wells and Brandon 1992; Wilshusen et al. 2002). One strategy with the potential to address the dual goals of conservation and sustainable development is ecotourism. Ecotourism is a market-based conservation strategy that combines conservation and community development and generates direct net benefits to both (Buckley 2009; Weaver and Lawton, 2007; Ceballos-Lascurain 1996; Honey 1999).

A central premise of ecotourism is that economic revenues from tourism can be an incentive for local residents to conserve the natural resources tourists pay to see. Studies that evaluate ecotourism's social, economic and environmental achievements demonstrate that this premise does not always hold true (e.g. Buckley 2003; Stronza and Pegas 2008). In some cases, despite local support, ecotourism has generated few jobs and income, as in the case in Papua New Guinea (West and Carrier 2004) and in Mexico (Barkin 2003). Ecotourism has also been shown to increase local economic dependency on tourism rather than maintaining a diversified economy (Honey 1999; Stem et al. 2003). Other ecotourism shortcomings include further degradation rather than the conservation of resources. In the case of Gales Point (Belize) Belsky (1999) found that in addition to providing only a few and seasonal jobs, ecotourism also negatively impacted local land tenure systems and created dissatisfaction among the community, leading to further resource degradation. Therefore, understanding the factors that contribute to ecotourism success remains a pivotal component in ecotourism research. Despite these shortcomings, ecotourism ventures are prolific and support for their use as a tool for conservation and community development remains strong (e.g. Buckley 2003; Stronza and Durham 2008).

The aim of this chapter is to provide the reader with an insight into ecotourism as a tool for protecting marine turtles and community livelihoods in Brazil. The study evaluates the relationship between economic benefits from ecotourism and sea turtle conservation in the fishing village of Praia do Forte, Bahia. Local beaches are important nesting sites for four species of sea turtles, including the critically endangered hawksbill turtle (*Eretmochelys imbricata*) (IUCN 2011), and have the highest density of loggerhead (*Caretta caretta*) nesting activities in Brazil (Marcovaldi *et al.* 2007). The abundance of meat and eggs contributed to the diet of local residents, who traditionally harvested sea turtles and their eggs on a constant but subsistence basis (Marcovaldi and Marcovaldi 1999). Since 1982 conservation strategies aimed to protect marine turtles have been implemented by the Brazilian Sea Turtle Conservation Programme, TAMAR. TAMAR's strategies are threefold: monitor for activities that violate sea turtle protection laws, provide economic benefits via ecotourism, and promote awareness via education. Empirical studies on sea turtle populations in Praia do Forte show an increase in the number of sea turtle hatchlings released and an increase in the number of sea turtle nests since early 1980s (Marcovaldi and Chaloupka 2007; Marcovaldi et al. 2007; Santos, Marcovaldi and Godfrey 2000). These records suggest TAMAR's strategies are working. This chapter examines whether employment and income from ecotourism influence values and uses of sea turtles from the community perspective.

Background: sea turtles and ecotourism

Sea turtles have inhabited the world's oceans for millennia but their numbers have dramatically declined mainly due to unprecedented human exploitation, death as bycatch in fisheries, and habitat loss from coastal development (IUCN 2011). Conservationists have implemented different strategies to control, or at least reduce, the impact of these practices on species survival and on the ecosystems they live in. One strategy is to establish sea turtle protection laws that prohibit harvesting. Sea turtles can be legally harvested in Cuba, in the community of Ostional in Costa Rica (i.e. egg harvesting) (Campbell, Haalboom and Trow 2007), and in the British Caribbean island states but harvesting is illegal in all countries along the Pacific coast of the Americas (Nichols and Palmer 2006). In Brazil, harvesting is prohibited by federal law and punishable by imprisonment and a fine (Domingo et al. 2006).

The establishment of laws has succeeded in some locations but failed to halt illegal and legal harvesting in others. Among the key factors for these failures are the combination of existing cultural values, which create a demand for turtle products, and a lack of effective law enforcement (IUCN 2011). In northwest

Mexico, Nichols and Palmer (2006) estimate that approximately 15,600 to 31,200 sea turtles are consumed annually. In Brazil, sea turtles have been traditionally harvested by many coastal communities for their meat, eggs, fat and shells (Marcovaldi and Marcovaldi 1999). In the state of Espírito Santo there is greater demand for eggs (Almeida and Mendes 2007), while in the states of Maranhão and Paraíba, sea turtle fat is used as traditional medicine to treat illnesses like rheumatism and earache (Alves 2006). In Praia do Forte residents consumed the meat and eggs for food purposes and use the head and the flippers for shark bait (Grando 2003). Although harvesting in Praia do Forte was at the subsistence level, it occurred frequently and without a pre-established selection ritual (Marcovaldi and Marcovaldi 1999).

Another strategy to control harvesting and increasing sea turtle survival is ecotourism. A fundamental premise of ecotourism is to deliver net positive contributions to environmental conservation and community livelihoods. For Pearce and Moran (1994), the loss of access to resources via protection can be minimized only if the value of protecting these resources outweighs the benefits forgone by conservation. In order to outweigh the costs, ecotourism ventures have used economic benefits to improve infrastructure, promote economic development, and provide alternative sources of income and employment (Buckley 2003; Honey 1999; Stronza and Durham 2008; Weaver and Lawton 2007).

In the realm of sea turtle conservation, ecotourism is particularly popular where resource degradation, illegal harvesting and other human activities threaten species survival (Wilson and Tisdell 2001). In Costa Rica, ecotourism is a source of income and employment for families who live near Tortuguero National Park (Troëng and Drews 2004). In Indonesia, it was introduced to reduce local pressure on illegal turtle harvesting by providing employment opportunities (Putra and Bailey 2007). In Tanoliu, in the South Pacific Islands, economic benefits from ecotourism provide income alternatives to the community (Petro 2007). At Mon Repos, Australia, ecotourism is also generating economic returns for conservation via income from entrance fees (Wilson and Tisdell 2003). As presented in this chapter, ecotourism has been used to protect marine turtles in Brazil for over three decades (TAMAR 2011).

The TAMAR project and sea turtle conservation in Brazil

The Brazilian Sea Turtle Conservation Project (TAMAR) was established in 1980 by the Brazilian government, the former Brazilian Institute of Forest Development (IBDF), with the mission to protect sea turtles in Brazil (Marcovaldi and Marcovaldi 1999). Since 1988, TAMAR has also been co-managed by the non-profit organization Fundação Pró-TAMAR (Pró-TAMAR Foundation). The headquarters of TAMAR and the foundation are in Praia do Forte. The research station in Praia do Forte, one of TAMAR's first, was opened in 1982. The visitor centre, opened in the mid-1980s, is now the most popular of TAMAR's centres with 600,000 visitors annually (TAMAR 2011).

TAMAR operates in nine Brazilian states, monitors 1,100 km of coastlines, promotes conservation via 23 research stations, employs approximately 1,300 people, runs visitor centres and promotes ecotourism in 13 communities that have a strong tourism component (TAMAR 2011). While the staff of TAMAR monitors actions that violate laws, the staff does not have the legal authority to make arrests or confiscate gear. This task is a responsibility of the agents of the IBAMA, Brazil's environmental agency (IBAMA 2011).

TAMAR's conservation approach incorporates enforcement of sea turtle protection laws with socioeconomic incentives via ecotourism. Three decades of initiatives have generated some positive conservation indicators, such as the release of more than 10 million hatchings nationwide (TAMAR 2010). In Praia do Forte, 1,156 were released in 1982–83. Twenty-five years later, 40,890 hatchlings were released (TAMAR 2008). These numbers illustrate that TAMAR's strategies have curbed traditional egg-harvesting practices. For some, these achievements are examples of TAMAR's excellence as a conservation programme (Mast 1999; Spotila 2004).

Study site

The village of Praia do Forte is located 80 km north of Salvador in the state of Bahia and it can be reached via the Estrada do Coco Highway, also known as BA-099 Highway (Figure 8.1). The region where the village is located is a thriving tourism destination in Brazil, with tourism development in the form of secondary luxury homes and apartments now occupying most of the village's urban area.

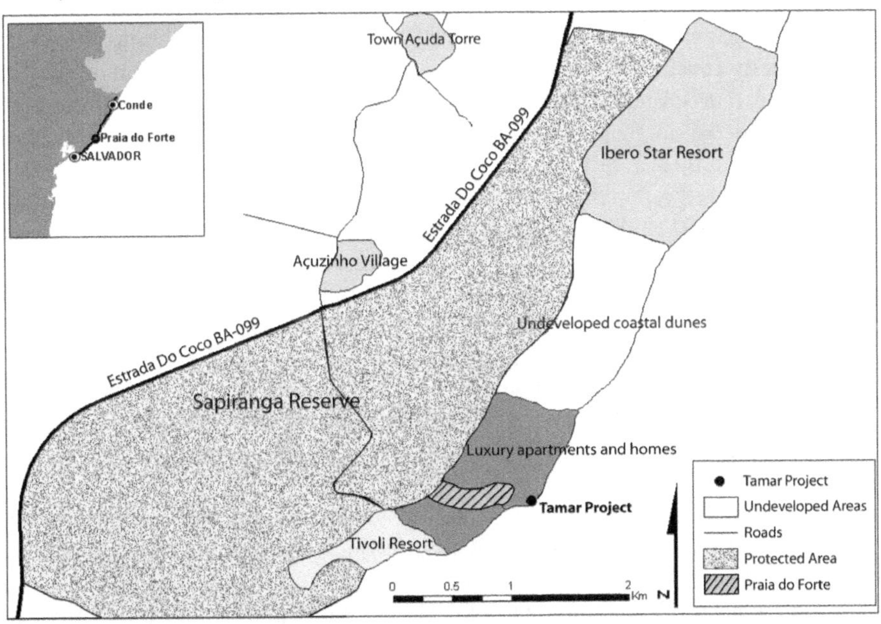

Figure 8.1 Location of the Praia do Forte (both historical and newer tourism development areas) and TAMAR's visitor centre and research station

The region has historical roots back to Garcia D'Ávila's settlement in 1551 (FGD 2005). The village, which has an approximate permanent population of 2,000 inhabitants (Prefeitura Municipal de MSJ 2004), was formed when the first families migrated to the area in the nineteenth century to work at the coconut plantation (FGD 2005). These families and their descendents form the native residents of today's Praia do Forte. During the plantation period families raised domestic livestock such as chicken, ducks and pigs to complement the main meat sources: fish and sea turtle. Income sources during the plantation period were limited to jobs at the plantation and income from fishing (Pegas and Stronza 2008).

Klaus Peters, a businessman from the state of São Paulo, purchased the plantation in 1970 and ceased the plantation operation a few years later (FGD 2005). The end of the plantation led to the outmigration of many families due to employment shortages (Pegas and Stronza 2008). Peters aimed to transform the newly acquired 12 km of beachfront property into an upper-scale tourist destination with the local fishing village and scenic beaches as main tourist attractions (FGD 2005). In 1983, Peters opened the Praia do Forte EcoResort, which is now owned by the Portuguese chain of hotels Tivoli and renamed as Tivoli Ecoresort Praia do Forte.

The region's potential for tourism development was also noticed by the state and federal governments. In 1994, the federal government launched the Tourism Development Project (PRODETUR) to promote tourism in Bahia and other states in the northeast region (PRODETUR 2005) – see Chapter 2. The projected growth of the local and regional tourism industry as result of the PRODETUR led to the establishment of the Area of Environmental Protection (APA) of the northern coast in 1995 (APA 1995). While the APA has been pivotal in monitoring tourism and coastal practices, it has not been able to control some of the projected impacts, like rapid immigration into the small fishing and coastal communities like Praia do Forte, Açuzinho and Açú da Torre. Between 1980 and 2000, the population of Praia do Forte increased four-fold (Prefeitura Municipal de MSJ 2004). The tourism industry has also bloomed over the past two decades. While local tourism *per se* started with a bed and breakfast owned by Peters in the early 1980s (Pegas and Stronza 2008), by 2009 it had extended to more 3,000 hotel rooms (Pereira, 2008). In 2007, the village was voted one of Brazil's best beach destinations (Veja 2007), establishing the area as one of Brazil's pre-eminent tourist destinations.

Methodology

Qualitative and quantitative data related to values, uses and perceptions about sea turtles and ecotourism were gathered during nine months of ethnographic research between May 2006 and September 2008. Data collection was divided into three phases of three months each. This segmentation allowed the author to witness ecotourism activities across time and during the sea turtle nesting period, which overlaps with the peak tourism summer season. The author conducted, transcribed and translated all interviews. When possible, interviews were tape-recorded. Detailed note-taking and participant observation also occurred throughout the study.

The author interviewed seven TAMAR research staff members and reviewed published material on historical land tenure and resource uses practices (e.g. FGD 2005), sea turtle conservation and consumption (e.g. Marcovaldi, Patiri and Thomé 2005), fishing culture and practices (e.g. Grando 2003), and tourism development (e.g., Bahiatursa 2008) to ensure data validity about the relationship between ecotourism at TAMAR and sea turtle conservation (Schensul, Schensul and LeCompte 1999). Data from this exploratory phase formed the baseline of the questionnaire administered in 2007.

In the first data collection (May to September 2006) the unit of analysis was the individual. Information was gathered via face-to-face interviews using open-ended and closed-ended questions. Thirty-five residents were interviewed using a snowball approach. This approach gave the author the opportunity to develop a relationship with the native fishing families and gain their trust. Detailed historical information about traditional land use practices, the fishing culture, livelihood conditions and perceptions about TAMAR and tourism in general were gathered during this phase from different family members. Of the 35 respondents, 28 were native to the village, 17 were fishermen, 12 women, and 8 worked for TAMAR. Their age ranged from 20 to 67 years old with an average of 34 years.

The second data collection phase (September to December 2007) provided the statistical data presented in this chapter. Face-to-face interviews were conducted with 77 residents. The unit of analysis was the household. Specific socioeconomic and environmental indicators used to analyse the relationship between employment and income from ecotourism with sea turtle conservation were residents' perceptions about and impacts of TAMAR, sea turtles, ecotourism, tourism in their lives and for the overall community; household income and expense by types and amounts; monthly income of the respondent and for each household member; and perspectives about quality of life across time. Questionnaires included both closed-ended and open-ended questions. Interviews lasted approximately 90 minutes. The snowball method remained the chosen method because not all fishermen and residents approached by the author agreed to participate in this study. There were also safety concerns which stemmed in part because the author was considered an outsider. This made some people suspicious because of the type of questions asked and, as a woman, the researcher challenged local perceptions of gender roles within the fishing culture. Nonetheless, this study includes representatives of the main social groups for this study: 32 native and 45 non-native residents of different age groups and gender (34 women, 43 men); TAMAR workers (n=25); fishermen (n=15); and native residents (n=34).

In 2008, the author returned to many of the families interviewed in 2006 and 2007 to assess whether values, uses and perceptions had changed since 2006 and to report changes associated with ecotourism or other tourism development initiatives in the village. A total of 15 residents were interviewed in this phase.

Results

Sea turtle use and income from conservation

Older native residents (n=14) said that prior to TAMAR's arrival in the village in 1982, sea turtle meat and eggs were consumed on a regular basis in great part because turtles were an abundant source of food. As stated by a fisherman, 'a turtle is big, feeds many people in the family, and the nest is also big with lots of food'. Harvesting increased during the nesting season because of the ease of catching nesting females and their eggs and when fish catch was low, which often occurred during rough seas. Despite frequent consumption, respondents preferred fish over sea turtle meat. The staff of TAMAR explained that such practices posed the greatest threats to the turtles since almost all nests and many nesting females were harvested during the nesting season. This traditional practice to harvest and consume turtles was also known and cited by 71 respondents (92.2 per cent).

Upon establishing the research station in 1982, the staff of TAMAR monitored the beaches for illegal turtle harvesting. One fisherman recalled that process and said that the community was told that they 'should no longer harvest sea turtles and that they [TAMAR] would offer jobs ... It was at that time that the opportunity of getting jobs from sea turtle conservation started.' Economic incentives from sea turtle conservation came in different forms: income and jobs. In an interview conducted in 2006, Gui Marcovaldi (Director of the TAMAR Project) said that as an incentive to stop the consumption of sea turtle eggs they (TAMAR) traded chicken eggs for sea turtle eggs and paid residents for harvested sea turtle eggs. Though the exact amounts and prices paid were not available at the time of this study, the author was told that residents were paid more for sea turtle eggs than if they were sold at the local market.

Economic opportunities and livelihoods

Alongside income alternatives were employment opportunities. At first, employment at the research station was low in numbers and limited to the fishermen. The fishermen helped TAMAR by sharing traditional knowledge about sea turtles, monitoring nesting beaches, testing fishing techniques, and promoting the idea of sea turtle conservation within their community. Among the respondents, 65 (84.4 per cent) said TAMAR helped and continues to support the fishermen in some way, providing them with benefits like fish bait and petrol for their boats.

With the expansion of the research station and opening of the visitor centre, job opportunities at TAMAR increased from 15 in 1990 to 110 in 2007. Opportunities also extended to non-fishermen and to the women in the community. Sixty-one (79.2 per cent) respondents said TAMAR is also a good place to work. The 25 respondents who worked for TAMAR held positions as receptionists, caretakers, housecleaners, drivers, mechanics, guides, sales representatives and educators. Their salaries ranged from US$262.20 to US$731.71 per month, with an average of US$355.31 per month (US$1.00 = R$1.64). Of the 45 respondents (58 per cent) who found employment at other locations, 33 (43 per cent) worked for the larger tourism industry (i.e. sales clerks at the retail stores, waiters, and receptionists), and 14 (18 per cent) worked in the service industry (i.e. drivers and security guards). Only three (3.9 per cent) made a living from fishing. Among those who reported their salaries (n=36), monthly income ranged from US$152.44 to US$1,219.51, with an average of US$451.96.

The number of sources of income per household ranged from one source (*n*=24) to five sources (*n*=5). The minimum reported household income was US$152.44 and the maximum was US$3,658.54, generating an average income of US$984.92 per month. This income was used to cover the costs associated with a series of household expenditures, such as cooking gas, food, education, clothing and medicine. The top three household expenditures were rent (US$195.63), food (US$178.06), and lease payments of household appliances (US$151.14).

Seventy-four (96.1 per cent) respondents said TAMAR benefits the community because it generates income and employment opportunities and promotes education for the children. 'TAMAR means work. Just take a look at the number of people who work for TAMAR. The more TAMAR grows, the more TAMAR needs people to work there,' explained a young local man. One resident found the presence of TAMAR 'a necessary component to bring tourism to the village. Everybody who comes to Praia do Forte goes to the Project, even if they do not buy anything from us, they go to the Project.' Economic benefits were also promoted for overall community quality of life, which included 'having a job' as an indicator of condition. Among the 77 respondents, 53 (68.8 per cent) said they had a good life. Although there was overall support for the larger tourism industry in the village, tourism also reportedly caused negative impacts to their lives and to the community. Fifty-one (66.3 per cent) respondents said tourism development introduced drugs, urban violence and prostitution, with 13 (16.9 per cent) stating that tourism degrades local natural resources and the fishing culture. For 72 (93.5 per cent) respondents, these impacts are the reason the overall quality of their lives is expected to decline within five years. Respondents did not associate ecotourism at TAMAR as responsible for these negative impacts, but the larger tourism industry promoted by the resort/hotel-type and secondary housing development (Figure 8.1).

Beyond economic benefits

TAMAR's efforts to engage the community in conservation, provide education opportunities for children, and foster the development of a long-term and positive relationship with the families since 1982 were acknowledged during the interviews. Native respondents, in particular, reported having positive associations with TAMAR and lasting ties with the founders. Fifty-eight respondents (68.8 per cent) said the fact that the founders of TAMAR have been in the village since 1982 positively influences the way the community views TAMAR and sea turtle conservation. For example, they stated that 'the fact that they [the founders of TAMAR] are here shows that they care about the protection of the turtles' and 'they are very important to the community'. For the remaining 21 respondents (27.3 per cent), their presence does influence behaviour because there is conservation awareness about the turtles. 'People here have become aware that there are other alternatives in getting a living without killing the turtles, like protecting them,' said a fisherman. For others, 'sea turtles should be protected because their numbers are low' and 'They can go extinct if we don't protect them.' A fisherman's daughter said the intensity of sea turtle harvesting will not return to the historical levels 'Because the situation today is different. In the past, when there were less financial resources so people were forced to kill them, but now it is different.' She warns, however, that although such opportunities are present and most people in the community do not consume or will not consume sea turtles, 'a group of people in the village would eat them again'. Thirteen respondents said they knew of at least one case of sea turtle harvesting within the last year, with non-local construction workers and non-local lobster fishermen identified as those responsible for these practices. Overall, 65 per cent of the respondents (n=35) who work for TAMAR and 68 per cent (n=36) of non-TAMAR workers said harvesting is likely to increase if TAMAR is no longer in the village.

Forty-eight respondents (62.3 per cent) said the presence of TAMAR in the village influences local uses and values of sea turtles. Seventy-two respondents (94.7 per cent) said sea turtles are valued differently from the way they were in the past because they are an essential component of the thriving local tourism economy. Fifty-nine respondents (76.6 per cent), regardless of their employment affiliation with TAMAR, said economic benefits (i.e. employment at TAMAR and income from ecotourism) were the main reasons they supported the protection of sea turtles. One statement provided by a native resident captures the overall changes in values and uses of turtles across time:

> People value turtles much more now than in the past. In the past, about ten to fifteen years ago, people here used to eat them. If TAMAR was not here the people here would continued eating turtles and they would all have been gone by now.

Discussion

Economic benefits and livelihoods

Ecotourism represents one example of a broader conservation strategy that uses alternative and more socially sustainable development approaches to achieve biodiversity conservation (e.g. Buckley 2009; Stronza and Pegas, 2008; Weaver and Lawton 2007). This socioeconomic and environmental potential makes ecotourism an approach that is compatible with sea turtle conservation programmes in many coastal communities around the world. In the village of Praia do Forte, Brazil, the Brazilian Sea Turtle Conservation Programme, TAMAR, has implemented ecotourism as a strategy to protect sea turtles for almost 30 years. A sharp decrease in sea turtle egg harvesting (e.g. Marcovaldi and Chaloupka 2007) indicates that TAMAR's strategies are generating some positive contributions to conservation.

Nine months of ethnographic fieldwork research and interviews with local residents indicate overall community support for sea turtle conservation and positive associations with TAMAR. Income and employment opportunities at TAMAR were, and continue to be, pivotal in gaining local support for turtle conservation. The majority of respondents said they supported conservation because sea turtles had a vital role in the local tourism industry, which benefited those who worked at TAMAR and the community in general. These statements indicate that economic benefits influence values, suggesting that sea turtles are perceived by the community as more valuable alive than dead. Such findings support the results obtained at other locations where ecotourism is a tool to protect endangered species (e.g. Stronza and Durham 2008).

As for economic returns to the community, employment records indicate that job opportunities at TAMAR increased over time, with many respondents finding TAMAR a good place to work. However, TAMAR workers earned on average, less than residents who found jobs outside TAMAR and at other tourism-based services. Therefore, from the individual salary income point of view, employment at TAMAR may not necessarily be more lucrative than other locally available employment options. If not as lucrative, what motivates residents to work at TAMAR? Factors that continue motivating residents' decision to work at TAMAR were associated with the long-term efforts of TAMAR to integrate, rather than exclude, the community in conservation efforts. The existence of a positive and long-term relationship between the community and the founders developed trust and fostered a family tradition that involved working at TAMAR. These findings support the claim that economic benefits are key if ecotourism is to alleviate economic hardship or create a financial incentive for conservation. However, economic benefits, though vital, seem to be insufficient to support conservation in the longer term if not integrated with other types of benefits (e.g., Stronza and Pegas 2008).

In the case of turtle conservation in Praia do Forte, the 'long-term' component is due to two main factors. First, the founders of TAMAR have been in the village since 1982. Second, promotion of economic benefits and implementation of non-economic incentives used as strategies to gain local support for conservation have been place since 1982. Other conservation programmes may be operating for a short period despite incorporating similar approaches to conservation, while others may have the time but not the strategies (e.g. Buckley 2003).

Despite successfully curbing harvesting and gaining local support for sea turtle conservation, threats to sea turtle survival and pressures on their habitat continue. Local tourism and coastal development can impact local natural resources, which include sea turtle nesting and feeding grounds (APA 1995). Tourists can damage nests by, for example, walking on top of them. New residents, unlike the native families, are unlikely to carry the same feelings of trust or have a long-term relationship with TAMAR. Also, respondents' perceptions that their lives will potentially degrade as a result of tourism illustrates the complex scenario ecotourism ventures encounter where ecotourism takes place parallel to other forms of tourism.

TAMAR's role as a strong stakeholder in the village and as a federal conservation organization has been vital in monitoring tourism development initiatives and in supporting the livelihood needs of coastal villagers. Incorporating local needs as part of ecotourism's livelihood-nature foundation has been criticized by some scholars who argue that such actions are not those of conservation projects but large-scale social interventions in complicated macropolitical settings (e.g. Brandon, Redford and Sanderson 1998). In the case of TAMAR and the community of Praia do Forte, providing for and addressing the needs of local residents has been as important for the community as having received economic returns. An example of this finding is demonstrated by the way residents value the positive and lasting relationship they have with the founders of TAMAR.

Existing cultural values and implications for conservation

Existing cultural values and uses of sea turtles that involve harvesting and consumption threaten their survival and the effectiveness of conservation strategies (IUCN 2011). In Praia do Forte, respondents stated that sea turtle harvesting was not done for religious purposes or specific cultural beliefs, but to supply families with a source of food. The use for food helps explain the effectiveness of the use of chicken eggs as a replacement for turtle eggs. The same concept holds true for sea turtle meat. Increased use of sea turtle meat was associated with shortages of fish and with the ease in harvesting nesting females. Unlike in Praia do Forte, the demand for turtle meat during the Easter period in Mexico persists despite the illegality of such actions (Nichols and Palmer 2006). These findings highlight the significance of understanding the reasons resources are used and their associated values. Such understanding is vital for effective management strategies that involve land use and tenure as well as whether resources should be allowed to be harvested or not. For ecotourism initiatives, existing traditional cultural values and uses can make or break an ecotourism venture (Buckley 2003; Stronza and Durham 2008).

Conclusion

Ecotourism ventures have the potential to generate net benefits for environmental conservation and minimize economic conditions of impoverished communities. For Buckley (2003: 245), ecotourism cases that have achieved these goals are 'still rare and most of them are very small in quantitative terms'. In Brazil, since 1980, TAMAR has used economic incentives, education, and monitors for activities that violate sea turtle protection laws to protect sea turtles in Brazil. In Praia do Forte, Bahia, local residents historically ate sea turtle meat and eggs on a constant basis. For almost 30 years, TAMAR has been providing income and employment via ecotourism as incentives to gain local support for sea turtle conservation. For Marcovaldi, Patiri and Thomé (2005), the greatest and most complex challenges to long-term sea turtle conservation is to change the habits of coastal communities in which intensive rates of natural resource use is a vital source of income and subsistence. 'Changing habits' implies changing both behaviours and values about these resources.

This chapter evaluated the relationship between economic benefits from ecotourism and turtle conservation in Praia do Forte. Results from this study indicate that economic benefits from ecotourism influenced local sea turtle values and uses. In Praia do Forte, income and employment from ecotourism have been able to change uses by providing support for livelihood needs. These achievements support the claim that economic benefits from ecotourism can become incentives for locals to support ecotourism's goals.

In emerging nations like Brazil, the desired short-term economic gain from development may come at high long-term environmental cost. There is also a belief that environmental conservation slows down development, leading to a 'develop now, fix later' attitude. Conservation of coastal and marine resources in tourism destinations like Bahia is not only important for species' survival but a crucial component of the industry's economic bottom line. In fact, ecotourism at TAMAR is one of the most popular tourist attractions in the region, attracting more than half a million visitors annually. As for the community, sea turtles have become the cash cow of the local tourism industry, providing economic and non-economic benefits that extend beyond those who work for TAMAR. In closing, the case of sea turtle ecotourism in the fishing village of Praia do Forte shows that conservation and economic development are compatible and can succeed in parallel.

Acknowledgements

The author is grateful to the families of Praia do Forte for their generosity and for sharing their life stories about their beautiful community. The author would like to thank TAMAR and its staff for their support and for providing a welcoming research environment throughout the study and the Fundação Garcia D'Ávila for sharing their archival data and Dr Amanda Stronza for the support and guidance during the study. This study was partially funded by the National Science Foundation Cultural Anthropology Programme (#0724347), the PADI Foundation, the Viillo and Gene Phillips Scholarships, and the Graduate Student Research Grant and The Centre for Socioeconomic Research and Education at Texas A&M University, USA.

References

Almeida, A. and Mendes, S. (2007) An analysis of the role of local fishermen in the conservation of the loggerhead turtle (Caretta caretta) in Pontal do Ipiranga, Linhares, ES, Brazil, *Biological Conservation*, 134: 106–12.

Alves, R. (2006) Use of marine turtles in zootherapy in Northeast Brazil. *Marine Turtle Newsletter*, 112: 16–17.

APA Area of Environmental Protection (1995) *Resolution N. 1,040 of 21 February 1995, Brazil*, Available at: www.semarh.ba.gov.br/conteudo.aspx?s=APALITOR&p=APAAPA (accessed 5 June 2011).

Bahiatursa (2008) *Invista no Turismo: Bahia, seu melhor destino – Dados Estatisticos Parte III*. Available at: www.setur.ba.gov.br/guia-do-investidor/o-turismo-na-bahia/dados-estatisticos/ (accessed 7 April 2011).

Barkin, D. (2003) Alleviating poverty through ecotourism: Promises amid reality in the Monarch Butterfly Reserve of Mexico. *Environmental, Development and Sustainability*, 5: 371–82.

Belsky, M. (1999) Misrepresenting communities: The politics of community-based rural ecotourism in Gales Point Manatee, Belize. *Rural Sociology*, 64: 641–66.

Brandon, K., Redford, K. and Sanderson, S. (eds) (1998) *Parks in Peril: People, Politics, and Protected Areas*, Washington DC: The Nature Conservancy/Island Press.

Brundtland, G. (1987) *Report of the World Commission on Environment and Development: Our Common Future*. New York: United Nations.

Buckley, R. (2003) *Case Studies in Ecotourism*. Oxon: Cabi International.

Buckley, R. (2009) Evaluating the net effects of ecotourism on the environment: a framework, first assessment and future research. *Journal of Sustainable Tourism*, 17 (6): 643–72.

Campbell, L., Haalboom, B. and Trow, J. (2007) Sustainability of community-based conservation: sea turtle egg harvesting in Ostional (Costa Rica) ten years later. *Environmental Conservation*, 34: 122–31.

Ceballos-Lascurain, H. (1996) *Tourism, Ecotourism, and Protected Areas: The State of Nature-based Tourism Around the World and Guidelines for its Development*. Cambridge: International Union for the Conservation of Nature and Natural Resources.

CITES (Convention on International Trade in Endangered Species of Wild Fauna and Flora) (2011) Available at: www.cites.org/eng/app/E-Apr27.pdf (accessed 3 June 2011).

Domingo, A., Bugoni, L., Prosdocimi, L., Miller, P., Laporta, M., Monteiro, D., Estrades, A. and Albareda, D. (2006). *The Impact Generated by Fisheries on Sea Turtles in the Southwestern Atlantic*. San José: WWF Programa Marino para Latinoamérica y el Caribe.

FGD – Fundação Garcia D'Ávila (2005) Ecoreport 2005: Comunidade ecoturística modelo de desenvolvimento sustentado. Praia do Forte, Fundação Garcia D'Ávila.

Grando, R. (2003) O conhecimento etnoecológico de pescadores da Praia do Forte – BA: Um saber ameaçado. Undergraduate thesis, Universidade Federal da Bahia, Salvador, Brasil.

Honey, M. (1999) *Ecotourism and Sustainable Development: Who Owns Paradise?* Washington, DC: Island Press.

IBAMA (Instituto Brasileiro do Meio Ambiente) (2011) *A Fiscalização do IBAMA*. Available at: www.ibama.gov.br/fiscalizacao/index.php/institucional/quem-somos/ (accessed 9 June 2011).

IUCN (2011) *IUCN Red List of Threatened Species Version 2010*. Available at: www.iucnredlist.org (accessed 3 June 2011).

Marcovaldi, M. and Chaloupka, M. (2007) Conservation status of the loggerhead sea turtle in Brazil: an encouraging outlook. *Endangered Species Research*, 3: 133–43.

Marcovaldi, M. A., Lopez G. G., Soares, S. L., Santos, J. B. A., Bellini, C., and Barata, P. C. (2007) Fifteen years of hawksbill sea turtle (*Eretmochelys imbricata*) nesting in northern Brazil. *Chelonian Conservation and Biology*, 6: 223–28.

Marcovaldi, M. and Marcovaldi G. (1999) Marine turtles in Brazil: The history and structure of the Projeto TAMAR-IBAMA. *Conservation Biology*, 91: 35–41.

Marcovaldi, M., Patiri, V. and Thomé, J. (2005) Projeto TAMAR: Twenty-five years protecting sea turtles through a community-based conservation programme. *MAST*, 3: 39–62.

Mast, R. (1999) Common sense conservation. *Marine Turtle Newsletter*, 83: 3–7.

Mast, R. and Princhard, P. (2006) Experts define the burning issues in sea turtle conservation. *The State of the World's Sea Turtles*, 1: 12–13.

Nichols, W. and Palmer, J. (2006) When reptiles become fish: on the consumption of the sea turtle during Lent. Frankfurt: WWF Germany.

Pearce, D. and Moran, D. (1994) *The Economic Value of Biodiversity*. London: Earthscan.

Pegas, F. and Stronza, A. (2008) 'The ecotourism equation: Do benefits for people equal benefits for conservation?, in A. Stronza and W. Durham (eds) *Ecotourism and conservation in the Americas: Putting Good Intentions to Work*. Wallingford: CABI.

Pereira, M. (2008) Ordenamento do território, densidades hoteleiras e seus efeitos sobre a paisagem no Litoral Norte do estado da Bahia, trecho Forte-Sauípe. Unplublished thesis, Universidade de Brasília. Available at: http://repositorio.bce.unb.br/bitstream/10482/4767/1/2008_MariaGracasBorjaGondimSantosPereira.pdf (accessed 7 September 2011).

Petro, G. (2007) One small bag for tourists brings big benefit. *SWOT Report*, 2: 38.

Portal Oficial de PF (2008) *História e Cultura de Praia do Forte*. Available at: www.praiadoforte.org.br/a_vila/historia.html (accessed 20 April 2011).

Prefeitura Municipal de MSJ (2004) Adequação do Plano Diretor Urbano de Mata de São João ao Estatuto da Cidade. Mata de São João: Prefeitura Municipal de Mata de São João.

PRODETUR (2005) *Relatório Final de Projeto – Programa de Desenvolvimento do Turismo no Nordestes – Primeira Fase*. Available at: http://www.bnb.gov.br/content/aplicacao/prodetur/downloads/docs/docum_10_pcr_ii. pdf> (accessed 2 June 2011).

Putra K. and Bayley, L. (2007) Curbing the Balinese sea turtle trade. State of the World's Sea Turtle. *SWOT Report*, 2: 30–1.

Schensul, S., Schensul, J. and LeCompte, M. (1999) *Essential Ethnographic Methods: Observations, Interviews and Questionnaires*. London: Altamira.

Spotila, J. (2004) *Sea Turtles: A Complete Guide to their Biology, Behavior, and Conservation*. Baltimore: Johns Hopkins University Press.

Santos, A., Marcovaldi, M. and Godfrey, M. (2000) Update on the nesting population of loggerhead sea turtles in Praia do Forte, Bahia, Brazil. *Marine Turtle Newsletter*, 89: 8–11.

Stem, C., Lassoie, J., Lee, D. and Deshler, D. (2003) How 'eco' is ecotourism? A comparative case study of ecotourism in Costa Rica. *Journal of Sustainable Tourism*, 11: 322–47.

Stronza, A. and Durham, W. (2008) *Ecotourism and Conservation in the Americas*. Oxfordshire: Cromwell Press.

Stronza, A. and Pegas, F. (2008) Ecotourism and conservation: Two cases from Brazil and Peru. *Human Dimensions of Wildlife*, 13: 263–79.

TAMAR (2008) Banco de dados do projeto Tamar. Praia do Forte, Brazil: Projeto Tamar.

TAMAR (2010) *Soltura nacional de filhotes marca os 30 anos do Tamar*. Available at: www.tamar.org.br/noticias1.php?cod=122 (accessed 7April 2011).

TAMAR (2011) *O Projeto TAMAR*. Available at: www.tamar.org.br. (accessed 1 May 2011).

Troëng, S. and Drews, C. (2004) Money talks: Economic aspects of marine turtle use and conservation. Gland WWF – International.

Veja (Veja o melhor do Brasil) (2007) *Praia: O Melhor Destino*. Available at: http://veja.abril.com.br/especiais/brasil_2007/p_018.html (accessed 5 March 2007).

Weaver, D. and Lawton, L. (2007) Twenty years on: The state of contemporary ecotourism research. *Tourism Management*, 28:1168–79.

Wells, M. and Brandon, K. (1992) *People and Parks: Linking Protected Areas with Local Communities*. Washington DC: Island Press.

West, P. and Carrier, J. (2004) Ecotourism and authenticity: getting away from it all?, *Current Anthropology*, 45: 483–91.

Wilshusen, P., Brechin, S., Fortwangler, C. and West, P. (2002) Reinventing a square wheel: Critique of a resurgent 'protection paradigm' in international biodiversity conservation. *Society and Natural Resources*, 15: 17–40.

Wilson, C. and Tisdell, C. (2003) Conservation and economic benefits of wildlife based marine tourism: sea turtles and whales as cases studies. *Human Dimension of Wildlife*, 8: 49–58.

9 Backpacker tourism in the Brazilian Amazon

Challenges and opportunities

Cristina Rodrigues and Bruce Prideaux

Introduction

The Amazon rainforest has the potential to become one of Brazil's most important ecological attractions based on the region's diversity of ecosystems. While there is strong domestic and international pressure for conservation and balanced development of the Amazon rainforest (Filho 2006; Ruschmann 1992; Wallace and Pierce 1996) including sustainable tourism development, the region's tourism potential is largely untapped. Surprisingly, even backpackers, usually one of the first groups to explore remote and interesting areas, are largely absent from the area.

This chapter discusses the current status of backpacking in the Brazilian Amazon, and explores the difficulties that are likely to be encountered in developing this tourism sector. The discussion will focus on aspects of the supply side of backpacker tourism in Brazil's two largest Amazonian states, Amazonas and Pará, with a specific focus on the lack of government support for the backpacker sector, access issues, cost, attractions and the natural environment. In many aspects Chapter 4 complements what is presented in this chapter, particularly in terms of analyzing tourism in Belém Marajó and river tourism trips between Manaus and Belém.

The specific objectives of this research are as follows:

1. Identify the existing scale and form of Brazilian Amazon tourism products marketed to backpackers, especially in the cities of Manaus and Belém.
2. Identify opportunities for local community participation in the backpacker sector.
3. Identify barriers to promoting the Brazilian Amazon as a backpacker destination.

Conceptualizing backpacker tourism

In the past backpacking represented a travel lifestyle beyond the industrialized mass tourism product that has been a feature of the tourism industry for many decades. For many participants it also represents an expression of identity and a search for meaning beyond the rigidly of contemporary careerism. Increasingly however, elements of the contemporary backpacking experience have assumed the characteristics of industrialized mass tourism that was the antithesis of early forms of backpacking (Ateljevic and Doorne 2004; Cohen 2004; Loker-Murphy and Pearce1995).

Older forms of backpacking, centred mainly on younger travellers, were characterized by travellers who sought to extend their journey beyond that of a brief annual holiday. It was done in a manner that maximized opportunities for social interaction with fellow travellers and in many cases with the members of the communities they were travelling through. To afford this style of travel, participants were generally very budget conscious and chose to adopt a lifestyle based on low-cost accommodation, consumption of local foods and travel using local transport networks. This form of travel utilizing locally available resources offered local enterprise the opportunity to participate in tourism at a low start-up cost (Loker-Murphy and Pearce 1995; Scheyvens 2002a).

Commenting on the backpacker phenomenon, Pearce (1990) defined backpacker from a social rather than demographic or economic perspective, based on the idea that backpacking describes an approach to travel that is not defined by the age of the participant or the level of their spending. Following this line of argument he suggested that there are a number of key social and behavioural characteristics that capture the essence of the backpacker phenomenon, including:

- a preference for budget accommodation;
- an emphasis on meeting other travellers;
- an independently organized and flexible travel schedule;
- longer rather than brief holidays;
- an emphasis on informal and participatory holiday activities.

Sorensen (2003) has defined contemporary backpacker tourism from a cultural perspective, where individual participants are viewed as representatives of the culture they are members of. As backpackers from different cultures mingle their norms, conduct and values are continuously negotiated, challenged, manipulated and either upheld or changed through social interaction. This perspective is useful for understanding changes in the backpacker travel system, although care needs to be taken not to eliminate individuals who view themselves as a backpacker but who may not conform to the accepted definitions of a traveller who prefers low-cost travel options.

There is general agreement in the literature that backpacking is a style of travel that is independent, spontaneous, based on low-cost travel and accommodation options and that has a significant social element, including interacting with the local community. This form of travel offers opportunities for local enterprises to invest in the provision of backpacker services. However, the expansion of the youth travel sector in recent years has seen a blurring of the former boundary between backpacker travel and industrialized mass tourism and today it is not uncommon to see elements of the self-identified backpacker industry offering products and experiences that are little different from the products offered by the industrialized mass-tourism sector. These constrictions can be seen in some areas of Brazil where the lack of specific backpacker bundled products has forced young budget travellers to use accommodation and participate in tours that in other areas they would reject.

Backpacker tourism in developing countries

While a growing number of researchers have focused on backpacking in developing countries including East Africa, India, the Middle East, North Africa and South East Asia (Hampton 1998; Scheyvens 2002b; Hampton 2003; Sorensen 2003; Visser 2004; Hottola 2005), there remains a need to extend the scope of backpacker research into new backpacker regions such as Latin America (Cohen 2004; Richards and Wilson 2004). In many of these regions a specialized backpacker sector based on hostels, restaurants and tours that target backpackers has yet to emerge, forcing young travellers to use accommodation and other facilities that do not allow them to identify strongly as a specific subculture of travellers. Key issues that need to be investigated in under-researched areas include the forms of backpacking that have developed, the degree of similarity or difference between backpacking in these regions and backpacking in the older established destinations such as Australia and Europe and the options for backpacking to support sustainable tourism, particularly in remote areas. This last point is particularly relevant in the Amazon.

A number of authors have argued that backpacking offers an opportunity for encouraging local development in developing countries. Scheyvens (2002b), for example, stated that backpacker tourists are able to contribute to local economic and social development in developing countries because they are generally predisposed to purchasing more locally produced goods and services than other categories of tourists, require basic rather than capital intensive infrastructure and do not demand luxury, minimizing the need for imported goods.

One significant contribution made by backpackers to local development is the empowerment of those communities to cater for the needs of backpackers while retaining control of their own enterprises. Where tourism relies on large investments in hotels and other infrastructure, local communities are often disempowered. Scheyvens (2002a), for example, argues that local participation is able to generate economic and social sustainable tourism while allowing local people to control their own backpacker businesses. Hampton (1998) also identified a number of economic benefits that backpacker tourism can provide, including job opportunities at backpacker enterprises, increased incomes for businesses supplying services to backpacker operators and facilitating local control of tourism enterprises. Hampton (2003) also suggested that the nature of such small-scale locally owned tourism businesses, and particularly their minimal capital requirements, is able to provide a useful component of local economic development in developing countries.

The Brazilian tourism industry

Before examining the potential to develop a backpacking sector in the Amazon it is useful to overview the Brazilian tourism sector to provide an understanding of the context. While there is widespread support for the tourism industry in Brazil both by the public and private sectors, this support has not yet extended to backpacking.

The most popular destinations for domestic tourists are São Paulo (7.5 per cent of domestic visitors), Brasília (3.3 per cent) and Rio de Janeiro (32 per cent). By comparison, Belém in the Amazon attracts only 3 per cent of domestic tourists and Manaus, also in the Amazon, attracts even less (FIPE 2009). The most popular Brazilian destinations for international visitors are Rio de Janeiro (30 per cent), Foz do Iguaçu (21.4 per cent) and Florianópolis (16.7 per cent). Manaus, by comparison, attracts 2.2 per cent of the nation's international visitors mainly from the business sector, while official statistics do not mention the number of international visitors in Belém (Ministério do Turismo 2010). Investment in tourism development has focused on mass tourism in the southeast cities and coastal areas (Hampton 1998; Oliveira 2008; Scheyvens 2002b) with relatively less support for tourism development of any substantive nature in the Amazon region (Parker, Morrison and Ismail 2003).

Currently, tourism is estimated to contribute about one per cent to the Brazilian Amazon region's overall GDP (Filho 2006). Neither the Brazilian tourism industry nor Brazilian tourists show any interest in visiting the Amazon region. Most domestic tourists who have the economic capacity to travel to the Amazon live in the south and southeast regions of the country and require flights of between three to six hours to travel to the Amazon (Amazonastur 2009). The high domestic cost of air travel to the Amazon is a major disincentive with lower fares on other sectors creating preferences for travel to the northeast and south of Brazil and even Argentina and the United States of America (Filho 2006; Ruschmann 1992). Research by Parker, Morrison and Ismail (2003) identified the Amazon jungle and Rio de Janeiro as Brazil's major inspirational destinations but for both destinations respondents indicated concerns about, crime, violence, poverty and personal safety.

Backpacking in Brazil

As a form of tourism, backpacking has not received a great deal of support from either the public or private sectors in the key tourism destinations of Rio de Janeiro and Foz do Iguaçu. While there are a large number of budget hotels in major cities and the popular mass beach resort regions of southeast Brazil, few have specifically orientated their accommodation offer to focus on backpackers although it is apparent that in some cases young budget travellers constitute a significant proportion of their guests. In the major cities of the Amazon the situation is even worse, with only three hostels identified in Manaus and two in Belém.

Tourism leaders in both the public and private sectors do not recognize backpacker tourism as an important element for the country's tourism development. Discussions with senior government officials in Pará and Amazonas and officials from the federal government indicated that there was little support for the development of the backpacker sector and almost no recognition of its potential to support local community development. As a consequence the backpacker sector in the Amazon is small and receives little support from either the public or local private sectors.

Methodology

This study adopted qualitative research methods including content analysis of printed information material, participant observation, semi-structured interviews with private stakeholders and governmental agencies at the local, regional and national levels and focus groups with local community. Fieldwork was undertaken over a five-month period, from November 2010 to April 2011, with a specific focus on the Amazon's two main gateway cities of Manaus and Belém.

The first element of the research involved a content analysis of the Brazilian national tourism plan, Amazonia and Pará state tourism plans and brochures issued by tourism promotion bodies and the private sector to identify content about backpacker tourism. The texts were coded using words, phrases and key themes that related to backpacker tourism, nature-based tourism and local development. According to Stepchenkova, Kirilenho and Morrison (2009), content analysis examines textual data for patterns and structures, singles out the key features that indicate specific issues and develops categories that can be aggregated into perceptible constructs out of which meaning can be developed.

The second element of the research involved participant observation, participation in backpacker tours, staying in backpacker accommodation, conversations with backpackers in a variety of locations to identify issues that were of concern to backpackers and two focus groups with members of the community who now work in Ararinha Jungle Lodge. This approach enabled the researchers to experience backpacker tourism infrastructure including tours and accommodation, conversations and complaints on a first-hand basis. Factors identified during these observations were later incorporated in the prompt list developed for the semi-structured interviews of key stakeholders.

The third element of data collection involved conducting ten semi-structured interviews with a range of private and public sector stakeholders (see Table 9.1). Each participant was selected on the basis of his/her involvement with tourism planning and marketing. Each interview was tape-recorded and on average lasted for one hour. The stakeholders identified for interviews in this part of the research included the presidents of government tourism agencies in Amazonas (Amazonastur) and Pará (Paratur). The interviews focused on participants' understanding of backpacker tourism, how they were contributing to this form of tourism, and what strategies they had implemented to develop this market. Other key public-sector stakeholders interviewed were the federal co-ordinator of the

Table 9.1 Interview participants

Participants	*Organization*	*City*
President	Amazonastur	Manaus
President	Paratur	Belém
Co-ordinator of the ecotourism programme	Ministry of Environment	Brasília
Director of Tourism Segmentation Planning	Ministry of Tourism	Brasília
Owner	Hostel Manaus	Manaus
Owner	Amazon Gero Tour and Ararinha Jungle Lodge	Manaus
Owner	Hostel Amazonas	Manaus
Owner	Amazonia Hostel	Belém
Owner	Hotel Amazonia	Belém
Owner	Hotel Fortaleza	Belém
Members of local community	Ararinha Jungle lodge	Manaus

Ecotourism Programme at the Federal Ministry of Environment and the director of the Tourism Segmentation Planning at the Federal Ministry of Tourism located in Brasília. The private-sector stakeholders interviewed were directly involved in the provision of backpacker services in Manaus and Belém.

The results of the interviews enabled the researchers to establish the current state of development of the backpacker market and identify the major pull factors that attract backpackers to the Brazilian Amazon region. The interviewer used a list of prompts about backpacker tourism to gain insights into specific issues related to tourism development. In many cases interviewees introduced new issues that were added to the prompt list. The objective of using a prompt list was to add structure to the interview, although the ordering of the discussion on the list varied between the interviews (Jennings 2001).

Findings

The structure of the Brazilian Amazon backpacker sector

One of the key objectives of the research was to identify the existing scale as a form of backpacker sector in the Brazilian Amazon. The Amazon region is remote, lacks tourist-standard hotels and offers relatively few tourism products such as river tours and jungle lodges. The region does have enormous potential to develop forest-based ecotourism products centred on the region's unique flora and fauna, its forest landscapes, indigenous culture and heritage, particularly in older cities such as Manaus and Belém. Most of nature-based tourism activities in the Brazilian Amazon region are found along the Amazon River, Solimões River, Negro River and Tapajós River, and in the cities of Manaus and Belém. These cities are surrounded by the rainforest and act as the gateways to nature-based tourism activities (Filho 2006; Unibanco Guides Amazon 2009).

Manaus, the capital city of Amazonas state with an estimated population of 1,802,525 (IBGE 2010), offers the largest range of nature-based tourism experiences such as jungle lodges, river cruises, sport fishing, bird watching and adventure tourism, which could be further developed to specifically target the backpacker market. Day cruises from both Manaus and Belém are also a major attraction as are longer Manaus–Belém overnight cruises.

Manaus is the main port of entry for travellers visiting the Amazon jungle and, apart from nature-based experiences, the city supports a small tourism sector based on accommodation, tour operators, restaurants and shops (Unibanco Guides Amazon 2009).While Amazonas state has significant potential to develop domestic and international tourism including backpacker products, the focus of both the private and public sectors has been on other forms of economic development, such as automobile and appliance manufacturing.

The top priority for most foreign backpackers visiting Manaus is to participate in an overnight jungle trip, usually from two to four days in duration spent in budget jungle lodges situated along the Negro and Solimões Rivers. Jungle trips are sold by tour operators located in the city centre, around the Amazon as Opera House. Backpacker jungle lodges are generally built with traditional materials, including wood and palm fronds and are modelled on native architecture. The lodges use low technology and supply their electrical energy through diesel generators. Collectively, the location, jungle-orientated activities and technology contribute to an authentic Amazon forest experience. Aside from the jungle lodges that target the backpacker market, there are a small number of high-end lodges in Amazonas state. These lodges are expensive and, in most instances, are priced at levels that put them beyond the reach of most domestic tourists.

Figure 9.1 Ararinha jungle lodge
Photo: (Prideaux 2011).

The physical structure of most backpackers' jungle lodges are very similar and, in most cases, feature a dining area, multi-room cabins with hammocks or beds, private or shared bathrooms and a lobby and lounge open to the forest (see Figure 9.1). The architecture of these lodges enables them to blend into the forest and most arelocated in the vicinity of river communities offering the inhabitants of these communities an opportunity for employment.

Most backpackers' jungle lodges offer similar attractions and trips, including the meeting of the Solimões and Negro Rivers to form the Amazon River; hiking in the jungle; bird watching including herons, parrots and macaws; canoeing in narrow river channels; fishing for piranhas; observation of pink dolphins; spotting caiman (freshwater crocodiles) at night; staying overnightin the jungle and visiting or staying overnight in a native family house. What differentiates one jungle lodge from another is the location and the local richness of wildlife in the vicinity of specific lodges.

The other major destination for backpacker activity is the city of Belém, the capital of Pará state. The city has a population estimated to be 1,392,031 (IBGE 2010) and is strategically located near the mouth of the Amazon River. First established as a fort by the Portuguese in 1616, the city has a rich historical and cultural legacy based on centuries-old colonial buildings in addition to ready access to the rainforest. In recent years Pará state authorities have embarked on strategies to develop the city as a major hub for Amazonian tourism (Prideaux and Lohmann 2009). This ambitious goal envisages Belém becoming a destination that provides nature-based tourism attractions, particularly along the Atlantic coastal area of the state. The major limitation for tourism development in Belém and other areas of Pará is poor tourism infrastructure, which can only be rectified with a strong collaborative partnerships between the private and public sectors. There is evidence that the public sector has begun investing in tourism infrastructure and, in recent years, has significantly upgraded the city's airport and supported restoration of some the city's large stock of heritage buildings. One fine example of what has been achieved is the Estação das Docas wharf refurbishment. The former goods warehouse has been successfully redeveloped as an up-market tourism precinct. Unfortunately, just across the road from Estação Docas wharf, a number of beautiful old heritage buildings continue to decay. One major gap in the city's' tourism infrastructure is accommodation. There is a very limited number of high-end and mid-range tourist hotels and only a very small number of backpacker hostels. Other deficiencies include shopping precincts and visitor attractions.

Pará's location in the eastern part of the Amazonian basin offers opportunities for Amazonian experiences based on the rainforest and wildlife as well as opportunities to develop coastal resort tourism along its Atlantic Ocean frontage. Other tourism resources that are currently under-utilized include river beaches along the Alter do Chão in Tapajós River and Marajó Island at the mouths of the Amazonas and Tocantins rivers. Marajó Island, the world's largest river-mouth island, has attracted growing domestic attention as an aspiration tourism destination based on its Círio de Nazaré religious festival and unique gastronomy.

To date, neither Marajó Island nor the coastal beaches have attracted significant interest from the backpacker market. However, as was the case with jungle lodges near Manaus there is opportunity for local communities to benefit from the backpacking sector. One example is Pesqueiro Village located on Marajó Island. The village is supported by an NGO called Instituto Peabiru and a tourism agency Turismo Consciente, and has targeted the backpacker sector. Services that are provided for backpackers are divided among a number of families, each of which specializes in one specific function. Examples include providing home stays, preparing and selling food and families who are responsible for the tourism activities. The result is that the families benefit from the tourism and no longer have to depend on fishing for their livelihood.

Compared with Amazonas, Pará state has invested more resources in tourism development, targeting both domestic and international tourists. In recent years tourism development has tended to focus on the state's coastal areas, specifically the main tourist locations of Mosqueiro, Salinópolis, Cotijuba, Agodoal, Bragança and Marajó Island. In general Pará has not focused on the jungle as a tourist product, but rather on beaches, culture and cuisine.

Both Manaus and Belém have environmental and cultural resources that are able to contribute to the backpacker tourism market, but in both cities tourism plays a minor role in the local economy. It is evident that there are substantial limitations that need to be overcome to achieve a considerable increase in the backpacker sector. Later in this chapter the difficulties and challenges of developing this market in the Brazilian Amazon region will be discussed.

One objective of this research is to investigate opportunities for community participation in backpacker tourism. To investigate this issue the researchers interviewed six tour operators and ten staff employed by a jungle lodge. Tour operators were identified as the basis of the promotional material that they used to attract backpacker tourist.

Ararinha Jungle Lodge case study

The involvement of the local community in the provision of tourism activities and in some cases involvement in management provides backpackers with an authentic experience in the forest. Most local communities first begin their engagement with the tourism industry when an NGO or private tour operator invests in the construction of a jungle lodge. From that point onward there are generally changes in the manner in which the community use the forest. This type of community involvement was observed at Ararinha Jungle Lodge located 100 km south of Manaus on Mamori Lake.

The lodge was built on private land by a Brazilian backpacker tour operator (Gero Tours) with a foreign partner and employs members of the local river community as guides, housekeepers, boat drivers, cooks and kitchen assistants. Other community members earn additional income from hosting guests either as day visitors or for overnight stays. The lodge owner is also assisting the local community develop their own lodge. Based on interviews held with members of the local community, it is now apparent that the community understands that conservation of jungle resources is critical if they are to continue to attract backpackers and benefit from the revenue stream they generate. Discussions with members of the local community indicate that trees and animals are now viewed as a tourist resource that adds value to their community and needs to be preserved rather than consumed for firewood and food. For example, the village leader stated that 'ten years ago, when the jungle lodge did not exist, most of the people in the community used to hunt, to fish and to sell timber. Nowadays, the forest is more preserved, we have more visibility of animals and the community understands that they need to preserve the rainforest to attract more tourists.'

Similar partnerships between private tour operators and local river communities are found in the Peruvian Amazon, one example being the native community of Inferno, which is involved with the management of an ecolodge (Pousada Amazonas). Stronza (2008) observed that by encouraging the local community to co-manage the ecolodge tourism has provided incentives for conservation in addition to contributing to building local capacity to manage environmental problems (Jamal and Stronza 2009).

In the case of Ararinha Jungle Lodge, interviews with local community members indicated that they were very satisfied with the lifestyle changes that tourism had brought. Previously, life had been difficult and based on slash-and-burn agriculture, hunting, fishing and extraction of timber. Focus group participants stated that tourism is now their main economic activity and life was less stressful, more profitable and more environmentally viable. All of the respondents complained about their difficult life before Ararinha Jungle Lodge. In the past they had to fish and plant manioc for their own consumption as well as for sale as a cash crop and had to wait between 10 and 12 months for the harvest. Now they can fish for pleasure and plant manioc for their own consumption without having to depend on it as a cash crop. They felt that tourism is a good way to make a living in the Amazon. One community member said 'tourism has benefited the community, in the past we had to work on the field to make manioc flour, which was good because our food is based on manioc flour, but at that time, life was more difficult because we had to plant to sell and to support us'. The cook confirmed the view by stating 'I prefer to work with tourism as well, because before the work was more stressful and we had to work in the sun, today everyone works in the shade and we have free days to go to Manaus.'

Other examples of this form of community–tourism sector partnership are limited but the success of the Ararinha Lodge partnership, from the perspective of both its owner and the local community, illustrates the type of benefits that backpacking can bring to local communities and importantly to the local ecosystems in which they are located. Given the size of the Amazon region there is enormous scope for more projects of this nature. However, given the current official apathy towards the backpacker sector it will be difficult for this type of tourism development to flourish, at least in the short term.

Impediments to the development of backpacker tourism

The Brazilian Amazon can be described as occupying a peripheral location for both the Brazilian and international tourism industry. For Asian, North American and European visitors, the major backpacker-generating countries, Brazil is not particularly accessible and the Amazon is less so. According to Prideaux (2003), contextualizing peripheral areas is difficult because the concept of distance is largely governed by spatial factors, human perceptions, time and transport technology. The concept of periphery is defined by a number of factors including distance, accessibility, visitor perceptions and scale, and can be measured on a scale from slightly peripheral to very peripheral (Prideaux 2003). Very remote areas situated in a location that is already classed as a periphery can be described as a periphery of a periphery. Thus for most overseas markets the Amazon is the 'periphery of a periphery' and exhibits characteristics including high travel cost, low levels of accessibility and limited infrastructure and services.

For many backpackers remoteness is a key element in the attractiveness of peripheral destinations. From a marketing perspective, as the degree of peripherality increases, the scale of uniqueness needs to also increase to give travellers a promise of value that is sufficient to entice them to discount other competing destinations in their travel decision set. Figure 9.2 illustrates how the degree or scale of distance from core to periphery operates in the Amazon. Weaver (1998) affirms that core–periphery models of this type provide a geographic framework for comprehending spatial disparities in power, levels of development and difficulties of access. In Figure 9.2 Europe is used to demonstrate one example of a core–periphery relationship. Europe was selected because it is a major source market for the backpackers. Within Brazil, the Amazon occupies

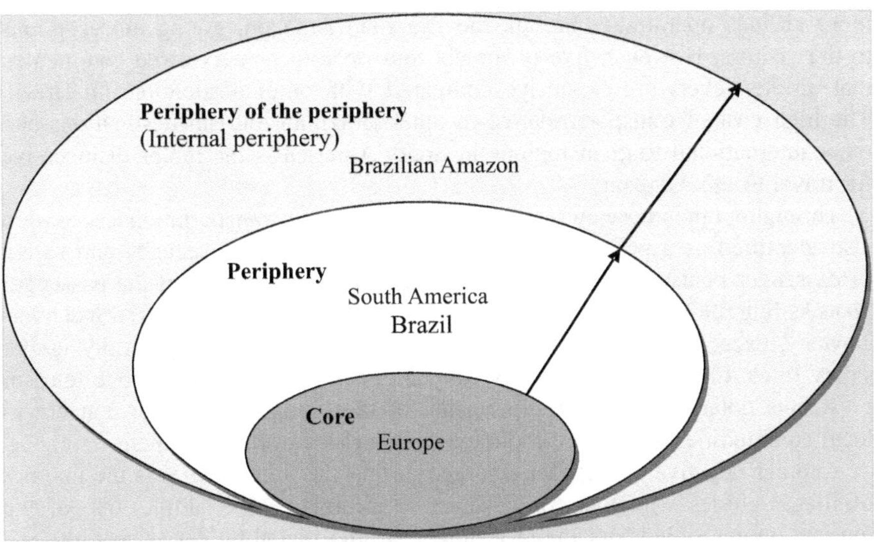

Figure 9.2 Core–periphery factored applying in the Brazilian Amazon model

a peripheral location while for Europeans the Brazilian Amazon region can best be described as a periphery of the periphery given it remoteness, difficulty of accessibility and absence from the holiday options offered in the catalogues of the world's travel agents.

As Prideaux (2003) noted in his discussion of the ability of destination in peripheral locations to attract visitors, the success of these destinations rests on their ability to offer attractions that are unique, perhaps even to the extent of having no substitutes in competing destinations. In addition, attractions in the periphery and even more so in the 'periphery of the periphery' need to attract investment in physical infrastructure and tourism infrastructureif they are to succeed (Prideaux 2003). Without supporting infrastructure, peripheral destinations face a difficult task in attracting visitors.

In the Brazilian Amazon, Amazonas and Pará states are more developed compared with the other seven states, but still suffer from a lack of electricity in some areas, poor communications infrastructure, transportation access and in some areas a lack of basic sanitation (Gouvea, Kassicieh and Figueira 2008). Commenting on the supply of electricity for example, the president of Amazonastur stated that 'Hotels cannot have blackout and visitors cannot stay without air conditioner.' This situation was experienced many times by the authors during their stay in Manaus and Belém.

Transportation is also a major issue. The distance between Amazonian destinations is a major challenge. Manaus has the only international airport in the Amazon and has direct flights from Miami and Buenos Aires while Belém is currently only serviced by domestic airlines. The other entry points to the Amazon region are by boat from Peru and Colombia or by land from Venezuela and Guyana.

Air transportation to Manaus and Belém has improved in recent years, with more airlines operating routes in the Brazilian Amazon, giving more options to the visitors. However, five of the six tour operators interviewed commented that airline tickets are expensive compared with other destinations in Brazil. The high cost of transport relative to other Brazilian tourism destinations and other international tourism regions in South America is the major disincentive for travel to the Amazon.

Throughout the interviews with tour operators, river transportation issues were also identified as a problem, particularly in relation to the security and safety of passenger boats plying the Amazon (see Figure 9.3). Many of the passenger boats sailing the Manaus–Belém route, locally referred to as recreios, travel over-capacity, exceeding the maximum recommended weight, and generally ignore safety rules. Enforcement of safety standards is very lax. As both state tourism presidents noted, the lack of supervision of these boats is a major concern to local communities and may discourage backpackers from using them.

Another negative aspect that emerged during the interviews was the number of illegal guides who tout for business at airports. For example, one of the tourism guides stated 'our major problem are the illegal guides, who often use the name of an existing tour operator to sell bad trips through the jungle'. This

Figure 9.3 Typical landing for boat passengers
Source: (Prideaux 2011)

was also mentioned by the jungle lodge owner, who stated 'the state government should give more attention to this issue. Illegal guides are a threat to tourism in the Brazilian Amazon.' Many touts target budget travellers, selling cut-rate tours that can become a nightmare for participants, when they find what they believed they paid for was not what they received. This concern has also appeared in the *Lonely Planet Guide to Brazil* – 'the backpacker bible' – which stated 'never pay for a tour anywhere except the agency's main office in town. Touts often pretend they are with a legitimate agency but steer you to a café or airport bench to make the deal. They even make phone calls to convince you the main office is closed, or that you must commit right away to get the best price or the last seat on the boat. These are all scams' (Lonely Planet Brazil 2010: 657). Tour operators interviewed during the course of the research emphasized that illegal guides use the names of existing tour operators in Manaus to attract tourists. The result has been a growing distrust of legal operators. This situation was discussed during interviews with tourism leaders in Manaus who said they are aware about this issue but do not know how to manage the problem, claiming it was an issue that the police needed to solve.

Collectively these issues affect the image of the Brazilian Amazon as a tourist destination. For this reason, it has been argued that it is very important for Brazil to address these concerns if it is to improve the images held by prospective and actual visitors so that the region can increase its competitiveness in the international market place (Parker, Morrison and Ismail 2003).

Information and marketing were two related issues raised by backpacker tour operators and by officials representing Amazonastur and Paratur. Tour operators criticized the lack of promotion undertaken by the DMOs in both states, stating that lack of information is one of the major causes for the low level of backpacker activity in the Amazon. Both DMOs affirmed that backpackers were not viewed as a potential market and this sector is absent from strategies developed at the national level. They argued that firstly it is necessary to invest in and develop backpacker tourism infrastructure and then invest in marking and information systems.

Not surprisingly, the backpacker component of the 'budget tourism' sector suffers from a poor image in Brazil. Interviewees from both the private and public sectors constantly repeated that backpacker tourists do not spend large amounts of money as they opt for cheaper accommodation, food, transportation and attractions. It was apparent that key stakeholders appeared to be unaware of the growing evidence of the contribution that backpackers can make to local economic development and to local communities in developing countries through the provision of goods and services to backpackers and the resulting increase in jobs opportunities and associated social and economic benefits.

Based on the evidence presented in this case study it is apparent that if the Brazilian Amazon region is to be developed as a new and competitive international and national backpacker destination, a number of issues must be addressed. These include:

- a reduction in fares by airlines servicing the region;
- enhancement of the quality of public transport in Manaus and Belém;
- improved safety standards of passenger shipping on the Amazon River;
- more effective marketing;
- a recognition by the public sector that backpacking can provide jobs and assist sustainable development;
- provision of relevant and accessible tourism information;
- improved human resources and skills;
- strategies aimed at enhancing Brazil's reputation as a tourist destination.

There is also a need for Amazonian backpacker operators to establish a collaborative marketing organization to develop marketing collateral, to undertake marketing initiatives and to lobby government on key issues such as infrastructure.

Opportunities to develop backpacker tourism

It is apparent that there are a number of major hurdles that must be addressed to develop backpacker tourism in the Amazon. The following discussionoutlines a number of strategies that could contribute to developing the Brazilian Amazon as a major backpacker destination.

Firstly, it would be desirable if the Amazon rainforest could be elevated in status to a tourism icon. The name Amazon evokes images of dense rainforest, indigenous tribes and abundant wildlife. The general use of the term 'icon' in the academic literature refers to activities, attractions and places that are unique while the scale of an iconic place or experience can range from local through national to global. Iconic destinations are easily recognized, well known and can attract consumers because they are so powerful that they have become juxtaposed and quasi-synonymous with the destination itself (Litvin and Mouri 2009). Given the reasonably small number of tourists visiting the area, the recognition of the Brazilian Amazon as an iconic destination has not yet occurred.

The Brazilian Amazon region has sufficient attractions that if effectively developed and marketed could be elevated to iconic status. Beginning with the region's current icon, the Amazon River, planning is required to develop a suite of associated iconic places and experiences. Candidates for iconic stature include river cruises between Manaus and Belém, visiting a jungle lodge, wildlife viewing, experiencing indigenous culture, built heritage such as the Amazonas Opera House, the revitalized water front in Belém and buffalos and handcraft in Marajó Island.

To date the potential of these attractions and experiences has received little attention, even in the domestic Brazilian market. During interviews with officials from state governments it became clear that official tourism data do not include the collection of information about available beds at backpacker hostels and budget jungle lodges (some of which are not registered). Jungle lodges that are included in the tourism statistics are the luxury lodges, although these are often outside the price range of the backpacker market. Moreover, current collection methodologies do not allow specific segments such as backpackers to be easily identified.

Secondly, the Amazon is a fragile environment with outstanding biodiversity and natural scenic beauty. Future development should be undertaken in a manner that ensures long-term social, economic and environmental sustainability. Backpacker attitudes and behaviours are characterized as gentle to the environment, interest in meeting and learning from local people, respect of the knowledge of the locals and respect for local regulations. According to Pearce (2008), backpacker tourism is an indicator group that reflects global consumer attitudes to sustainability. Backpackers form a globally interconnected international public, many members of which are aware of the needs for sustainability and in their own lives play out an ongoing battle between personal pleasure and their environmental responsibilities. Being able to offer sustainable tourism experiences provides destinations with the opportunity to tap into these concerns, while at the same time enriching the life of the individual backpacker provide new economic opportunities for local communities.

The third opportunity to develop backpacker tourism in the Brazilian Amazon region centres on Amazonian river communities and the potential they have to gain social and economic benefits from tourism. As backpackers do not demand luxury and prefer locally produced goods and services, local communities can promote their own business and tourism activities for the backpackers. Interviews conducted with the local community in Ararinha Jungle Lodge and in Pesqueiro Village at Marajó Island show that backpacker tourism is making a positive contribution to their quality of life. From the results of these interviews, it is apparent that the community employed by the Ararinha Jungle Lodge is satisfied with the change of life. Of particular note was their relief at not having to continue timber extraction. A similar finding emerged from interviews held with members of Pesqueiro Village located on Marajó Island.

Finally, backpacker tourism represents a new direction for tourism in the Brazilian Amazon region which has the potential to contribute to responsible environmental protection and of sustainable economic and social development to the host communities. Backpacker tourism is a great challenge to the Brazilian Amazon, but can be an alternative for the conservation of the rainforest and its inhabitants.

Conclusion

The Brazilian Amazon region has considerable potential to cater to the needs of the backpacker market but the public and private sectors need to recognize the potential of this market and take initial steps to develop strategies that will encourage the supply of backpacker-dedicated infrastructure. Initially, both the private and public sectors in each state (Amazonas and Pará) need to identify and profile the backpacker segments that are currently travelling to the Brazilian Amazon region. There is also a need to understand their behaviours, motivations and level of satisfaction. As previously discussed, Sorensen (2003) noted that it is essential to understand the socio-cultural aspects of backpacker tourism, for these characteristics influence financial decisions on infrastructure investment and attract the attention of government when policies are being developed. Understanding the characteristics of both domestic and foreign backpackers will also lead to increased understanding of the potential this market has for future growth.

It is also apparent that until governments change their views on the worth of backpacking as a tourism sector it will be difficult to encourage investment in the development of backpacker facilities, services and experiences such as backpacker hostels, cafes, telecommunications networks, tours and jungle guides, safe transportation and backpacker information centre. The Brazilian Amazon region is a destination that is still in the early stage of development but with appropriate incentives has the potential to become a backpacker destination of choice. The 2014 FIFA World Cup will have matches played in Manaus, offering Amazonian tourism a rare opportunity to gain access to the world stage. With appropriate support from the public sector the Amazonian backpacker sector will have a significant opportunity to promote its attractions.

The lack of marketing of the Amazon as a backpacker destination was identified by suppliers as a major challenge facing the industry. The Brazilian Amazon requires professional marketing to attract the backpacker tourism industry and to enable it to compete with other nature-based tourism destinations. Moreover, there is also an urgent need for existing operators to join together to lobby for public recognition of the worth of the sector. Until this happens it is likely that the public sector will continue to ignore the backpacker sector.

Finally, the backpacker sector offers significant opportunities for local economic development particularly in remote regions. There is growing recognition in official circles in Brazil that many of the problems faced by remote communities stem from lack of local economic opportunities. The backpacker sector offers some scope for promoting local economic development. But as previously noted, until there is a change in attitude towards the worth of backpacking as a sector there will continue to be few opportunities for local communities to take advantage of the economic potential of backpackers.

References

Amazonastur (2009) *Síntese dos indicadores de turismo do Amazonas 2003/2009*. Governo do Estado do Amazonas.

Ateljevic, I. and Doorne, S. (2004) Theoretical encounters: a review of backpacker literature, in G. Richards and J. Wilson (eds) *The global nomad: backpacker travel in theory and practice*. Clevedon: Channel View Publications.

Cohen, E. (2004) Backpacking: diversity and change, in G. Richards and J. Wilson (eds) *The global nomad: backpacker travel in theory and practice*. Clevedon: Channel View Publications.

Filho, J. M. (2006) *Livro de Ouro da Amazonia*, Rio de Janeiro: Ediouro.

FIPE (2009) *Caracterização e dimensionamento do turismo doméstico no Brasil – 2007*. São Paulo: Fundação Instituto de Pesquisas Econômicas.

Gouvea, R., Kassicieh, S. and Figueira, I. (2008) Sustainable strategies for the Brazilian Amazon region: an ecotourism perspective. *Competition Forum*, 6: 88–95.

Hampton, M. (1998) Backpacker tourism and economic development. *Annals of Tourism Research*, 25: 639–60.

Hampton, M. (2003) Entry points for local tourism in developing countries: evidence from Yogyakarta, Indonesia. *Geografiska Annaler*, 85, 85–101.

Hottola, P. (2005) The metaspatialities of control management in tourism: backpacking in India. *Tourism Geographies*, 7: 1–2.

IBGE (2010) Cities@. Available at hwww.ibge.gov.br/cidadesat/topwindow.htm?1 (accessed 14 May 2010).

Jamal, T. and Stronza, A. (2009) Dwelling with ecotourism in the Peruvian Amazon. *Tourist Studies*, 8: 313–35.

Jennings, G. (2001) *Tourism Research*. Brisbane: John Wiley and Sons.

Litvin, S. W. and Mouri, N. (2009) A comparative study of the use of iconic versus generic advertising images for destinations marketing. *Journal of Travel Research*, 48: 152–61.

Loker-Murphy, L. and Pearce, P. (1995) Young budget travellers: backpackers in Australia. *Annals of Tourism Research*, 22: 819–43.

Lonely Planet Brazil (2010) *The Amazon*. Lonely Planet Publications.

Ministério do Turismo (2010) *Anuário Estatístico de Turismo 2010*. Brasília: Departamento de Estudos e Pesquisas.

Oliveira, R. (2008) Turismo backpacker – estudos dos viajantes internacionais no Brasil. *Revista Cultura e Turismo*, 2: 90–104.

Parker, A. M. R., Morrison, A. M. and Ismail, J. A. (2003) Dazed and confused? An exploratory study of the image of Brazil as a travel destination. *Journal of Vacation Marketing*, 9: 243–59.

Pearce, P. (1990) *The Backpacker Phenomenon: Preliminary Answers to Basic Questions*. Townsville: James Cook University.

Pearce, P. (2008) Sustainability research and backpacker studies: intersections and mutual insights, in K. Hannam and I. Atelievic (eds) *Backpacker tourism: concepts and profiles*. Clevedon: Channel View Publications, pp. 38–53.

Prideaux, B. (2003) Creating visitor attractions in peripheral areas, in A. Fyall, B. Garrod and A. Leask (eds) *Managing Visitor Attractions*. Boston: Butterworth-Heinemann.

Prideaux, B. (2009) *Resorts Destinations: Evolution, Management and Development*. Boston: Butterworth-Heinemann/Elsevier.

Prideaux, B. and Lohmann, G. (2009) The Amazon: a river tourism frontier, in B. Prideaux and M. Cooper (eds) *River Tourism*. Wallingford: CABI, pp. 147–64.

Richards, G. and Wilson, J. (2004) Drifting towards the global nomads, in G. Richards and J. Wilson (eds) *The Global Nomad: Backpacker Travel in Theory and Practice*. Clevedon: Channel View Publications.

Rogerson, C. (2010) Towards strategic planning for an emerging backpacker tourism destiantion: the South African experience, in K. Hannamand A. Diekmann (eds) *Beyond Backpacker Tourism: Mobilities and Experiences*. Bristol: Channel View Publications.

Ruschmann, D. V. D. M. (1992) Ecological tourism in Brazil. *Tourism Management*, 13: 125–128.

Scheyvens, R. (2002a) *Tourism for Development: Empowering Communities*, London: Prentice-Hall.

Scheyvens, R. (2002b) Backpacker tourism and Third World development. *Annals of Tourism Research*, 29: 144–64.

Sorensen, A. (2003) Backpacker ethnography. *Annals of Tourism Research*, 30: 847–67.

Stepchenkova, S., Kirilenko, A. P. and Morrison, A. M. (2009) Facilitating content analysis in tourism research. *Journal of Travel Research*, 47: 454–69.

Stronza, A. (2008) Community views of ecotourism. *Annals of Tourism Research*, 35: 448–68.

Unibanco Guides Amazon (2009) *Amazon Guide*. São Paulo: Bei Comunicação.

Visser, G. (2004) The development impacts of backpacker tourism in South Africa. *Geojournal*, 60: 283–99.

Wallace, G. N. and Pierce, S. M. (1996) An evaluation of ecotourism in Amazonas, Brazil. *Annals of Tourism Research*, 23: 843–73.

Weaver, B. B. (1998) Peripheries of the periphery: tourism in Tobago and Barbuda. *Annals of Tourism Research*, 25: 292–313.

10 Sensual tourism in Brazil

The off-season carnival (*micareta*) experience

Miguel Moital and José Gândara

Introduction

People travel for many reasons, and attending events is one of the major motivations to travel. Events can be classified into cultural, sporting and business events and vary in form and size. From small village fetes to major expos, cultural events are sought after by tourists worldwide. Events bring about many benefits, both for tourists and for tourist destinations. For consumers, events provide the opportunity to satisfy a range of needs, whether personal (e.g. play) or interpersonal (e.g. affiliation, reputation) (Correia and Moital 2009; Getz 2007; Murray 1938). For destinations, hosting events can have a positive influence; events help maintain and strengthen a destination's image and act as demand stimulators (Edwards, Moital and Vaughan 2004). In Brazil, out-of-state travellers are one of the major drivers of domestic tourism. Besides Carnival events, some cultural events attract a substantial number of visitors. For example, Natal Luz in Gramado, southern Brazil, attracts approximately 800,000 visitors, of whom over 65 per cent are from outside the state of Rio Grande do Sul (Generosi 2011).

The culture of a people is reflected in their festivals, music, dance and other forms of cultural celebrations. In Brazil, many cultural festivals are associated with religious celebrations (SPPERT n/d). Some still contain a strong religious component, such as Festa do Divino, Folia de Reis and Cavalhada. Other events, such as the celebration of Carnival, have developed into having more of a 'profane' role. Festas Juninas (June celebrations), which also have religious origins, started as a means to honour St John, St Peter and St Anthony, Catholic saints whose celebrations happen in the month of June. Today, these celebrations are largely driven by profane celebrations involving music, food and dance. The Réveillon or New Year's Eve events are also very popular across Brazil. These celebrations have both religious (Christian or African) and non-religious elements and are associated with the search for prosperity in the New Year. There are also cultural events that do not have religious origins, for example, the Boi Bumbá events, which take place mainly in northern and northeastern regions, or *rodeos*.

Among the various types of cultural events, music-based events in Brazil have grown considerably over the past years, mirroring the trend in many other parts of the globe (Mintel 2008). While many of the aforementioned cultural events are not strictly music-based events, music is often the main component, or it has the same level of importance as the other key attractions of the event. Many of these events feature top performers in one or more of the music genres with large national appeal: Axé, Samba, Pagode, Funk, Forró, Sertanejo, Bossa Nova and Brazilian rock and Brazilian popular music (*Música Popular Brasileira*, MPB).

Irrespective of their origins, in general, cultural festivals are places where people from different backgrounds can be found and where social, physical and ideological differences are often forgotten (Bueno 2008; Barbosa 2005). Bueno and Barbosa further argue that the relaxed atmosphere transforms participants in a way that encourages communication and contact with others, which strengthens social ties. Events are oriented towards celebrating life, fostering happiness and challenging preconceived values and rules. In Brazil, carnival events are perhaps the type of event where such values are most reflected.

The celebration of Carnival in Brazil has taken many forms throughout the country (e.g. the parade of samba schools in Rio de Janeiro and in São Paulo, the street blocks in Olinda/Recife and the fancy dress (or not) balls and *blocos de sujo* across the country) (SPPERT n/d). In Salvador, the Carnival is celebrated through Trio Elétricos, which are live music parades.

The Carnivals in Salvador and Rio de Janeiro are the biggest in terms of participant numbers. The Rio Carnival involves samba music and theatre via parades all over the city, and the main Carnival takes place at the Sambódromo. The Salvador Carnival is very music-oriented. Salvador Carnival is one of the largest street carnivals in the world, with an estimated daily attendance of 1.7 million (Carnaval de Salvador 2011). The Carnival takes place every year in February or March, and it resembles a music festival. Although the range of music genres has expanded recently among carnivals, the music played at this Carnival is *axé*, a genre that originated in Salvador. The Salvador Carnival (and axé music) has become so popular in Brazil that many cities all over the country, inspired by its success, have started to organize off-season carnivals. These events first started in other northeast states and later spread to central and southern states (Gaudin 2000). *Micaretas*, as these off-season carnivals are known, attempt to recreate the Salvador Carnival, but at a smaller scale. However, this does not mean that these events are small. A typical three-day *micareta* featuring some of the major axé music artists will attract around 100,000 attendees, with the largest reaching one million attendees over four days (Diário de Natal 2010). These off-season carnivals attract a combination of locals and domestic tourists, and they have little, if any, ability to attract international tourists, mostly because they feature Brazilian music (with lyrics in Portuguese), which is presumably not attractive to foreigners.

A *micareta* is a cultural event that celebrates Brazilian music and values. Although music is a central driver for attendance at *micaretas*, it is not the only one. What is particular about the Salvador Carnival (and, consequently, *micaretas*) is a sensual practice called *pegação*. The *pegação* is the generalized (and accepted) practice of 'snogging' or 'French kissing'. While kissing is not uncommon at music events in Brazil (and elsewhere), what is unique about *micaretas* is that attendees can (and are encouraged to) engage in the *pegação* practice with several different participants.

Thus, the Salvador Carnival and its offspring, *micaretas*, have developed a unique culture whereby specific rules of seduction have been established. Physical contact is accepted even between those with minimal previous interaction (it is not uncommon for kissing to happen even before words are exchanged). Thus, one important element of *micaretas* is the opportunity to interact with individuals (of the opposite sex) at a quasi-sexual level. In other words, sensuality is materialized through several brief romantic relationships. During the event, these brief relationships encompass a 'flirting' stage, which can take merely seconds, followed by the kiss. Depending on this episodic romantic experience, things can be taken to the next level: continuation of the romantic relationship during or even after the event.

The popularity of *micaretas* results from the importance of sensual experiences as a basic human need (Murray 1938; Maslow 1943). Previous research dealing with the influence of sensuality on tourism clearly suggests that there is a segment of tourists who travel in search of sensual experiences (Ryan *et al.* 1996; Wickens 2002; Sonmez *et al.* 2006). The word 'sensual' has been used in many ways; however, in this chapter, a narrow definition was adopted. Sensuality refers to engaging in behaviours of a romantic and/or sexual nature. Therefore, sensual tourism refers to tourism motivated by travellers seeking engagement in sensual (i.e. romantic or sexual) behaviour. While sensual pursuit as a driver of tourism has been researched in the past, most previous studies have focused on sex tourism. There has been little research on sensual tourism practices not directly associated with (commercial) sex. Therefore, the study detailed in this chapter aims to explore sensual tourism in the context of *micaretas*. Its objectives are:

- to investigate the importance of sensuality as a motivation to attend *micaretas*;
- to explore sensuality in the *micareta* experience;
- to identify facilitators of the sensual experience.

To address these objectives, the chapter is divided into four parts. The first part provides background for the research, including an overview of a *micareta* and a review of the literature on both tourism motivation and sensuality in tourism. Next, the methodological steps that were taken to collect the data are explained, followed by a presentation of the results. Finally, the results are discussed, and conclusions about the role of sensuality in *micareta* tourism are drawn.

Background

The micareta concept

Micaretas are unique to Brazil, and therefore, a short explanation for international readers is necessary. *Micaretas* are off-season 'mini' carnivals that attempt to recreate the Salvador Carnival and take place all around Brazil. Although they are labelled as carnivals, *micaretas* resemble a music festival, but with some particularities. Singers perform on top of trucks travelling along a circuit at a very low speed (approximately one km per hour). Thus, the event resembles a parade, albeit one in which participants can walk in rather than just watching the parade pass by. Most *micaretas* last three or four days and usually feature two or three of the five axé-music headline artists: Chiclete com Banana, Ivete Sangalo, Banda Eva, Claudia Leitte and Asa de Águia. A number of other lesser-known artists also perform at the event. There are three forms of participation at *micaretas*.

Bloco or pista (block)

These participants travel along with the truck (called *trio elétrico*) carrying their chosen artist. In public spaces, the boundaries of the block area are defined by a rope circling the truck held by security personnel. To access the area, a participant needs to hold a ticket in the form of a t-shirt (or *abadá*).

Camarote (VIP box)

A *camarote* is a tribune overlooking the circuit. Access to these VIP boxes follows the same rules as the block – entry is granted by showing the correct T-shirt. Tickets usually include drinks (on an open-bar basis), and many have now started to offer food as part of the ticket price. Besides providing an opportunity to watch the parade, these VIP boxes recreate the nightclub experience when no artists are parading.

Pipoca (popcorn)

These attendees do not hold a ticket and watch the event for free. Initially, most *micaretas* were located in town/city centres; however, recently, many of them have started moving to specialized temporary venues, where this type of participant does not feature.

Motivation

Motivation is a central concept in studying consumer decision-making. Previous studies on tourist motivations have focused on the entire set of motivations (Beard and Ragheb 1983; Cohen 1972; Correia and Crouch 2004; Crompton 1979; Dann 1977; Iso-Ahola 1982). A different strategy has been adopted by some researchers, who alternatively look at individual motivations. For example, Correia and Moital (2009) developed a model to examine the motivation of prestige in travel. While a broad analysis of tourist motivations is important, examination of specific needs is required for a more detailed understanding of travel motivation. This chapter aims to contribute to this body of research by examining desire for sensual experiences in the context of event tourism.

Two types of motivation theories can be found in the literature (Mullins 2009). Process theories focus on how certain variables motivate behaviour, whereas content theories examine what motivates people. Vroom's (1964) expectancy theory is one of the widely accepted process theories of motivation. According to the theory, three variables interact in motivating behaviour: expectancy, instrumentality and valence. Valence refers to the importance of the outcome, instrumentality to the expectation of achieving the outcome (performance) and expectancy to the extent to which the person believes that his/her effort will lead to achieving the outcome. Based on Vroom's theory, the stronger the expectancy, the instrumentality and the valence, the greater the motivation is to perform the behaviour. In tourism, the valence and instrumentality components have been researched under the label of 'push' and 'pull' factors (Crompton 1979). Push motivations are the individual needs of the consumer, while pull motivations are the attributes of the destination/tourism product. The means–end theory (Gutman 1982) further suggests how the two ends of motivation (push/valence and pull/instrumentality) come together. According to this theory, products (and their attributes) are a means to an end, in which the end is the satisfaction of the needs.

Sensuality in tourism

Sensual tourism practices have traditionally been investigated by examining romantic and sexual relationships between tourists and locals. Most of this research has focused on 'sex tourism', which is defined as relationships of a commercial nature involving an economic exchange (in cash or in kind) between a seeker and a provider (Ryan and Kinder 1996; Dahles 2008). When the relationship does not involve monetary exchange, it is labelled as 'romantic tourism'. While, initially, these two types of sensual tourism were conceptualized as distinct categories, Herold, Garcia and DeMoya (2001) considered them as two ends of a continuum of motivations rather than as distinct categories. Based on gender studies, some authors have argued that sex and romance should be viewed not from an economic point of view but from a motivational point of view. Sex tourism involves entering a sensual relationship with the main purpose of having sex, while in romantic tourism priority is given to affection and companionship (Dahles 2008). In other words, sex tourism is mainly driven by physical needs, whereas affection/psychological needs drive romantic tourism. Research suggests that men are more explicit about sex as a motivation, whereas women tend to look for romance (Dahles 2008; Sonmez *et al.* 2006).

References to sensual tourism have typically focused on the relationship between elements of the inner travel group, i.e. other tourists known to the tourist (Sirgy 2010; Trauer and Ryan 2005) and other tourists not known to the tourist before departure (Wickens 2002), and locals (Ryan and Kinder 1996; Herold, Garcia and DeMoya 2001; Meisch 1995). Earlier studies have focused on host–tourist interaction, but more recent studies have started to examine sex and romance among tourists themselves (Trauer and Ryan 2005). The clear identification of who is involved in the romantic or sexual encounter is important. According to Trauer and Ryan (2005), there are two types of relationships based on who is involved: relationship development or relationship reinforcement. The tourist decision-making process is likely to be different according to the type of relationship. For example, in relationship development, tourist decision-making is likely to incorporate considerations about the extent to which a suitable potential romantic or sex partner is likely to be found. In relationship reinforcement, this would not be a relevant consideration. The identification of the parties involved also leads to moral assessments by those not directly involved in the relationship (Oppermann 1999); interaction with locals is usually viewed negatively, while that between tourists is considered adventurous. One of the reasons why the host–tourist relationship is often viewed negatively is due to the assumed differences in economic power between the two parties (Herold, Garcia and DeMoya 2001). This, in turn, leads to concerns about exploitation. Such exploitation is not thought to exist when the relationship is between tourists because it is generally assumed that there is no power differential.

There are a number of characteristics related to sensual tourism encounters involving someone new that make them different from those that take place at home. First, these encounters are likely to be driven by experiencing the moment without much concern about the future (Trauer and Ryan 2005). Trauer and Ryan related these encounters to situational involvement, which is characterized by superficial (rather than profound) emotional investment and are, consequently, more selfish. As they are temporally bounded by the holiday period (Ryan and Kinder 1996), these relationships imply a minimal level of responsibility (Trauer and Ryan 2005). A particular characteristic of the relationships between hosts and tourists, especially if monetary exchange is involved, is a tendency to desire secrecy (Ryan and Kinder 1996).

Methodology

This section reviews the main methods used to collect and analyse data. To examine sensual tourism in the context of attending *micaretas*, a mixed-method approach was adopted, whereby the researchers' partial, historically derived, embodied experiences are brought together with a 'data collecting' approach (Daymon and Holloway, 2011). Data were collected through participant observation and a participant survey. Participant observation is a data-collection technique that involves studying subjects within their environment (Sarantakos 1998). It involves taking 'part in the daily activities, rituals, interactions and events of a group of people as a means of learning the explicit and tacit elements of their life routines and culture' (Dewalt and Dewalt 2002: 1). The majority of the data reported in this chapter was derived from a purposive observation that took place at one of these *micaretas*, namely, Carnabeirão, in 2008. Carnabeirão takes place in Ribeirão Preto (in the state São Paulo), around 300 km from the São Paulo city centre (see Figure 1.1). In this instance, one of the authors bought a package and joined a trip party of around 30 attendees. The trip started in São Paulo on Friday afternoon and returned on the Sunday evening after the show. The package included transportation (by bus) to and from the event, accommodation (Friday and Saturday), tickets to the event (Friday, Saturday and Sunday) and a barbeque on Saturday.

The observation focused on participants' behaviour during the trip (from São Paulo to Ribeirão Preto and return) and the conversations, either between participants themselves or between the author and participants. A diary was kept during this trip to record observations and conversations. Participant observation focused on identifying elements of the *micareta* experience through observing topics of conversation, body language and the interaction between participants and the environment (e.g. singers, venue). Data collection was undertaken through informal interviewing in the form of conversation (Dewalt and Dewalt 2002: 1). In conversation, each interaction between the participant and informant is unique because the flow of the discussion does not follow a predefined or uniform set of questions. Participants in the trip were informed of the research and of the fact that data were being collected about their experience of the *micareta.* To ensure anonymity, at no point in this chapter were names or detailed personal information presented.

The same author has attended a range of *micaretas* over the years. While formal observations were made only at Carnabeirão in 2008, perceptions developed through informal participant observations at these other *micaretas* were also used in this chapter. In fact, the idea of undertaking participant observation came from first attending the Salvador Carnival in 2005 and one *micareta* in 2006 (Fortal in Fortaleza, northeast Brasil). Previous experience from attending the Salvador Carnival and *micaretas* contributed to developing sensitization with the field, which is an important element in participant observation (Dewalt and Dewalt 2002). In addition, being an experienced *micareta* attendee facilitates acceptance by the group, which permits the researcher to take on a 'full membership' role and thus enables a greater level of immersion in his/her experience (Dewalt and Dewalt 2002: 21). Since the formal observations in 2008, the author has participated in two other *micaretas*, Carnabeirão and CarnaRioPreto (São José do Rio Preto, São Paulo), which were both held in 2010 and have helped the author to consolidate reflections on the *micareta* experience.

Participant observation clearly identified sensual motivations as a critical element of the *micareta* experience. However, because the exact importance of sensuality was unknown, an online survey of past and present *micareta* tourists was undertaken in May 2011. This survey, which had a broader aim of profiling the *micareta* tourist, asked past and current *micareta* tourists a range of questions. The results of the following three questions that indicate the importance of sensuality in the *micareta* experience are reported: what the best *micareta* they had travelled to was, and why it was the best; what *micareta* they had not been to yet but would like to travel to and why; and a general motivation question asking the tourists why they travel (or travelled) to *micaretas*. The answers to these three open-ended questions were used to draw conclusions about the role of sensuality in the decision to travel to *micaretas*. Responses were analysed for content and meaning, followed by coding and aggregation into major categories. The results are displayed in Table 10.1, which contains the frequency (in count and percentages) for each category.

The online questionnaire was advertized using a variety of methods. Posts were made on *micareta*-related communities within social networks (Facebook and Orkut). A simple message containing the information about who should answer, the academic (non-commercial) nature of the survey, and the time it took to complete the questionnaire (around eight minutes) was included. In addition, because a number of past and present *micareta* tourists were known to the researchers, snowball sampling was employed. These individuals were asked to fill in the survey (via an Orkut scrap or a Facebook wall post) and were also encouraged to invite others that they knew had travelled to *micaretas*. The survey was also promoted in an online discussion board consisting of over 400 tourism academics predominantly from Brazil. The Brazilian academics were also asked to promote the survey among their students, which are part of the age group that tends to attend *micaretas*.

Table 10.1 Reasons to travel to *micaretas**

Why they travel to micaretas (n=158)			*Why they liked the micareta and thought it the best they had been to (n=165)*			*Why they would like to travel to the micareta they have not been to (n=98)*		
	n	%		*n*	%		*n*	%
People	33	20.9	People	44	26.7	Tourist attractions	16	16.3
Music	30	19.0	Music	33	20.0	Famous	15	15.3
Pleasure	23	14.6	Sensuality	27	16.4	Music	13	13.3
Sensuality	21	13.3	Atmosphere	20	12.1	Word-of-mouth	12	12.2
Entertainment	20	12.7	Structure	14	8.5	Size of event (large)	9	9.2
Tourist attractions	10	6.3	Tourist attractions	9	5.5	Sensuality	8	8.2
The trip	8	5.1	Event organization	9	5.5	Desire and curiosity	8	8.2
Escape/ relaxation	5	3.2	Price	5	3.0	Traditional	6	6.1
Other	8	5.1	Other	4	2.4	People	4	4.1
						Other	7	7.1

*The total number of answers is greater than the number of questionnaires collected (92) because the respondents could provide more than one answer/reason.

Findings

Participation

The responses from 92 past and present *micareta* tourists were used. The age of the respondents varied from 18 to over 60 years, with an average age of 25 years. The sample contained residents in 15 Brazilian states and was evenly divided by gender. Half of the respondents were not in a relationship, eight per cent were not in a serious relationship, 31 per cent were in a serious relationship and 10 per cent were married. The mean number of trips to *micaretas* taken by the sample was 11, and the median number of trips was five. The difference between the median and mean is explained by a group of respondents who had attended a fairly high number of *micaretas*. While more than half had not travelled to more than five *micaretas*, 10 per cent of the sample had travelled to between 20 and 50 *micaretas*, and five respondents reported having travelled to more than 50 *micaretas*.

The 'sensuality' motivation

Table 10.1 shows the results of three open-answer questions contained in the survey, which focused on understanding why the tourists travel to *micaretas*, which *micareta* they thought was best and why they would like to travel to a desired *micareta* that they had not been to before. According to the results, the motivation to attend *micaretas* is driven by a range of reasons, with people and music being among the most important ones. The sensual elements were also cited frequently: it was the fourth most frequent reason for travelling to *micaretas* and the third most frequent reason for choice of the best *micareta*. Sensuality was also mentioned as a reason to travel to the *micareta* that they had not been to before. A number of answers were related to the act of travelling, such as the existence of other tourist attractions and undertaking a trip, while the rest were related to the event itself. Tourist destination reasons were particularly important in explaining why they wanted to travel to the *micareta* that they had not been to yet.

How did respondents refer to the sensual component of the event? Several respondents indicated the presence of 'beautiful' people at the event as a key motivation to travel to the event. It has also emerged as a key factor among the decisions of which *micareta* to travel to. For example, several respondents mentioned 'a lot of beautiful women' to explain why they travelled to *micaretas* or why they considered a certain *micareta* to be the best that they had ever travelled to. Two respondents explained that there are regions in Brazil known to have beautiful women and that this factor has a lot of influence in the selection of the event to travel to. Several answers were more overt in their recognition of the sensual component. For example, one respondent said that the reason behind his choice of the best *micareta* was due to the number of women that he could kiss (in Portuguese *pegar*, which can be translated as 'catch'). Other respondents mentioned conquests (*conquistas*), girlfriends (*namoradas*), lots of dating (*muito namoro*), the quantity of women (*mulherada*), to flirt (*paquerar*) and romantic relationships (*amores*). All of these answers suggest the opportunity to engage in sensual interactions with more than one partner.

A small number of respondents also mentioned sex. The reasons for considering a certain trip to be the best included 'fascinating sexual experiences' and 'ease in engaging in sexual intercourse'. One respondent said that he was driven to travel to *micaretas* by the opportunity to engage in adventurous behaviour, including sex. Another set of answers was much more abstract and thus more subjective in its interpretation. However, an understanding of their meanings in the context of attending events (which is usually different from the standard definitions in a dictionary) further suggests the importance of the sensual component. Answers that were understood as encompassing sensual elements included *farra*, *animação* and *festa*. One respondent answered '*rsrsrsrsr nem vou falar*', which means 'lol, I won't even mention it'.

Sensuality in the micareta experience

Participant observation contributed to identifying a number of behaviours and conversations related to sensuality. From the outset, the *pegação* (kissing) topic was a topic of conversation between members of the trip. The short journeys between the hotel and the event venue and return also included discussions about *pegação*. On the way to the venue, the topic was about expectations and tactics, and on the return journey, the discussion was about successes. The topic of *pegação* continued till breakfast the following morning, with the conversation often centred on how many people each person had kissed. A low number of 'hits' led to condemnation and pressure to change one's behaviour. Implicit in this behaviour was a sense that not partaking is 'uncool', and therefore, talking about *pegação* worked as a pressure tactic to lead everyone who was not travelling with a partner to conform and do the 'right thing'. On the last day of the event, one of the topics of discussion was anticipating what was likely to happen that day. One group of participants in the trip compared the last day of the *micareta* to the last day of the Salvador Carnival, arguing that the *pegação* on the last day was much more frequent and forceful than in the previous days. Because it was the final day, it was the last opportunity to engage in such behaviour. The forcefulness element was also evident through observations at the event of many men insisting on a kiss, sometimes using physical strength to do so.

During the event, there were many behaviours adopted by both men and women that were associated with sensual interactions. The men showed the most overt behaviours. As the crowd slowly moved along with the carnival truck, several men faced the direction of the crowd, enabling them to make eye contact with potential girls they could kiss. Several men had no shirt on for the purposes of emphasizing their physical attributes. Some girls also engaged in overt flirting behaviours by dancing, sometimes effusively. This was to attract the attention of men. It was also very common for women to carry lipstick and to use it while in the middle of the crowd.

Drivers of the sensual experience

Sensual encounters do not happen by chance, and a number of drivers could be identified. To start with, the *pegação* was well embedded in the culture of the event. As illustrated earlier, this topic was very much discussed throughout the trip. The extent to which the sensual element was an expected feature of the event is illustrated in the views of one male participant who, right at the beginning of the trip before departure from São Paulo, asserted that people were also attending the event for romantic reasons. He further suggested that 'no one was joining the trip without expecting to kiss/stay with someone'. According to him, snogging was unique to *micaretas*, and this was influenced by the Carnival spirit, which is embodied by sheer happiness. He further noted that *micaretas* are more social than other events, such as raves, in which people tend to stay within their own groups.

The presence of alcohol was also a driver. Alcohol was widely available throughout the journey, either for free or at relatively low prices. Alcohol intake started even before the bus departed from São Paulo and was consumed throughout the entire journey to Ribeirão Preto (300 km away). Most of the trip participants carried alcohol with them, while beer and some spirits were freely available to be consumed on the onward bus trip as a part of the travel package. On Saturday and Sunday, there was an *esquenta*, which involved starting to drink alcohol a few hours before travelling to the event venue so that participants arrived at the event 'warmed up'. On Saturday and Sunday, men carrying cooler boxes mixed with the crowd in the block, which meant that event participants did not have to walk to a bar to buy alcohol – the bar 'came' to them. This is common practice at both the Salvador Carnival and at *micaretas*. Unlike the Saturday and Sunday events, which were strictly open to participants 18 years of age and older, 16- and 17-year-old participants were also allowed to attend the first day (Friday). By law, alcohol cannot be sold to participants under 18 years of age; hence, the organization made sure that alcohol was only sold and consumed in an area not accessible to those under 18 years of age. This meant that no alcohol could be consumed in the circuit area (close to the carnival truck). Several participants voiced their dissatisfaction with the fact that they had to leave the centre of the party (around the truck) to buy and consume alcohol.

There were other general elements of the event that appeared to be drivers of sensual interaction:

- The event concentrated a large number of people in a relatively small area. This led to a physical proximity that, it could be argued, drives sensual encounters.
- Because many people were engaging in the activity, there was an element of 'anonymity' through not 'standing out' in the crowd.
- Within each area (VIP box or block), everyone used the same T-shirt (*abadá*). However, participants are allowed to change the shape of the T-shirt as long as they keep the event's hologram in the centre front. The overwhelming

majority of women made changes to the T-shirt to make it more feminine (and sexy). Many men also modified their T-shirts to uncover more of the upper body.

- Many axé-music songs have an associated choreography, with several of these actually involving physical contact such as hugging in small groups and holding hands. For example, one song required the crowd to open an aisle in front of the truck, with men and women separated to either side. At the command of the singer, the men and women would run towards each other, closing the aisle. At this moment, there was intense body contact.
- Many of the lyrics of the songs also appeared to encourage sensual behaviours. For example, one song portrayed the story of a young man arriving in Salvador to attend the Carnival, saying that he is single in Salvador and asking where his love is. There were also songs dedicated to short-lived carnival romances. Some lyrics also focused on kissing.
- Singers also frequently encouraged kissing and romance between attendees. For example, they asked the crowd to be happy and to enjoy the moment through an intense kissing activity. During the last day, they asked if anyone had not kissed yet. This further shows that the attendees faced an intense external pressure to partake in sensual behaviour.

Although the above drivers are common to all of the participants in the event, they are more intense in the 'block' area than in the VIP or popcorn areas. Additionally, some drivers are specific to certain parts of the event. Notably, for block-ticket holders (those enjoying the event along with the truck), the dynamic/moving stage facilitated a frequent change in the people around block-ticket holders, providing them with the opportunity to interact with a greater number of people when compared to those at other areas of the event.

Discussion and conclusions

This chapter sought to explore sensual tourism in the context of *micareta* events. An underlying assumption of this endeavour is the existence of 'sensual tourism', defined as tourism motivated by the desire to engage in sensual behaviour. The results suggest that sensuality is an important element associated with the motivation to travel to *micaretas*. Using the means–end theory principles, which argue that a product (or its attributes) is a means to an end (the needs or values), the results suggest that participants travelling to *micaretas* perceived the event as containing a range of attributes that are able to satisfy their need for sensuality (the end). These attributes refer to both tangible and intangible elements. The tangible elements include the extent to which beautiful people attend the event, the constant physical contact often encouraged by lyrics/singers, a similar dress code (*abadá*), which is often adapted to show more of a participant's body, and the widespread availability of alcohol; the intangible elements include the 'culture' associated with the *micareta* event. Culture refers to the 'accumulation of shared meanings, rituals, norms and traditions among the members of an organization or society' (Solomon 2006: 542) and informs the members of a culture about what is expected and what should be accepted and rejected. The results of this research suggest that the culture of the events was one geared towards the expectation that participants engage in sensual behaviours (notably, the *pegação*).

While research on tourism and sensuality is not new, most of it has focused on (paid) sex tourism involving hosts and guests. This chapter has documented a different perspective on sensual tourism whereby a relationship, whether at a romantic or a sexual level, does not have a commercial nature. While both the hosts and the guests engaged in sensual behaviour at *micaretas*, most of the time, it is not possible to distinguish between locals and tourists because all the participants were in the same place with important physical cues removed (all are wearing the same T-shirt). While the event is unlikely to be attended by lower classes due to its cost, the removal of physical/symbolic barriers between participants through the wearing of a common t-shirt led to reducing any differences in the social background of participants (i.e. between those of the middle and upper classes). Hence, all of the participants tended to be at the same compatible social levels.

As suggested by Piorkowski and Cardone (2000), there are four levels of intimacy: physical intimacy (actual body contact), communication intimacy (verbal and non-verbal communication), spiritual intimacy (sharing values and beliefs) and intellectual intimacy (sharing knowledge). The results of participant observation suggest that there are three levels of sensual encounters in the *micareta* travel experience, which are conceptualized in terms of progression: flirting, passionate and sexual. These three levels can be looked at in terms of the type and amount of intimacy that they involve. The research also suggests that both the types and amount of intimacy vary according to the type of ticket held: VIP box or block. Table 10.2 provides a tentative profile of each type of sensual encounter based on the types of intimacy that they encompass (spiritual and intellectual were merged into one category, as their separation is not thought

Table 10.2 Intimacy according to the three levels of sensual encounters

	Block			*VIP Box*		
	Physical	*Communication*	*Spiritual and Intellectual*	*Physical*	*Communication*	*Spiritual and Intellectual*
Flirting	No	Non-verbal, possibly verbal	Inexistent or minimal	No	Non-verbal and verbal	Limited
Passionate	Yes	Non-verbal, possibly verbal	Inexistent or minimal	Yes	Non-verbal and verbal	Limited
Sexual	Yes	Non-verbal and verbal	Minimal	Yes	Non-verbal and verbal	Limited

to be relevant in this analysis). They reflect the minimum levels of intimacy required at each sensual encounter level.

Unlike flirting, the passionate and sexual levels involve physical intimacy. The main difference between passionate and sexual sensual experiences is that the latter involves sexual intercourse. Within the block experience, communication intimacy at the flirting and passionate levels can be non-verbal only. It is not uncommon that physical contact (a kiss) happens without the exchange of words. In the VIP box, both verbal and non-verbal communications usually involve all three levels, as encounters tend to last longer. At the sexual level, both verbal and non-verbal communication intimacy exist, irrespective of the type of ticket held. While spiritual and intellectual intimacies are not intense during the event itself, they are less likely to exist within the block experience, given the episodic nature of many sensual interactions. Travelling as part of an organized trip provides an experience closer to the VIP box, as participants travelling in the same coach are able to interact throughout the whole trip. This greater interaction leads to greater levels of intimacy – communication, spiritual and intellectual – as it is possible to 'get to know' more about the participants in the trip. Those who joined the trip tended to be in their late twenties or thirties, which is at the higher end of the age range of the typical attendee (18 to 40 years).

Besides economic reasons, one plausible explanation for the preference for travelling in a group is that, as people grow older, they are keen to experience higher levels of knowledge and intellectual intimacy along with physical intimacy. Based on observing the participants, this chapter has provided evidence of a different form of sensual tourism, which is mainly driven by 'passion' (physical contact without intercourse). While sex appears to be involved and is likely to be an important element, it does not appear to be the driving motivation. *Micareta* tourism is centred on the opportunity to interact with individuals of the opposite sex at a quasi-sexual level, where the need for sensual experiences is materialized through several brief sensual relationships underpinned by the practice of kissing. Using the three-factor model of satisfaction (Fuller and Matzler 2008), for the sensual tourist attending *micaretas*, relationships at the sexual level are likely to be viewed as an 'excitement factor' (they increase satisfaction if materialized but do not cause dissatisfaction otherwise), while relationships at the passionate level are considered to be a 'performance' factor (they lead to satisfaction if performance is high and to dissatisfaction if performance is low). This contrasts with sex tourism, in which the extent to which the relationship happens at the sexual level functions as being a 'performance' factor.

Depending on the 'satisfaction' with the episodic sensual experience, the relationship can then be taken to the next level: continuation of the romantic relationship during the event/trip or even after the trip. In other words, for those who were not in a relationship (the vast majority of attendees), there was an element of enjoying the moment, but there was also the possibility of developing a post-trip relationship with individuals that they met at the event. In fact, there were plenty of examples of long-term relationships that developed between people who met at these events. In a sense, *micaretas* appear to work as a mega-speed-dating event, albeit one in which the 'two minutes' of interaction involve mainly physical contact. This long-term perspective is usually not associated with romantic or sex tourism (the labels used previously in the literature refer to sensual tourism). Sex tourism is short-term oriented, in the sense that relationships are unlikely to develop at the destination after the trip has ended, even those of a non-commercial nature.

While similar forms of sensual tourism have been identified, such as clubbing tourism, *micareta* tourism is different. Sensual behaviour at *micaretas* is highly visible, accepted and encouraged, whether subtly through lyrics or overtly by singers during the shows. Event organizers also understand this sensual component and have used it in marketing *micaretas*. A recent update on the 'Folianópolis' Facebook page (Folianópolis is the off-season carnival in Florianópolis in Santa Catarina state) said 'good morning, greetings from the most beautiful *micareta* in Brazil'.

This chapter reported an exploratory study of sensual tourism in Brazil. The findings suggest that there are different types of *micareta* tourists, one type of which appears to be driven largely by sensual needs. However, not everyone is likely to seek sensual tourism. In fact, a proportion of attendees appear to reject the 'episodic romance' component of the event by not engaging in the kissing behaviour. Even within the sensual tourist group, there appear to be sub-groups. For example, those who go to the VIP box, while still looking for romance, do not want to undergo the intense kissing pressure that occurs in the block area. Therefore, future research should examine in more detail not only the different types of *micareta* tourists but also the existence of different types of sensual tourists.

Another possible future research direction is to explore the relationship between one's sensuality and *micareta* attendance career. The results appear to suggest not only that sensuality is strongly related to *micareta* attendance but also that it is related to how people experience the event. It appears that behaviours associated with travelling to *micaretas* change according to changes in personal circumstances (e.g. age, relationship status and past *micareta* attendance). This suggests the existence of an event career directly anchored in the sensual element. Finally, a close examination of differences in sensual motivation across genders could also be made. Preliminary evidence from this study appears to support findings from previous studies that suggest that men and women are different when it comes to engaging in sensual behaviour while travelling (Dahles 2008; Sonmez *et al.* 2006).

References

Barbosa, F. M. (2005) O evento como contraponto do cotidiano. *II ANPTUR*, Balneário Camboriu. Available at: www.anptur.org.br/anais/seminario2005 (accessed 16 May 2011).

Beard, J. G. and Ragheb, M. G. (1983) Measuring leisure motivation. *Journal of Leisure Research*, 15: 219–28.

Bueno, M. S. (2008) Lazer, festa e festejar. CULTUR – Revista de Cultura e Turismo, vol. 2 (online).

Carnaval de Salvador (2011) *Números do Carnaval*. Available at: www.carnaval.salvador.ba.gov.br/2011/servicos/numeroscarnaval.asp#festa (accessed 16 May 2011).

Cohen, J. B. (1972) *Behavioural Science Foundation of Consumer Behaviour*. New York: Free Press.

Correia, A. and Crouch, G. (2004) A study of tourist decision processes: Algarve, Portugal, in G. Crouch, R. Perdue, H. Timmermans and M. Uysal (eds). *Consumer Psychology of Tourism, Hospitality and Leisure*, Vol.3, in Oxford: CABI Publishing. pp. 121–34.

Correia, A. and Moital, M. (2009) The antecedents and consequences of prestige motivation in tourism: an expectancy-value motivation. in M. Kozak and A. Decrop (eds) *Handbook of Tourism Behaviour: Theory and Practice*. New York: Routledge, 16-30.

Crompton, J. L. (1979) Motivations of pleasure vacation. *Annals of Tourism Research*, 6: 408–24.

Dahles, H. (2008) Romance and sex tourism, in M. Hitchcock, V. T. King and M. Parnwell (eds) *Tourism in Southeast Asia: Challenges and New Directions*, Copenhagen: NIAS Press, pp. 222–35.

Dann, G. M. S. (1977) Anomie, ego-enhancement and tourism. *Annals of Tourism Research*, 4: 184–94.

Daymon, C. and Holloway, I. (2011) *Qualitative Research Methods in Public Relations and Marketing Communications*, 8th edn. London: Routledge.

Dewalt, M. and Dewalt, B. (2002) *Participant Observation: A Guide for Fieldworkers*. Lanham: Altamira Press.

Diário de Natal (2010) Segurança do Carnatal terá 1,5 mil policiais. Available at: www.diariodenatal.com.br/2010/12/01/cidades4_0.php (accessed 16 May 2011).

Edwards, J., Moital, M. and Vaughan, R. (2004) The impacts of mega-events: the case of EXPO'98 – Lisbon', in M. Robinson and P. Long (eds) *Tourism and Cultural Festivals and Events: Marketing, Management and Development*. Sunderland: Business Education Publishers, pp. 195–215.

Fuller, J. and Matzler, K. (2008) Customer delight and market segmentation: An application of the three-factor theory of customer satisfaction on life style groups. *Tourism Management*, 29: 116–26.

Gaudin, B. (2000) Da mi-careme ao carnabeach: a história da(s) micareta(s). *Tempo Social*, 12: 47–68.

Generosi, A. (2011) Natal Luz em Gramado (RS), tradição e inovação: um olhar sobre os fatores que determinam o retorno dos turistas ao evento. MSc thesis, Universidade de Caxias do Sul.

Getz, D. (2007) *Event Studies. Theory, Research and Policy for Planned Events*. Oxford: Butterworth-Heinemann.

Gutman, J. (1982) A means-end chain model based on consumer categorisation process. *Journal of Marketing*, 46: 60–72.

Herold, E., Garcia, R. and DeMoya, T. (2001) Female tourists and beach boys: romance or sex tourism? *Annals of Tourism Research*, 28: 978–97.

Iso-Ahola, S. (1982) Towards a social psychology of tourism motivation – a rejoinder. *Annals of Tourism Research*, 9: 256–61.

Maslow, A. (1943) A theory of human motivation. *Psychological Review*, 50: 370–96.

Meisch, L.A. (1995) Gringas and Otalaveros: changing tourist relations. *Annals of Tourism Research*, 22: 441–62.

Mintel (2008) *Music Concerts and Festivals – UK – August 2008*, Mintel International.

Mullins, L. (2009) *Management and Organisational Behaviour*, 8th edn. London: Prentice Hall.

Murray, H.A. (1938) *Explorations in Personality*. Oxford: Oxford University Press.

Oppermann, M. (1999) Sex tourism. *Annals of Tourism Research*, 26: 251–66.

Piorkowski, G. K. and Cardone, S. S. (2000) *Too Close for Comfort: Exploring the Risks of Intimacy*. Boulder: Perseus Publishing.

Ryan, C. and Kinder, R. (1996) Sex, tourism and sex tourism: fulfilling similar needs? *Tourism Management*, 17: 507–18.

Ryan, C., Robertson, E., Page, S. J. and Kearsley, G. (1996) New Zealand students: risk behaviour while on holiday. *Annals of Tourism Research*, 17: 64–9.

Sarantakos, S. (1998) *Social Research*. New York: Palgrave.

Sirgy, M. J. (2010) Toward a quality-of-life theory of leisure travel satisfaction. *Journal of Travel Research*, 49: 246–60.

Solomon, M. (2006) *Consumer Behaviour: Buying, Having, Being*, 7th edn. Harlow: Pearson Education.

Sonmez, S., Apostolopoulos, Y., Yu, C. H., Yang, S. and Mattila, A. (2006) Binge drinking and casual sex on spring break. *Annals of Tourism Research*, 33: 895–917.

SPPERT (n/d) Festas Populares Brasil. Available at: www.sppert.com.br/Brasil/Cultura/Festas_populares/ (accessed 16 May 2011).

Trauer, B. and Ryan, C. (2005) Destination image, romance and place experience – application of intimacy theory. *Tourism Management*, 26: 481–91.

Vroom, V. (1964) *Work and Motivation*. New York: Wiley.

Wickens, E. (2002) The sacred and the profane: a tourist typology. *Annals of Tourism Research*, 29: 834–51.

11 Staged indigeneity and the Pataxó

Rodrigo de Azeredo Grünewald

Introduction

Indigenous societies in Brazil have resorted to various survival strategies to guarantee their social reproduction. Since the 1970s, the emergence of tourism as an economic alternative for indigenous societies has been seen not only through Indian handicraft sales volume but also through academic publications (Aspelin 1977). Highly acculturated native populations in different areas of Brazil have developed various tourism activities, including trade shows, exhibits, museums and other types of cultural activities. These societies have invested in intense processes of cultural production, which, reaching beyond the instrumentality of tourism exhibition, emphasize their ethnicities through a movement running counter to the acculturation pattern imposed by colonial expansion and global capitalism.

Based on research materials collected among the Pataxó, an indigenous group living along the southernmost coast of the state of Bahia, the attractions most required by tourists are commoditized handicraft or material culture, such as dances and other performances, including body painting and shamanism. For that reason, these are the elements that have been renovated or reconstructed by the Pataxó. Most aspects of so-called 'indigenous tourism' appear in the classification proposed by Smith (1996), which is based on four characteristics known as 'the 4Hs': habitat, heritage, history and handicraft. Chambers (2000) adds a fifth H – healing – which is also present in such contexts.

By examining tourism among the Pataxó, the objective of this chapter is to verify which particular tourism patterns have prevailed in this case and the socio-cultural implications of those patterns. Globally oriented economic flows and social perspectives, along with the resulting private and governmental investment, helped to configure two facets of tourism in the region: first, a form of tourism that did not specifically strengthen the ethnic aspects of the Pataxó people; and, second, a form of tourism with a model consolidated from an ethno-developmental logic that ensures sustainability for part of the population under consideration. Based on such duality, this chapter intends to assume the stage perspective (MacCannell 1973) and to re-elaborate it in a positive way, focusing on the indigenous social dynamics that legitimately recreate the reference culture for exhibition in what it is called ethnotourism arenas.

In particular, this chapter aims to examine the creation of tourism arenas associated with social spaces demanded by a post-modern perspective that encourages natives to reconstruct their ethnicity (MacCannell 1992) and to renovate their reference culture. In the background, however, the general reader can detect the existence of a large polyphonic arena moulded by the hegemonic society where indigenous ethnicity is minimized.

Theory, field and method

According to Max Weber's classic sociological work (1991), to comprehend the notion of an ethnic community means to perceive it as a characteristic commonality, as its members subjectively sense it. A common feature (a common origin, for instance) can establish contrast with other groups that do not possess it and allow communal action from already established boundaries. As in classic sociological thought, the subject of ethnicity arose as a political unity with boundaries that mark contrastivity among groups. Through the subjective, contextual criteria of ethnic identity that feature such notions of contrastivity, a particular group perceives and defines itself in opposition to every other group. Therefore, it is the ethnic self-ascription of collectivity agents that provides an operational definition and an inherent understanding of the ethnic group.

Like Weber, Barth (1969), substantiating the notion of ethnicity in a classic formula, argues that the self-ascription of an identity is based on the rhetoric of ancestrality, which serves as the basis to establish an ethnic group. Ethnicity would thus reflect the positive trends of identification and inclusion in an ethnic group whose perception is usually based on a common culture, history and origin.

This leads to another basic issue, namely, the definition of indigenous peoples. According to Smith (2002: 6), 'the term "indigenous" is problematic in that it appears to collectivize many distinct populations whose experiences under imperialism have been vastly different'. In turn, the term 'indigeneity' emerges as a concept that international organizations try to establish transnationally, despite its embeddedness in local characteristics. In the context of this chapter, indigeneity positions Indian peoples as those who, although situated within a nation-state, claim continuity with their past pre-colonial societies (i.e. pre-Columbian societies in the case of the Americas). Furthermore, the construction of their ethnic identity and self-determination as a people is fundamentally connected with their basic territory.

In Brazil, indigenous populations in general – as differentiated from Indian peoples – are those who have experienced culturally and historically specific forms of land takeover and natural resource appropriation. There are currently at least 225 Indian peoples speaking some 180 different languages throughout Brazil, living on both Indian lands and urban centres, totalling 734,000 indigenous individuals, according to the census performed in 2000 by the Brazilian Institute of Geography and Statistics (Instituto Brasileiro de Geografia e Estatística, IBGE).

Graburn (1976) points out that ethnic identities may be perceived as under constant change as a result of their global and local interactions. As far as cultural change is concerned, so-called ethnic tourism (van den Berghe and Keyes 1984; MacCannell 1992; Grünewald 2001, 2002, 2006) fulfils its role by privileging an analysis of the dynamics, whereby group identities are changed by the expectations of tourism. Their ethnicities are emergent and localized movements of social actors in subordinate positions, trying to say something about themselves against a background of impersonal, anonymous globalized forces present in a (post)-modern, diversified world. Ethnic tourism arenas function as social spaces where the reconstruction of ethnicity is unique, whereas tourism itself promotes restoration and preservation, often recreating ethnic attributes as commodities.

However, not every individual from a given ethnic community can engage in 'ethnicity-for-tourism' (MacCannell 1992), and those who do end up creating another community, the tourism community, which, for the purposes of this chapter, is called an 'ethnotourism community' (Grünewald 2006). Ethnicity is present therein, and the ethnic identity constructed on such a stage is legitimate and authentic from the perspective of those engaged in creating these social spaces.

As far as the process of cultural renovation is concerned in such arenas, it is worth reconsidering the notion of culture as applied to indigenous population scenarios. The acculturative view sees the cultural change resulting from tourism in a negative light, and the mingling product as the loss of ancestral, legitimate Indian purity. In contrast, when viewed positively, the mestizo or hybrid elements are perceived in terms of their cultural complexity and as a starting point for new traditions (whether artefacts, dances, or story plots) to be exhibited in tourism arenas.

Gruzinski (2001: 51) reminds us that culture is still understood as a 'complex ensemble, a coherent, stable whole with tangible contours, able to condition behaviours'. However, cultures ought not to be considered as exclusivist, substantive entities because the cultural contents of groups must be seen as dynamic and co-extensive and the attribution of ethnic diacritics prevails even when culture is clearly shared. Another complicating factor can be detected: the notion of identity, which is usually referred to as the stable and invariable substratum of the individual. Identity, however, is defined based on multiple relations and interactions, and, just as identities are fragmented, cultures are dynamic and not automatically limited to specific societies; rather, their constituent elements have roots that are as uncertain as their future.

In regard to the indigenous experience of cultural re-updating in tourism arenas, Sahlins (1997: 58) points out that the rising of 'syncretic, multicultural, translocal or neo-traditional forms' must lead to a renovation of anthropology whenever it faces the emergence of 'human culture original patterns' and reaches unexpected forms of a unique existence. In Brazil, tourism demands the presentation of a pristine Indian culture, with an expectation that it has survived the advance of modernity. In addressing this demand, the past is recreated as fiction in an interpretive construction (see Geertz 1978). The Indians are acculturated, but they retain some native elements, which they may exhibit to those interested. These native elements, however, become mixed with the commercial dynamics of the tourism context in processes of commodification. Tourism involves different modes of native culture commoditization, and the issue of authenticity is important to anthropologists because it is a founding factor in the ways of thinking exhibited by individuals, especially in situations of interculturality (Grünewald 2009a).

To address the social processes (diachrony) that moulded Pataxó tourism arenas, the notion of 'social field' (Gluckman 1987) has been valuable in exploring the interdependences among actors in the case presented in this chapter. By employing a 'perspective that focuses on strategies rather than structures' (Sjöberg 1993: 30), this case study examines the relationships between individuals and their actions and the existing dialogue between Indians and broader segments of society. The multiplicity of strategies under dispute, particularly between Indians, entrepreneurs and NGOs, has been noted in the construction of social spaces where concrete social interactions take place. There is herein an essential preoccupation with the processes of change and cultural mobilization.

Still under Sjöberg's direction, the research presented in this chapter was concerned with establishing the Indians' vision of themselves and the image that several social agents hold of them in public arenas (or social fields). In this case, the Indians' interactions and the process of cultural production, which was intended for tourist consumption, became a central process in the conscious reconstruction of their identity. The investigator's engagement in the research was characterized by the use of multi-sited ethnographic work (Marcus 1995), obtained through observation, interviews and conversations from multiple positions, including the Indians themselves and other actors, especially tourists.

Indigeneity tourism

Bunten and Graburn (2009: 2) emphasize that 'indigenous peoples have been involved with tourism since they first hosted guests through exploratory and early colonial encounters, yet Indigenous ownership and control of such venues is a relatively new phenomenon worldwide'. This chapter considers that indigenous tourism implies managing at least part of the products and services available to tourists; therefore, the idea of commoditization is already implicit. That is, it exists whenever an Indian society commercially arranges elements of its culture or nature for tourism. This is even more remarkable because currently 'ethnicity is *also* becoming more corporate, more commodified, more implicated than ever before in the economics of everyday life' (Comaroff 2009: 1). However, in spite of globalization, differences in local contexts exist. For example, as North Americans strived to assimilate natives into capitalism (Bodinger de Uriarte 2003), the ethnicity of businesses in that part of the world should not be considered so strange. The same issue arises in the context of emerging ethno-corporations in Africa analysed by Comaroff (2009). In Brazil, however, there is a broad national rejection, particularly by the government and society as a whole, of capitalist enterprizes on Indian lands. Finally, although tourism appears to be a new form of imperialism or colonialism (Nash 1989, 1996), this chapter argues that, as a form of imperialism, tourism can facilitate a counter-hegemonic rhetoric as it projects native discourse onto global tourists who visit indigenous peoples who listen to them, and who often endorse their longing for self-determination.

In the United States, tourism events have included native participation since the early twentieth century (Gleach 2003; Nesper 2003). In Central and South America, tourism has affected several indigenous peoples. Van den Berghe (1994), for instance, examined ethnic tourism in the area of Chiapas (Mexico); he regarded the natives (related to Mayan people) as indigeneity performers. In a different research project in Peru, the same author perceived a new 'Incanism' as a marketing strategy destined to commodify the Inca tradition for consumption by national and foreign tourists (van den Berghe and Ochoa 1999). Furthermore, tourism in native Amazonian societies, which promote ethnic tourism, shamanic tourism and ecotourism in general, has also become the subject of research.

Most ecotourism in the Amazon region is not based on indigenous tourism (see Chapter 9); that is, Indians do not participate in management. In many cases, even when carried out under the label of ecotourism, tourism activities often negatively impact Indian communities. There are countless cases of jungle hotels and large resorts promoting ecotourism or sport fishing wherein the management disrespect and marginalize indigenous ways of life, territorialities and the traditional use of the environment and resources. Though some governments have attempted to address this disregard, these plans are seldom successful. As a result, capitalist ecotourism – a contradictory phrase, with equally contradictory results for the Indians – eventually prevails. However, community-based tourism (Bartholo Júnior, Sansolo and Bursztyn 2009) has been a rural alternative to enhance indigenous participation, though it has not been an opportunity for the Indian peoples who are under the tutelary regime of the Brazilian government (Grünewald 2009b).

Indigenous tourism in Brazil has not been well regarded by Brazilian indigenism nor has it found backing from the National Indian Foundation (FUNAI). It seems that indigenism is the primary power that tourism must face to reach Indian peoples in Brazil. However, Indian populations in all regions of the country have become more and more involved in tourism, despite government attempts to define and control the flow of external agents into Indian territories. Finally, despite the fact that tourism in Indian villages is still scarce, tourism has existed for almost forty years in the Pataxó Indian lands in the state of Bahia.

The Pataxó case

The Pataxó population consists of approximately 9,000 individuals divided among 25 villages spread across five Indian reservations along the southernmost coast of the state of Bahia. Currently, the two main reservations of the Pataxó are Barra Velha, on the southern border of Porto Seguro municipality (see Figure 1.1), and Coroa Vermelha, on the southern border of Santa Cruz Cabrália municipality. Barra Velha has an approximate population of 2,300, and Coroa Vermelha has 3,000 people.

The Pataxó reservations lie where Pedro Álvares Cabral anchored his ships when he 'discovered' Brazil in 1500. Many native groups who lived in the region were expropriated from their lands during settlement processes. Barra Velha is regarded as the Pataxó 'mother village'. It has been the original Indian settlement since 1861. Today, the Pataxó are a Portuguese-speaking group who are still fighting for land in the region. In 1961, the Monte Pascoal National Park was created, and the most important indigenous activities – hunting, gathering and farming – were banned. Not surprisingly, the Indian population had difficulty living off their own lands. With the creation of a tourist hub in the city of Porto Seguro in the 1970s, the Pataxó began to make and sell necklaces (and later other pieces made of wood, seeds and straw), as crafts were becoming an important economic alternative.

Barra Velha began to receive sporadic visits from backpackers as early as the end of the 1970s. Even today, Barra Velha has just been reached by alternative tourism due to its distance from the mass tourism flow of Porto Seguro. Even so, the Indians see interaction with tourists as important because it provides them with a way of earning money for basic goods such as clothes, food and medicine.

It is worth noting that a cultural revival has occurred in Barra Velha encompassing not only craftwork but also dances and songs and relying on both Indian names and a language still under construction. It grew from the 1970s into the 1990s through a process of 'collecting the pebbles spread out by tradition' (i.e. 'cultural revival'), with the purpose of rebuilding cultural heritage. However, because those cultural elements had only recently been created, Brazilian neighbours did not see them as authentic. That is, these cultural elements did not match the imaginations and expectations of unchanged heritage or 'genuine' traditions passed on through generations since ancient times.

The commercialization of Pataxó crafts started in the early 1970s, when the federal government facilitated entry to the region by providing road access to Porto Seguro and Santa Cruz Cabrália. Along with the roads, the historic markers at the sites of the discovery of Brazil and the first mass celebrated in Brazil were also inaugurated at Coroa Vermelha. In this context, in November 1972, Indian families began to move from Barra Velha to the area, establishing themselves with the goal of developing commercial activity, including tourism. Coroa Vermelha grew demographically during the 1970s and 1980s, as did Porto Seguro, which enjoyed an economic boom at the beginning of the 1980s. Despite the fact that Pataxó Indians have always been present in the region, interest in promoting them as a tourist attraction has not been high. Rather, the Pataxó always featured as a casual attraction at tourist outings.

Indians in this village earn a living almost exclusively from crafts sold to charter or mass tourists (Smith 1989), who generally come by bus or car. Most tourists are part of an outing to the historical site of Cabral's discovery of Brazil or on a recreational beach tour, which includes stops at various restaurant stalls selling food and drinks. In this village, some Indians still produce a rustic form of crafts with products sourced exclusively from the forest. However, the production of wooden serving bowls has dominated Indian commerce in this village since the end of the 1980s, when they started to be made with electric machines rather than sanded by hand with leaves from the imburana tree. Through the summer of January and February of 1998, the Indians sold around 35,000 wooden serving bowls in Coroa Vermelha and surrounding areas, which reveals the scale of production. The Pataxó also sell such crafts on the roadside, at 'hippie' fairs and on busy beaches. Lastly, although this is an Indian village, many points of sale for crafts were leased to non-Indian merchants, who sell an enormous range of souvenirs and other craft and non-craft items. The Indians have also begun to sell a wider range of items, including many goods that do not belong to their traditions.

Despite the mixed commercial approach described above, cultural renewal took place in a much broader way than simply the commercialization of items for tourists, strengthening the Pataxó ethnicity at that location. Tourists and their interest in tradition seem to have motivated the Pataxó to reinvigorate their cultural heritage. Craftwork opened the way for social interaction, and tradition-building to promote Pataxó ethnicity followed. At the early stages of crafts practice, the Indians did not use Indian names, nor did they speak a Pataxó language. When viewing Indian crafts for sale, many tourists asked the vendors their names and were surprised to hear Christian names spoken in Brazilian Portuguese. The Indians suddenly became aware of the relevance of bearing Indian names and started using them as a marketing strategy, especially on their tents while selling crafts at Coroa Vermelha. Tourists also wanted to know about Indian languages. As the Indians spoke Brazilian Portuguese, they decided to start using words that were allegedly Pataxó to impress visiting tourists at their points of sale. Finally, tourists also asked about dance and music, which led the Indians to create new traditions in those spheres as well. Such cultural demands were important for the Pataxó, as these requests helped them to value their ethnic identity in an arena where they were formerly treated with prejudice by local residents, guides, and even by tourists, who had considered them civilized and therefore fake Indians or former Indians.

By the mid-1970s, the Pataxó region was visited almost exclusively by hippies. During the following years, there was a concentration of investments in tourism such that, in 1996, Porto Seguro had a population of 65,000 inhabitants and was the seventh most visited destination in the country, receiving 600,000 tourists per year. In the summer of 1996, there was a daily average of 700 people visiting Coroa Vermelha. The great majority were Brazilian charter tours and mass tourists. As of 2008, Porto Seguro could count a population of 113,000 individuals, receiving over a million tourists yearly.

For over twenty years, the Pataxó from Coroa Vermelha were little more than a craft attraction at the historic sites of the discovery of Brazil and the first

Catholic mass, where they had formed an urban, almost exclusively commercial village. As the village expanded and faced expectations that it would be demarcated by FUNAI, its population also needed agricultural land and wood for crafts. Therefore, two sections of forest close to the shore were occupied in 1997: one for agriculture and the other for environmental preservation and natural resources renewal. This second section of the forest was prepared for the development of what the Pataxó called 'ecotourism'. In 1999, the Pataxó Association for Ecotourism (ASPECTUR) and the Jaqueira ('Jackfruit') Ecological Reserve were created, with the explicit objective of offering tourists the opportunity to experience and display the beauty of their culture as well as preserving the environment.

As of late 1999, the Jaqueira Reserve has been open to tourists who arrive by private automobiles and organized coach tours. These visitors park in assigned places at the welcome gate of the reserve where there are instructions about sightseeing opportunities. In the reserve, tourists can see the sacred river and take walks along a narrow trail in the jungle as far as the core of Jaqueira, where tourist huts are located. Huts for dwelling and for sacred rituals are located in more private places.

Tourists' visits start with a lecture about the history of Jaqueira and Pataxó. Other attractions include an indigenous museum with pictures, crafts and the handicraft hut that sells Coroa Vermelha Indian products for inflated prices. While visitors enjoy another trail in the forest, they attend lectures about trees, replanting, medicinal plants and hunting traps. There is a field for inter-tribal games, such as soccer, log rides and corporal fighting. There is a school for Patxohã language learning and a hut that displays a typical indigenous dwelling in forest conditions. The tourists move into another hut to taste traditional fish and tea, and there is a hut for learning about rituals where they can perform dances with the Indians. The interpretative speech by the native guide relates to the search for lost traditions. Facilities include toilets, and visitors are able to try their skills at firing a bow and arrow at a target. Finally, tourists are shown the Jaqueira symbol: the trunk of an apparently dead jackfruit tree from which four new jackfruit trees spring up. This metaphorically represents the indigenous revival after colonization.

Indians living in the reserve have become more deeply involved in Indian culture, with 30 families becoming engaged in Jaqueira's activities. Tourism is no longer called ecotourism but rather 'ethnic tourism'. Jaqueira Indians are now exclusively devoted to cultural activities. They must learn and re-create their own language and dances, the process of which incidentally involves strenuous rotating shift work. However, everything consumed at Jaqueira is bought at Coroa Vermelha, even the very handicrafts resold at Jaqueira. This patronage gives aid to the Indians' relatives in Coroa Vermelha.

Tourism is considered to be a way of life for the Indians in Jaqueira, and tourists are encouraging the Indian cultural revival. As a result, it can be argued that tourism has not affected the pre-existing culture of the Pataxó but has encouraged the revival of traditional practices and the (re)creation of other elements to display to tourists. As for handicrafts, some of the items used are known to the elderly, but they have undergone modifications for the new context of tourism. Other items have been recently created. The iconography and drawings in crafts and body painting have transformed Pataxó standards. The creation of new myths has also been reported in Jaqueira. Some of these myths are important in entertaining tourists along the sightseeing trail, but others are reserved for the Indians themselves. As for songs and dance, the Indians in Jaqueira state that these are their own creation, but everything follows the Pataxó 'traditional style'. Jaqueira is also considered to be sacred land. From the forest, the Pataxó get energy for their cultural and spiritual reinforcement, as their intent is to transmit good energy in a joyful manner to tourists through dancing. Incidentally, at the end of one of the tour walks, if a tourist happens to be interested in shamanism or healing, a prayer takes place to bestow spiritual cleansing on the tourists. The visit lasts three hours; tourists are then led back to their cars or buses and usually take Pataxó souvenirs along.

Finally, we noted that at the Jaqueira Reserve, the process of updating culture for display in tourism arenas involves creating, choreographing and mixing old Pataxó elements with cultural traits from other peoples, even from the 'white man'. The Jaqueira Reserve became the primary site for the Pataxó from Coroa Vermelha, where new traditions created through the intense work of Indian 'cultural revival' are displayed to tourists through ecotourism or ethnotourism. This project incorporates ideas and actions that contribute to the sustainability of a part of the Indian community.

It is also worth noting that Jaqueira contributed to the strengthening of the Coroa Vermelha community in the celebration of Brazil's 500th anniversary in April 2000. During this time, the Pataxó received Indians from many ethnic groups from other parts of the country along with national authorities, social movements and the media. This provided the Pataxó with the opportunity to reinvigorate their culture in accordance with the national image as to what an Indian should be (i.e. according to indigenism). For the anniversary celebrations, Coroa Vermelha was re-urbanized, and innumerable problems resulted. The federal administration built an indigenous museum, a shopping area and monuments. However, the problems related to diverse commerce and the leasing of shopping stalls have been the same. That is, such re-urbanization does not strengthen ethnic tourism nor does it bring sustainability to the Pataxó people, who must compete in a crafts market with 'white men'. The latter, having established factories for wooden serving bowls and other items, sell replicas of Pataxó pieces (along with crafts of other indigenous origins) at competitive prices on a site adjacent to the indigenous shopping centre where tourist buses now park. The site of the discovery of Brazil is on Pataxó land. However, the Pataxó have remained under the shadow of a tourism management regime, which, as a form of colonialism, seeks to maintain control of Indian tourism production and to integrate the Pataxó into a global capitalist order, with significant implications for their ethnic and cultural production.

Only in Jaqueira, far from an imposed Indianness, have the Pataxó created an ethnic tourist arena through an ecotourism project. It is worth emphasizing that the neighbouring woods of Jaqueira have been totally devastated by their owners, who have extracted timber and sand; the Indians, however, have maintained the value of their forest. The Jaqueira Reserve promotes the sustainable development of part of an Indian community, adding cultural and environmental value. The idea of ethnodevelopment (Grünewald 2003) should be reserved for situations like this; the concept refers to a process that aims to sustain an Indian society's development with a certain ethnic autonomy. Perhaps indigenism can legitimize tourism in societies that are subjected to strong colonial impact and help to strengthen their ethnicities when subjected to the gaze of contemporary tourists.

The vigour of the ethnic work performed on Jaqueira has been so successful that it has recently expanded towards other Pataxó villages. Jaqueira eventually received Indian visitors from other villages, who learned how to manage their own tourism based on the experiences of the Pataxó. The same process also happened with Imbiriba and Aldeia Velha, two former agricultural villages that now rely on tourism performances focusing on indigeneity. More importantly, the mother village itself, Barra Velha, has changed its approach to tourism in the last ten years. Tourists used to travel on foot from the hamlet of Caraíva to become acquainted with life in the village where the Pataxó produced and sold their craftwork. The men usually worked with raw materials, while the women and children finished and wove the items. The Pataxó themselves sold the goods to tourists visiting the village. Typically, women and children offered items to the tourists or simply had them on display at their home entrances. They frequently agreed to exchange their craft pieces for tourists' possessions, such as shorts, sunglasses or T-shirts.

Currently, tourists who visit the hamlet of Caraíva, next to the Indian land, are no longer interested in seeing a 'village of acculturated Indians'; consequently, there is hardly any craftwork production or direct sales to tourists. Realizing the change of orientation in local tourism, the natives formed an association and bought 16 carts, which they use to promote recreational rides for tourists between the hamlets of Caraíva and Corumbau, thus entertaining tourists in a coastal environment that includes the self-controlled Indian land. A number of tourists do not even realize that the people leading the tours are Indians. At an Indian land area in Barra Velha called Porto do Boi, one of the natives embraced the performative model of indigeneity tourism and established, along with his family members, an arena similar to Jaqueira to attract visitors coming from Caraiva. This is the only venue where Indian culture has been commercially exposed.

These three new Pataxó tourism arenas emulated the Jaqueira pattern in every way they could: apprenticeship of a language under construction, native names, dances, songs, body painting, adornments and explanations of the environment and Indian culture. There is already a project underway to interconnect all four arenas into a package tour focused on Pataxó culture.

Conclusion

Ethnic tourism and the Pataxó stage model

This chapter has sought to define a model of indigeneity tourism based on the Pataxó case that has only recently emerged in Brazil. This research, carried out by the author for a doctoral thesis in anthropology during the late 1990s, recorded the presence of backpackers in Barra Velha and the domestic dynamics of welcoming those tourists, who searched out indigenous crafts. Most importantly, the research highlighted the urban and commercial village of Coroa Vermelha with its socio-cultural multivocality. There, the Pataxó presence imposed itself territorially, and local Indian culture was renewed by the demand from a global society for a tourist experience that provided an Indian distinctiveness. Note that Indian distinctiveness does not necessarily mean ethnic distinction, as what really matters to tourists in Coroa Vermelha is the availability of Indian elements in the market of cultural goods, irrespective of any ethnic belonging.

Such a comprehensive tourism arena, which still prevails in the locality in question, is characterized by the presence of tourists who, however interested in beach entertainment and Brazilian history, are clearly not attuned to the Pataxó presence or territoriality. Finally, although the Pataxó can commercially perform their indigeneity in that arena – a very large stage – they do not possess the rights to manage the tourism market. Everything is negotiated with difficulty between the Pataxó, the entrepreneurs, the marketers, the government and other groups, depending on often contrasting interests. Script, direction, costumes, scenery, and everything else making up the play are not set by the Indians themselves because of the hegemonic socio-cultural and economic flows that surround them on such a stage.

More important, however, is to view the ten years since the creation of the Jaqueira Reserve as an exclusive sustainability project for a part of the Coroa Vermelha population, with a focus on ethnic distinction. The ethnodevelopment perspective initiated at the reserve did renew the tourists' approach not only to the Pataxó but also to every other social segment with which they interact. Tourists now go there to be acquainted with Indians of Pataxó ethnicity and their lifestyles. However, the Pataxó only see Jaqueira as a 'job'. They are not necessarily interested in exhibiting their current way of life to tourists but rather in performing the play, which the Pataxó built for themselves, on the Jaqueira 'stage'.

Such ethnodevelopment dynamics, based on indigenous tourism, have been replicated in other Pataxó villages, where they now prevail over older forms of tourist activity and even other forms of economic production. It is ultimately in the creation and shaping of these small Pataxó tourism arenas that we find the vigour of their current cultural renewal, although this does not come without criticism from within the Pataxó community. The present research sees this form of cultural re-creation as legitimate and positive, as it not only encourages Indians to reflect on their culture but also leads them to value their own environment. The recording of cases parallel to the Pataxó's (especially in Brazil) should be interesting in advancing the discussion of empirical cases; such cases may also test academic perspectives on the staging of ethnic tourism. This chapter's final considerations remind us of how transient the empirical and the theoretical (native and academic) fields are. Heretofore, we will move from parallel cases to the Pataxó.

In the late 1990s, this research established a parallel between the case studies of tourism among the Pataxó and the Ainu of Japan (Grünewald 2001). Just as the Pataxó needed to exhibit a distinctive culture to stand out as Indians within the Brazilian scenario, the Ainu also created a tourism arena to maintain their traditional ways of life and affirm themselves as a legitimate yet separate people in Japan. Both the Pataxó and the Ainu turned to craftwork production a means of 'emphasising the distinctive content of their culture for tourists' (Sjöberg 1993: 187), which became a central process in the conscious reconstruction of their identities.

With the recent developments apart from craftwork in Pataxó tourism, the display of cultural elements to tourists is gaining specialization. Ethnic tourism has been linked to specific arenas, where the Pataxó market themselves as the 'first Brazilians' or the 'Indians of the discovery' (Grünewald 2001, 2002, 2009c). The movement of re-creating and displaying traditions that satisfy the tourists image about Indianness can be found in other places of the world. In some cases, even the establishment of indigenous enterprises destined to manage such tourism is detectable. Such is the case of the Cherokee of North Carolina, USA, who, unlike the Ainu, display a made-for-tourism indigeneity in public arenas and keep their way of life far from the stares of the tourists (Beard-Morse 2009). Under such a perspective, the Pataxó seem farther from the Ainu and more like the Cherokee in their specialized professionalism, as they conduct tourist activities far from their private homes and closer to the social arenas where they perform and stage an indigeneity proper to ethnic tourism. In accordance with a number of records (particularly newspaper articles and information from indigenist organizations) concerning tourist activities on Indian lands throughout Brazil, this paper supports the hypothesis that the above trend is relevant, as far as indigeneity tourism in Brazil is concerned.

In a purely theoretical analysis, however, it is worth recollecting a particular discussion about the specificity of ethnic tourism. MacCannell (1992) employed the phrase 'constructed ethnicity' with reference to the various ethnic identities that emerged in opposition to colonialism. However, constructed ethnicity would only be a 'conceptual springboard to a more complex phenomenon'. According to MacCannell (1992: 158–9), 'the global diffusion of White Culture, internal colonization, and the institutions of modern mass tourism are producing new and more highly deterministic ethnic forms than those produced during the first colonial phase. The focus is on a type of ethnicity-for-tourism in which exotic cultures figure as key attractions.' Furthermore, 'the concern here is not with the often bizarre results of the tourists' efforts to "go native". Rather, it is with the natives' efforts to satisfy the tourism demand, or to go native-for-tourists.'

These new forms of ethnicity require a methodological reorientation because, unlike the typical interactions of classical colonialism, tourism promotes the restoration, preservation and re-creation of ethnic attributes. In this way, a 'reconstructed ethnicity' emerges in response to pressures exerted by the 'white culture', resulting in the preservation of ethnic elements that now have persuasion and/or entertainment effects for 'a general other'. Although still dependent on former strategies of ethnic identity, reconstructed ethnic forms are appearing as a more or less automatic response in all groups that enter into the global network of commercial transactions. Therefore, rather than simply serving as rhetorical weapons, cultural elements can be re-signified as commodities; they can be a form of symbolic expression with a function or exchange value in a larger system (MacCannell 1992).

The conception of social spaces for the performance of tourism is vital. MacCannell (1973) worked with the idea of staged authenticity in tourism arenas (Grünewald 2001), suggesting that, in moments such as the performances of Pataxó culture, the Indian objective should be to show a façade such as a 'back region' (Goffman 1959) and to show the invented and produced experience for tourists as if it were an intimate, authentic tradition. Van den Berghe and Keyes (1984) also denied authenticity to such performances, stating that in such a process the natives falsify their culture and, generally speaking, the tourist's search for Indian authenticity is frustrated because the ethnic tourist would destroy the intact native, the very thing the tourist desires to see. For Van den Berghe and Keyes (1984: 347), 'the touree is the native when he begins to interact with the tourist and modify his behaviour accordingly. The touree is the native-turned-actor – whether consciously or unconsciously – while the tourist is the spectator.'

This chapter stands against such a negative way of facing the issue of authenticity. Researchers must not deny that authenticity is an ideal and relational construction elaborated by distinct social actors (Grünewald 2009a). Concerning the Pataxó, this research has considered that the Jaqueira Reserve is now the site of Coroa Vermelha Indian land, where such new cultural configurations of traditions built through intensive Indian 'cultural revival' are being exhibited to tourists through a sustainable development project. The reserve is not a show like *Fantasy Island*, and it does not seem to be productive for anthropology to consider such a situation as if it were a construction of the unreal. It would be ungenerous towards the social actors to relegate their creativity to the realm of farce and to fail to perceive that this inventive dynamic belongs to the realm of tourism activity and to authentic tourism arenas, where new objects are available in a post-modern *bricolage* that is no less authentic (Grünewald 2009a).

Until the 1990s, Indians were unanimously consensual in connection with a Pataxó cultural pattern in terms of body painting, dance and adornments. In recent years, however, the elders, the Indians who began shaping the culture for tourist show and those who are still not linked to tourism unanimously, deny that the cultural elements presented to tourists are inherent to the Pataxó. They argue that a pattern has been discontinued and that in the service of becoming more appealing to tourists, and in their political exhibition of indigeneity, the Pataxó, who perform culturally on tourist stages, are producing 'a fantasy'.

The issue of cultural authenticity would hardly fit into this chapter, but throughout this text, an underlying idea ought to be reinforced. Because our discussion centres on the staging of indigeneity rather than authenticity, we must emphasize the robustness of the stage model, referring to an agency rather than an idea. The largely profitable stage model found in the Jaqueira tourism arena, which has been steadily spreading to other villages, is the only successful model as far as this research has shown. It is the prevailing model in terms of ethnic tourism promotion managed by the Indians themselves. Such a model can be extended to learn more about other tourism arenas in Brazilian Indian societies or in other countries. However, this remains a difficult task, because in the specific case of indigeneity tourism in Brazil, we still do not have sufficient academic studies to justify an investigation of the recurrence of such a model. It is arguable that, once this pattern has been established, interdisciplinary approaches will be fundamental. In the domain of anthropology, theoretical studies on performance may well contribute to the construction of such a model, which, like a theatre stage, ought to emphasize the creativity and agency of the Indian actors.

References

Aspelin, P. L. (1977) Anthropological analysis of tourism: indirect tourism and political economy in the case of the Mamainde of Mato Grosso, Brazil. *Annals of Tourism Research*, 4: 135–60.

Barth, F. (1969) Introduction, in F. Barth (ed.) *Ethnic Groups and Boundaries: The Social Organisational of Culture Difference*. London: Allen & Unwin, pp. 9–38.

Bartholo Júnior, R. S., Sansolo, D. G. and Bursztyn, I. (eds) (2009) *Turismo de Base Comunitária: Diversidade de Olhares e Experiências Brasileiras*. Rio de Janeiro: Letra e Imagem.

Beard-Moose, C. T. (2009) *Public Indians, Private Cherokees: Tourism and Tradition on Tribal Ground*. Tuscaloosa: The University of Alabama Press.

Bodinger de Uriarte, J. J. (2003) Imagining the nation with house odds: representing American Indian identity at Mashantucket. *Ethnohistory*, 50: 549–65.

Bunten, A. C. and Garburn, N. (2009) Guest editorial: current themes in indigenous tourism. *London Journal of Tourism, Sport and Creative Industries*. 2: 2–11.

Chambers, E. (2000) *Native Tours. The Anthropology of Travel and Tourism*. Long Grove, Illinois: Waveland Press.

Comaroff, J. L. (2009) *Ethnicity, Inc*. Chicago: University of Chicago Press.

Geertz, C. (1978) Uma descrição densa: Por uma teoria interpretativa da cultura, in C. Geertz (ed.) *A Interpretação das Culturas*. Rio de Janeiro: Zahar, pp.13–66.

Gleach, F. W. (2003) Pocahontas at the fair: crafting identities at the 1907 Jamestown exposition. *Ethnohistory*, 50: 419–45.

Gluckman, M. (1987) Análise de uma situação social na Zululândia moderna, in B. Feldman-Bianco (ed.) *Antropologia das Sociedades Contemporâneas*, São Paulo: Global, pp. 227–344.

Goffman, E. (1959) *The Presentation of Self in Everyday Life*. New York: Anchor Doubleday.

Graburn, N. H. H. (1976) Introduction: the arts of the Fourth World, in N. H. H. Graburn (ed.) *Ethnic and Tourist Arts: Cultural Expressions from the Fourth World*. Berkeley: University of California Press, pp. 1–32.

Grünewald, R. A. (2001) *Os Indios do Descobrimento: Tradição e Turismo*. Rio de Janeiro: Contra Capa.

Grünewald, R. A. (2002) Tourism and cultural revival. *Annals of Tourism Research*, 29: 1004–21.

Grünewald, R. A. (2003) Etnodesenvolvimento indígena no nordeste (e leste): aspectos gerais e específicos. *Anthropológicas*, 14: 47–71.

Grünewald, R. A. (2006) Tourism and ethnicity. *Horizontes Antropológicos*, 1, no. se.

Grünewald, R. A. (2009a) The contingency of authenticity: intercultural experiences in indigenous villages of Eastern and Northeastern Brazil. *Vibrant*, 6: 225–53.

Grünewald, R. A. (2009b) Indigenism, tourism and cultural revival among the Pataxó People in Brazil. *London Journal of Tourism, Sport and Creative Industries*, 2: 21–7.

Grünewald, R. A. (2009c) Os Pataxó e a construção social dos índios do descobrimento, in D. A. Reis, H. Mattos, J. P. Oliveira, L. E. de Souza Moraes and M. Ridenti (eds) *Tradições e Modernidades*. Rio de Janeiro: Editora FGV, pp. 77–91.

Gruzinski, S. (2001) *O pensamento mestiço*. São Paulo: Companhia das Letras.

Harkin, M. (2003) Staged encounters: postmodern tourism and aboriginal people. *Ethnohistory*, 50: 575–85.

Hinch, T. and Butler, R. (1996) Indigenous tourism: a common ground for discussion, in R. Butler and T. Hinch (eds) *Tourism and indigenous peoples*. London: International Thomson Press, pp: 3–19.

MacCannell, D. (1992) Reconstructed ethnicity: tourism and cultural identity in Third World communities, in D. MacCannell (ed.) *Empty Meeting Grounds*. London: Routledge, pp. 158–71.

MacCannell, D. (1973) Staged authenticity. *American Journal of Sociology*, 79: 589–603.

Marcus, G.E. (1995) Ethnography in/of the world system: the emergence of multi-sited ethnography. *Annual Review of Anthropology*, 24: 95–117.

Nash, D. (1989) Tourism as a form of imperialism, in V. Smith (ed.), 2nd edn. *Hosts and guests: The anthropology of tourism*. Philadelphia: University of Pennsylvania Press, pp. 37–52.

Nash, D. (1996) *Anthropology of Tourism*. Kidlington: Pergamon.

Nesper, L. (2003) Simulating culture. Being Indian for tourists in Lac du Flambeau's Wa-Swa-Gon Indian bowl. *Ethnohistory*, 50: 447–72.

Sahlins, M. (1997) O 'pessimismo sentimental' e a experiência etnográfica: por que a cultura não é um objeto em vias de extinção (Parte I). *Mana Estudos de Antropologia Social*, 3: 41–73.

Sjöberg, K. (1993) *The return of the Ainu: cultural mobilization and the practice of ethnicity in Japan*. Chur: Harwood Academic Publishers.

Smith, L. T. (2002) *Decolonizing Methodologies: Research and Indigenous Peoples*. London and New York: Zed Books Ltd.

Smith, V. L. (1989) Introduction, in V. Smith (ed.), *Hosts and Guests: The Anthropology of Tourism*. 2nd edn. Philadelphia: University of Pennsylvania Press, pp. 1–17.

Smith, V. L. (1996) Indigenous tourism: the four Hs, in R. Butler and T. Hinch (eds) *Tourism and Indigenous Peoples*. London: International Thomson Press, pp. 283–307.

van den Berghe, P. L. (1994) *The Quest for the Other: Ethnic Tourism in San Cristóbal, Mexico*. Seattle and London: University of Washington Press.

van den Berghe, P. L. and Keyes, C. F. (1984) Introduction: tourism and re-created ethnicity. *Annals of Tourism Research*, 11: 343–52.

van den Berghe, P. L. and Ochoa, J. F. (1999) Tourism and nativistic ideology in Cuzco, Peru. *Annals of Tourism Research*, 27: 7–26.

Weber, M. (1991) Relações comunitárias étnicas, in *Economia e sociedade vol. 1*. Brasília: UnB, pp. 267–77.

12 Tourism education and research in Brazil

Sérgio Rodrigues Leal, Alexandre Panosso Netto and Luiz Gonzaga Godoi Trigo

Introduction

Since the 1970s, higher education institutions in Brazil have been offering tourism programmes (Trigo 2002). This chapter discusses the current provision of post-secondary tourism education and the status of tourism research in Brazil. Because tourism education is a key element contributing to the development of the tourism industry (WTO 1997), this chapter examines how tourism education has evolved and influenced the tourism sector in Brazil. Accordingly, this chapter is divided into four main sections. First, an overview of the Brazilian education system is provided. Second, drawing on earlier work by Ansarah (2002), major phases in the development of tourism education in the country are analyzed. The opportunities and barriers for the internationalization of tourism education and the obstacles that Brazilian researchers face are also discussed. Third, postgraduate programmes are reviewed with the goal of understanding the 'pipeline' that produces and has shaped the community of academic educators. Finally, the characteristics of the tourism academy are presented to better understand the challenges of addressing the teaching-research nexus. In addressing the aims of this chapter the importance of vocational education is acknowledged, however the main focus is on undergraduate and postgraduate tourism and tourism-related programmes offered at higher education institutions. These programmes include concentrations in hospitality, leisure and events management.

The Brazilian education system

To begin discussing the provision of tourism studies in higher education in Brazil, it is first important to understand Brazil's education system. The provision of education in Brazil is highly regulated. The primary entities are the Ministry of Education and the Federal Council of Education. Pre-university education is provided mainly by the government, and only a small share is attributed to private education providers. In contrast, the provision of university-level education by private providers of higher education has increased significantly since the passage of the New Education Principles and Guidelines Act (Lei de

Diretrizes e Bases). This Act was sanctioned in 1996 by the Brazilian government and delineates the structure of the Brazilian education system (Brazil 1996), which is broadly divided into basic education and higher education with several subdivisions (see Figure 12.1). According to the Act, education should be seen as a means of developing students as citizens and future professionals. Therefore, access should be made available to all Brazilians. To achieve this goal, the government determined that the provision of education in Brazil was to be shared between the state and private institutions. This strategy has led to an increase in private education providers across the country in several fields of study, including tourism.

Higher education is generally more didactic in Brazil than in other countries, consisting of more modules and course hours. Undergraduate higher-education programmes require four years of study, and two-year industry-oriented technological programmes are also offered. These technological programmes come under the rubric of 'further education' in many other countries, which differentiates them from higher education. However, these programmes are also taught in the university setting. The core curricula in both higher education undergraduate programmes and technological programmes are fixed and defined by official government bodies. Although this method of definition facilitates the organization, standardization and evaluation of programmes, the local characteristics of some regions of Brazil can influence the roll-out and outcomes of programmes, and these local characteristics tend to be overlooked in the curricula (Leal 2010b).

At the postgraduate level, programmes are available in two formats. They are labelled in Figure 12.1 as *lato sensu* and *stricto sensu* programmes. *Lato sensu* programmes are essentially vocational programmes directed at the development of professional skills; they require a minimum of 360 course hours and award certificates rather than degree titles. *Stricto sensu* programmes are research-based programmes equivalent to the MPhil and PhD programmes in most English-speaking institutions; these programmes require an average of two and four years of study, respectively, and are aimed at academic and scientific development.

Another offering in postgraduate education in Brazil is a master's degree *(Mestrado profissionalizante),* which is intended to enable students to conduct and apply specific knowledge derived from research in the professional world. These degrees are not considered academic master's degrees and generally attract people who are already well established in their careers and are looking for new educational opportunities.

Tourism education in Brazil in the international context

From an international perspective, initial interest in tourism as an academic field of study emerged between the 1940s and 1960s and mirrored the expansion of mass tourism in some regions of the world. From the late 1960s through the early 1980s, mass tourism consolidated in parallel with the academic study of tourism (ANECA 2004). However, the predominant focus of both programmes

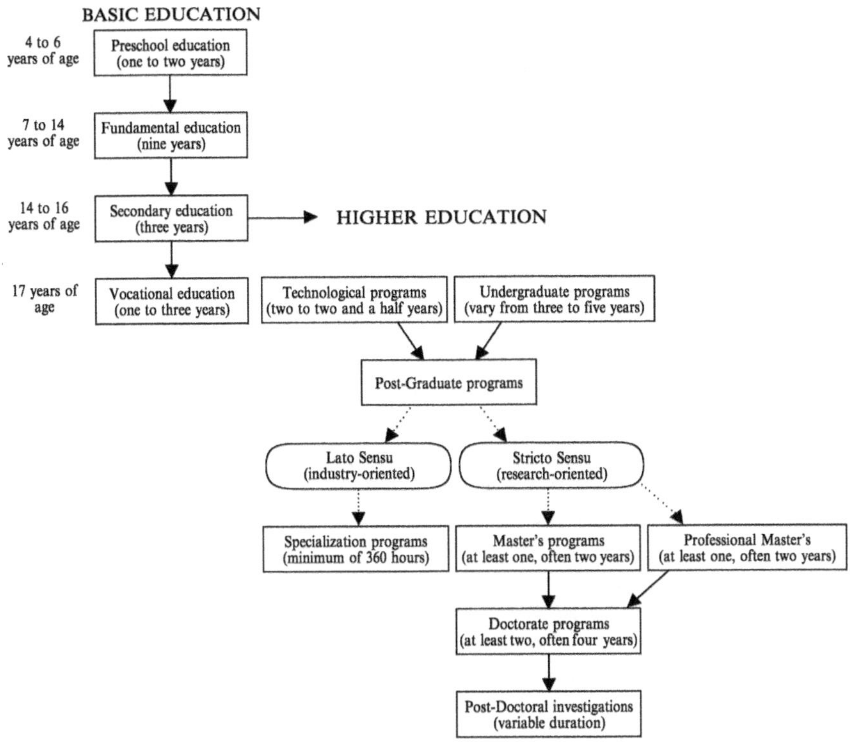

Figure 12.1 The Brazilian education system

and research at the time was on the economic aspects of tourism. Recently, globalization, technological advances and concerns about the environment, among other issues, have impacted how tourism activity is managed. As a result, tourism education and research has evolved to incorporate a more holistic approach.

According to Formica (1996), hospitality programmes have existed globally for many decades. Hospitality education began as early as 1893 in Europe and 1922 in the United States. The United Kingdom started offering hospitality programmes in the early 1960s (e.g. the University of Surrey in 1964 and Strathclyde University in 1965). In Brazil, tourism-related education, with few exceptions, was initiated with the creation of tourism-specific programmes. This approach can be contrasted with that of other countries, i.e. the United Kingdom, Australia, the United States and Germany, where tourism programmes emerged from disciplinary foundations, such as anthropology, economics and geography (Castillo Nechar *et al.* 2010; Castillo Nechar 2005; Fayos-Solá 1995; Vera Rebollo 1995).

Because of the introduction of tourism programmes without precedent in other disciplines, tourism education in Brazil is different to other countries. In

Iberian and Latin American countries, such as Brazil, Mexico, Spain, Argentina and Portugal, initial programmes were generalist in nature, featuring a broad curriculum and no specialization (Castillo Nechar *et al.* 2010; Rejowski 2010; Gómez Nieves 2008, 2010; Sakata 2002). In other cases, the programmes specialized in tourism as a 'discipline', which remains the subject of heated debate (see Leiper 1981; Beni 2001). In general, tourism programmes in Brazil were weak and superficial, and they were successful only because tourism was a fashionable topic of study at the time. Few programmes had well-defined themes such as events management, recreation or ecotourism in their curricula (Leme 2009; Rejowski 2010). Other than in a few centres of excellence, especially in São Paulo and in the southern states, tourism programmes in Brazil have never established themselves as the primary source of qualified workers for the tourism industry in either private or public sectors. Instead, tourism professionals generally came from several different fields of study, such as business administration, marketing and geography. After a sudden expansion of tourism education from 1996 to 2003, the number of programmes fell as a result of insufficient student enrolments.

Recently, a new generation of tourism students has chosen to conduct their master's and doctoral research at international institutions, especially in Portugal, Spain, the United Kingdom, Australia and New Zealand. Many of these researchers return to Brazil to inject their international experiences into tourism education programmes and to create networks with Brazilian and international researchers. Other researchers work internationally but remain closely connected to the Brazilian tourism research and teaching community. Therefore, tourism education in Brazil has begun to reach a new level of maturity and internationalization. During the 1990s, few Brazilian researchers were concerned with and aware of the international literature and key debates in tourism studies. Those researchers were considered the exception, and they interacted with the international academy almost exclusively through the International Association of Scientific Experts in Tourism (AIEST). Moreover, the arrival of the worldwide web in Brazil and its rapid expansion from 1996 were fundamental to the establishment of regular contact and engagement with the international tourism academy.

It has been forty years since the first institution of higher education began offering tourism programmes in Brazil (Trigo 2002). By the time the first postgraduate research programme was launched in 1993 (Rejowski 1996), a major outlet for tourism research had already been launched: the academic journal *Turismo em Análise*, which the country's top university the Universidade de São Paulo, began publishing in 1990. USP was also the first university to offer a postgraduate research programme on tourism in Brazil. Although São Paulo is the country's largest city and its financial and industrial heart, it is important to emphasize that other regions of Brazil also invested heavily in tourism, and, consequently, tourism education spread rapidly on a national scale.

Hotel management and events management programmes in Brazil have developed differently from tourism programmes. The first Brazilian hotel management programme was initiated in 1978 with a strong focus on hotel operations (Ansarah 2002). Events management programmes, on the other hand, have been available only as technological programmes, especially in the federal education institutes. As shorter programmes, they are focused on practical knowledge, and research is not a priority. Further, gastronomy programmes at both the vocational and the undergraduate level have also become popular in Brazil in recent years. However, the curricula for those programmes do not include tourism topics and the focus is exclusively on restaurant food and beverage management.

Development of tourism education and research in Brazil

In the early 2000s, Ansarah (2002) identified four initial phases in the development of tourism education in Brazil. Today, a fifth phase can be included to reflect the most recent developments in the area.

The beginning: 1970–80

The 1970s represented the first phase of tourism education in Brazil when the original undergraduate programmes were created. During the early part of that decade, the country was experiencing a moment known as 'the Brazilian miracle', which was characterized by significant investment in infrastructure, availability of foreign capital and the understanding that development meant economic growth. In addition, a military dictatorship was in power, which restricted many liberties, including freedom of speech. At that time, images of Brazilian women, Carnival and soccer were stereotypical images of the country abroad. During this period, a small number of tourism programmes were created, and in 1978, the first hotel management programme was launched at the Universidade de Caxias do Sul (UCS) (Ansarah 2002).

It is difficult to measure the scope of tourism education in the country during this initial phase of development because no studies were published on the subject during that time. Barretto (1996) notes that there were 31 books on tourism published by Brazilian authors and publishing houses during the 1970s, indicating growing academic interest in tourism during that decade. There are also no official data on the number of educational programmes for that period. In a historical account of tourism education in Brazil Matias (2002), lists 19 undergraduate programmes launched during the 1970s. These programmes reflected the government's investment in tourism and the optimism of a new and growing area of economic development. Institutions of higher education offering tourism majors at the time were limited to those in the country's largest cities, such as São Paulo, Rio de Janeiro, Recife and Curitiba.

In parallel with the official higher education programmes, in the 1970s the National Service for Commercial Learning (SENAC), an organization with representation across the country, offered comprehensive and sophisticated programmes of study in gastronomy and hospitality in São Paulo. In line with the focus of SENAC, the programmes were initially directed towards young people from lower socioeconomic backgrounds and focused on basic vocational education. Later, in the 1990s, these programmes were expanded to other parts of the country and were incorporated into secondary and higher levels of education.

The stagnation phase: 1980–90

The 1980s represented the second phase of development of tourism education in Brazil. During that decade, Brazil and its neighbouring countries faced economic and political instability. As a consequence, only a few new programmes were created during this period, and several existing ones were discontinued (Ansarah 2002). Once again, the limited official data and publications for the period indicate the minimal importance of tourism in higher education at that time. Matias (2002) identifies only nine programmes that were launched in Brazil during that decade.

In the economic and political history of Brazil, the 1980s were considered 'the lost decade' because the promises of the Brazilian miracle did not materialize. High inflation, unemployment, illiteracy and poverty created a range of profound socioeconomic problems that demanded increased attention by governments and policy-makers. This instability meant that tourism slipped lower in the government's list of priorities (Gaspari 2002).

Similar to the previous periods identified by Ansarah (2002), little information is available about the number of programmes launched during the 1980s, although there are indicators of how tourism research was developing. Barretto (1996), for example, comments that only 15 books on tourism were published in Brazil during the 1980s. Because the number of books published in any given area is often directly related to the number of educational programmes and students interested in the subject (Panosso and Calciolari 2010), the decrease in the number of books might indicate a downturn in the development of tourism education. In addition, Teixeira, Fletcher and Westlake (2001) observe that less than 30 per cent of the tourism and hotel management programmes that existed in 2001 were operating before the end of the 1980s, illustrating the uneven development of tourism and hospitality programmes.

The expansion phase: 1990–2000

To understand how tourism education developed in Brazil during the third phase of development, it is important to consider how broader socioeconomic factors have influenced the development of Brazil since the 1990s. After three decades of cyclic economic crises, inflation was contained in the 1990s, and the economy stabilized. Democracy was also strengthened. Domestic tourism benefited from a rise in social, political and economic confidence and the country was increasingly opened to overseas visitors (see Figure 1.2). Investment in infrastructure, products and services, especially in hotels and new airports, improved both the quality and the range of tourism experiences that were available. Foreign cruise ship companies were allowed to explore the Brazilian coast (see Chapter 4), and several projects in the services sector, especially in the accommodations sector, were funded by foreign capital.

In terms of tourism and hospitality education, Brazilian programmes reached a peak in terms of student enrolments during the 1990s. Teixeira (2001) notes that there was a boom in the number of tourism programmes offered in Brazilian institutions of higher education. She highlights that there were 156 undergraduate tourism programmes, in 1999, compared with 32 programmes, in 1994. Several reasons can be cited for the increase in tourism programmes during that period.

First, in 1995, the Brazilian government made a decision to open the national higher education system to the market by allowing private institutions to establish new programmes in all areas. The rationale behind the liberalization of higher education was that the government could not meet the growing demand for free public higher education. The higher education sector needed to expand, and the best way to achieve this was through private sector involvement. It is worth mentioning that the early 1990s was a period of expansion in higher education worldwide (Karapetrovic, Rajamasi and Willborn 1999). This expansion was characterized by growth in the number of institutions and the number and diversity of programmes and the growing importance of higher education in Brazil. This expansion also led to higher levels of public expenditure. As Barnett (2000) points out, the shift towards a global knowledge economy has led to a change in how societies view education, and globalization and neoliberalism have also changed how universities operate. Therefore, higher education has become a highly competitive and commercialized sector worldwide. Higher education in Brazil has been transformed by these trends.

Second, the growth of the Brazilian tourism industry, especially in the northeastern states, has created demand for high-quality human resources. To meet the requirements of the industry, tourism programmes were launched in all five geographical regions of Brazil. It is important to note that the emphasis during this stage was on higher education programmes and not on technological programmes and vocational training. As a result, the number of professionals with undergraduate degrees in tourism grew significantly, while the number of professionals with vocational training did not. This imbalance meant that there were few qualified professionals for the day-to-day operations of businesses and an overwhelming number of professionals who were skilled in tourism management.

Because undergraduate education provided the pipeline for postgraduate study and academic career progression, this imbalance led to a situation in which most tourism academics in the 1990s lacked relevant industry experience. Therefore, academic publications by Brazilian scholars were theoretical or conceptual in nature. With few exceptions, new academics had never worked in the development of tourism destinations. In addition, approaches to teaching also lacked an entrepreneurial and creative approach which has, in turn, influenced a whole generation of Brazilian scholars (Espíndola 2009). At the time of graduation, students were able to identify business opportunities but did not know how to act, reflecting the lack of entrepreneurship and creativity in their educational experience. As a result, a large portion of tourism research in the country today focuses on theoretical and conceptual studies of tourism planning (Rejowski 2010).

Third, the minimal investment required to mount new tourism higher education programmes stimulated private investors in higher education to prioritize such low–investment opportunities. Therefore, the number of tourism programmes in private higher education grew significantly. As evidence, Teixeira, Fletcher and Westlake (2001) observe that, in the early 2000s, 94 per cent of tourism programmes in Brazil were offered by private institutions.

Public higher education institutions in Brazil are responsible for the majority of tourism research because they host most of the postgraduate programmes in the country. Private institutions tend to focus on undergraduate education, which does not require their faculty to publish in high-ranking journals to receive a favourable evaluation. This scenario is similar to those in other countries, such as Mexico, Spain and Portugal, where the market liberalization of higher education policy has led to a growth in the number of private providers with emphases on teaching to fee-paying students (e.g. Castillo Nechar *et al.* 2010).

Fourth, tourism programmes in higher education became fashionable in the 1990s, especially for young students. The word 'tourism' suggested that the programme would be based on field trips with subsequent employment opportunities in exotic domestic and international destinations and the chance to meet and mix with beautiful, young and rich people. This artificial imagery continued until 2004–5, when the country began to develop a more comprehensive view of the complexity and potentialities of tourism.

One sign of the growing maturity of tourism education and research in Brazil in the 1990s was the increase in the number of academic books and journals and regional, national and international conferences (Leal 2006). Panosso Netto (2005), for example, noted that between 1990 and 1997 no more than two academic books on tourism were published each year. In contrast, in 2002 alone, more than 80 titles were published. From the establishment of the first tourism journal in the country in 1990 to the second, *Turismo: Visão e Ação*, published by Universidade do Vale do Itajaí (UNIVALI), eight years had passed. The growth in tourism research probably mirrored the boom in the provision of tourism education in Brazil and the subsequent demand for teaching literature, but it also reflected the maturation of the academic workforce. Leal (2010a), for example, identified 16 Brazilian academic journals (see Table 12.1) that were favourably evaluated by the CAPES Foundation (Brazilian Ministry of Education) with the word 'tourism' in their titles.

The main criticisms of the boom in the number of institutions establishing tourism programmes during the expansion phase are that: (1) there was little concern for the sustainability of such programmes in terms of the quality of education and their financial stability; (2) there was little attention given to the real needs of the industry and to filling labour-force demands; (3) there was

Table 12.1 List of academic journals with the word 'tourism' in their titles and their respective rankings according to the 2008 CAPES evaluation

Journal	*Ranking**
Boletim de Estudos em Hotelaria e Turismo	–
Caderno Virtual de Turismo	B4
Cultur: Revista de Cultura e Turismo	C
Dialogando no Turismo	C
Patrimônio: Lazer & Turismo	B5
Pesquisas em Turismo e Paisagens Cársticas	–
Revista Acadêmica Observatório de Inovação do Turismo	B4
Revista Brasileira de Pesquisa em Turismo	C
Revista Científica Eletrônica de Turismo	–
Revista de Turismo Matogrossense	–
Revista Eletrônica de Turismo Cultural	C
Revista Turismo & Desenvolvimento	B5
Revista Turismo em Análise	B2
Revista Unibero de Turismo e Hotelaria	–
Turismo & Ciência	–
Turismo e Sociedade	C

(*)Due to the interdisciplinary nature of tourism, the journals in this field are ranked in areas as diverse as "history", "geography", "economy" and "urban and regional planning." The rankings presented here (in descending order from A1, A2, B1, B2, B3, B4, B5 to C) are those in the 'business administration, tourism and accounting' area only.

minimal high-quality research in the private sector, and thus a teaching-research nexus was nonexistent; (4) and there were not enough qualified academics to fill the needs of institutions, especially the private ones, which were subject to high growth in enrolments (Lohmann 2004). As a result, this growth phase was short-lived, and a decline in the number of programmes started to take place in the mid to late 2000s.

Regarding labour force industry needs, it is important to stress that universities lie between two paradigms that are difficult to reconcile: education to perform specific work and tasks, i.e. a vocational/professional orientation, and education through critical thinking, i.e. a liberal education orientation. The liberal orientation is more dominant in tourism education in Brazil, although it reflects in research outcomes in only a few centres of excellence across the country.

There are criticisms, especially from within the tourism industry, that students are not receiving sufficient practical knowledge in tourism programmes in Brazil. Although managerial and economic views of tourism are important for future professionals, it is also necessary to question these views in light of critical perspectives on tourism. A balance between the two is needed. This has been a point of debate in both left and right-wing intellectual groups, but a common understanding has not been reached. This is not a problem because having a common understanding can result in a lack of attitude and change. It seems that Brazil is not suffering from this stagnation, because the debates continue (Santos and Almeida Filho 2008; Santos and Paula 2009).

Consolidation and internationalization: 2000 and onwards

Ansarah (2002) predicted a fourth phase in the evolution of Brazil's tourism and hospitality education beginning in the mid-2000s. The significant increase in offerings in higher education programmes in the 1990s proved unsustainable (Leal 2004) and the number of programmes began to decline toward the end of the 2000s. Ansarah (2002) predicted that this phase would be marked by a search for a balance between quantity and quality, and these predictions have largely been proven accurate. There are indications, such as the establishment of postgraduate research programmes, the promotion of national and international academic conferences and the creation of academic associations, that the quality of tourism education has improved. To date, very few studies have addressed the internationalization of Brazilian tourism research. However, the internationalization process is evident in the number of papers written by academics in the field of tourism in which they report on their experiences at international conferences and in the establishment of partnerships with international academics and institutions.

At the same time, the number of tourism and hospitality programmes has decreased. A simple search for the term 'tourism' in the names of programmes on the official website of the Ministry of Education (http://emec.mec.gov.br/) resulted in 475 matches in September 2011. This result can be compared to a peak of 834 programmes found in 2005 (Leal 2010b). It is important to note that the large number of programmes combines the traditional four-year bachelor programmes with the two to two-and-a-half-year post-secondary technological education programmes and distance learning initiatives. Although not a straightforward comparison, these figures indicate how offerings in tourism education have dwindled over the years.

One significant development that took place beginning in 2000 was the creation of the National Association of Tourism Research and Postgraduate Education (Associação Nacional de Pesquisa e Pós-Graduação em Turismo, ANPTUR). ANPTUR is the prime organization for tourism and hospitality educators, and its activities include publication of the double-blind refereed journal *Revista Brasileira de Pesquisa em Turismo* (Brazilian Journal of Tourism Research, first published in September 2007) and hosting of an annual conference (first held in November 2002) during which researchers from all over the country have the opportunity to meet and discuss emerging issues in tourism research and education.

Fifth phase: present and future

Building on the quality improvements from the previous phase, new challenges for tourism education in Brazil have become closely tied to the imperative of internationalization (Morosini 2011). Under related initiatives, individual researchers and institutions have developed partnerships with foreign universities that have resulted in student and academic exchanges in centres of excellence in other countries. Brazilian academics have also been successful in bids for international scholarships, and there is currently a trend towards studying abroad. Prominent international researchers have been invited as keynote speakers at conferences throughout Brazil. This exchange has proved to be positive for both Brazilian researchers and international researchers, who are benefiting from the cross-pollination of ideas and exchange. Increasingly, global attention is turning to Brazil because it has one of the fastest-growing economies in the world, as well as its role in hosting the 2014 FIFA World Cup and the 2016 Summer Olympic Games. Further examples of the internationalization of tourism education in Brazil are increases in the number of academic articles published by Brazilian researchers in international journals (often in Spanish and English) and the number of scholars attending international tourism conferences. In July 2011, a group of researchers based both in Brazil and overseas launched the International Academy for the Development of Tourism Research in Brazil (Academia Internacional para o Desenvolvimento da Pesquisa em Turismo no Brasil, ABRATUR), which aims to foster more international collaboration among scholars studying tourism in Brazil.

There is at least one hurdle to be overcome if Brazil is to play a stronger role in the international tourism academy: the language barrier. Few students and researchers have published in the highly ranked international outlets for tourism research because they are impeded by the necessary command of English. However, in the Latin American and Iberian countries, Brazilian scholars have continued to increase their participation in publications, conferences and research groups and projects. One outcome of these partnerships was the launch in 2011 of the Ibero-American Tourism Journal (*Revista Iberoamericana de Turismo*, RITUR), which is a joint publication of Brazilian and Spanish universities. These universities were able to collaborate because the Spanish and Portuguese languages are, to some extent, similar, which facilitates communication among researchers.

In the next decade, another significant shift in tourism education in Brazil is expected. Universities are now allowed to create shorter 'fast-track' programmes, known as technological programmes, which are often two or two-and-a-half-year programmes but have the same legal and educational value as the traditional four-year bachelor's programmes (see Figure 12.1). This shift has forced most private education providers to convert traditional programmes to shorter ones, which offer rapid return on investment to their students. A similar situation is occurring in other countries, such as the UK, where shorter programmes, known as foundation programmes, have become popular.

The impact of these changes has yet to be assessed, and there are questions regarding whether shorter programmes will compromize the provision of higher education. Barnett (1992) comments that critical dialogue, self-reflection, conversation and continuing redefinition of theories and frameworks are closely linked to the concept of higher education, and these didactic activities require time. Reducing the number of academic semesters from the standard eight to four or five, suggests that higher levels of understanding and critical thinking might be replaced by more operational-related content. In that case, there will be less time for critical analysis, self-reflection, conversation and continuing redefinition in institutions, which might in turn lead to a departure from the original values of higher education. A policy-oriented solution might be that the responsible government agencies should encourage the creation of tourism programmes in institutions that offer vocational education.

Postgraduate tourism education in Brazil

The creation of the first master's degree programme focusing on tourism in 1993 was an indication that the field was starting to mature. It meant that tourism had begun to establish a sufficiently large and cohesive body of research and researchers to deserve a place in an increasingly multidisciplinary world. In 2011 there were 11 postgraduate research programmes in Brazil, eight master's programmes with the word 'tourism' in their names, two programmes in related areas (leisure and hospitality) and only one doctorate programme in business administration and tourism were listed on the government's official agency for postgraduate research education (CAPES) (see Table 12.2). In 2004, Lohmann (2004) observed that the number of research degree programmes was still inadequate for the country's needs, especially in terms of the need for qualified active research-teaching academics to staff the numerous undergraduate programmes.

Regarding academic conferences related to tourism, there were no major outlets to disseminate research for many years. This deficiency has been addressed via postgraduate programmes that organize, promote and host academic conferences directed towards their own academic staff and students. Table 12.3 presents the major tourism conferences held in Brazil today.

The conferences presented in Table 12.3 attract large audiences. However, it is important to stress that a number of smaller academic conferences are organized across the country and have a local and/or regional scope. What matters is that the sum of all initiatives increases the interest and attention of researchers, government officials and those in the private business sector and builds awareness and capacity to understand the phenomenon of tourism in Brazil.

Conclusions

This chapter presented an overview of the development of tourism higher education in Brazil since the creation of the first programmes in the 1970s. The origins and development of tourism and hospitality education programmes have been influenced by broader socio-political and economic developments and shifting national and global priorities. Within this context, higher education in tourism has received uneven attention and has been characterized by phases of growth, decline and regeneration. Nevertheless, decisions to host the FIFA World Cup in 2014 and the Summer Olympic Games in 2016 suggest that Brazil is emerging as a powerful player on the world stage with a bright future. Higher

Table 12.2 Postgraduate programmes in tourism and related areas in Brazil in 2011

Programme name	Institution	Ranking*
PhD in Business Administration and Tourism	*Universidade do Vale do Itajaí* (UNIVALI) (Itajaí, Santa Catarina)	*4*
Inter-institutional Master's in Business Administration and Tourism	UNIVALI and *Centro Universitário do Norte* (Manaus, Amazonas)	**
Master's in Culture and Tourism***	*Universidade Estadual de Santa Cruz* (UESC) (Ilhéus, Bahia)	–
Professional Master's in Management of Tourism Business	*Universidade Estadual do Ceará* (UECE) (Fortaleza, Ceará)	*3*
Master's in Hospitality	*Universidade Anhembi Morumbi* (UAM) (São Paulo)	*3*
Master's in Leisure	*Universidade Federal de Minas Gerais* (UFMG) (Belo Horizonte, Minas Gerais)	*4*
Master's in Tourism	*Universidade de Caxias do Sul* (UCS) (Caxias do Sul, Rio Grande do Sul)	*3*
Master's in Tourism	*Universidade Federal do Rio Grande do Norte* (UFRN) (Natal, Rio Grande do Norte)	*3*
Professional Master's in Tourism	*Universidade de Brasília* (UnB) (Brasília, Distrito Federal)	*3*
Master's in Tourism and Hotel Management	UNIVALI (Balneário Camburiú, Santa Catarina)	*5*
Master's in Tourism and the Environment***	*Centro Universitário Una* – (UNA) (Belo Horizonte, Minas Gerais)	–

Sources: Rejowski (2011) and CAPES website (www.capes.gov.br)

(*) The highest ranking is 7, which indicates an international centre of excellence. The lowest acceptable ranking is 3, which indicates that the minimum requirements have been met.

(**) Inter-institutional programmes are a relatively recent innovation in the provision of postgraduate education in Brazil. At present, no ranking for this programme is available on the CAPES website.

(***) Programmes in the process of closure because of the non-achievement of the minimum quality requirements imposed by the CAPES Foundation (Brazilian Ministry of Education).

education programmes focusing on tourism and hospitality will certainly figure prominently in this scenario.

However, this chapter has also raised issues about the quality of programmes, the balance between vocational and liberal education and the development of the academy. Those involved in charting the future course for tourism education need to become active members in the academic 'tribe' of international tourism (Becher 1989). Language barriers will have to be overcome, and theoretical and methodological innovations will have to be prioritized and improved by

Table 12.3 List of the major tourism conferences in Brazil

Conference name	*Year of first meeting*	*Description*
National Association of Tourism Research and Postgraduate Education's (ANPTUR) Seminar	2002	This is an annual conference organized by ANPTUR and directed towards the professors and students of postgraduate tourism programmes. Participants from other programmes are welcome
Tourism Research Seminar of Mercosur (SEMINTUR)	2003	SEMINTUR started as an annual conference and now takes place every two years. The conference is organized by the Tourism Master Programme of the *Universidade de Caxias do Sul* (UCS) and attracts undergraduate and postgraduate students as well as professors from diverse fields of study
International Tourism Seminar (SIT)	1999	SIT was an annual event organised by the Tourism Observatory of the *Universidade Federal do Paraná* (UFPR) and the *Universidade Positivo.* The last meeting was held in 2009
National Meeting of Local-based Tourism	1997	This meeting started as an annual conference and now takes place every two years. The first meeting was an initiative of the *Universidade de São Paulo's* (USP) Department of Geography. Since then, each edition has been hosted by a different institution. It is a multidisciplinary conference that attracts researchers from several fields of knowledge

the Brazilian tourism academic community if it is to find its place among its international peers. To this end, the establishment and consolidation of tourism journals and conferences indicate the maturation of the field, and the increasing engagement of academics in international forums is a positive development. However, if Brazil is to play a significant role in the future, the quality of tourism education and research must be the focus of scholars, institutions and the government.

Acknowledgements

The authors would like to thank Dr Wayne Thomas Enders of the *Universidade Federal do Rio Grande do Norte* for his comments on an early draft of this chapter.

References

ANECA – Agencia Nacional de Evaluación de la Calidad y Acreditación (2004) *Título de Grado en Turismo*. Spain: Universitat de Girona.

Ansarah, M. G. R. (2002) *Formação e Capacitação do Profissional em Turismo e Hotelaria: Reflexões e Cadastro das Instituições Educacionais no Brasil*. São Paulo: Aleph.

Barnett, R. (1992) *Improving Higher Education: Total Quality Care*. Buckinghamshire: SRHE/Open University Press.

Barnett, R. (2000) *Realizing the University in an Age of Supercomplexity*. Buckinghamshire: SRHE/Open University Press.

Barretto, M. (1996) Produção bibliográfica em turismo no Brasil. *Turismo em Análise*, 7: 93–102.

Becher, T. (1989) *Academic Tribes and Territories: Intellectual Enquiry and the Culture of Disciplines*. Milton Keynes: SRHE/Open University Press.

Beni, M. C. (2001) *Análise Estrutural do Turismo*, 2nd edn. São Paulo: Senac São Paulo.

Beni, M. C. (2003) *Globalização do Turismo*. São Paulo: Aleph.

Brazil (1996) Lei nº 9.394, de 20/12/1996. *Estabelece as diretrizes e bases da educação nacional. Diário Oficial da União*. Brasília: Gráfica do Senado, nl. 248, 23/12/1996.

Carneiro, M. C. R. (1999) *O Governo Fernando Henrique 1995–1998*. São Paulo: Editora Três.

Castillo Nechar, M. (2005) La modernización de la política turística en México: tendencias y perspectivas, unpublished thesis, Centro de Investigación y Docencia en Humanidades del Estado de Morelos, Mexico.

Castillo Nechar, M., Tomillo Noguero, F. and García Gomez, F. J. (2010) *Principales Tendencias de la Investigación Turística en España y Europa*. Valladolid: Universidad Europea Miguel de Cervantes.

Espíndola, P. G. (2009) O empreendedorismo no curso superior de turismo: uma proposta metodológica para o seu ensino, paper presented at the VI Seminário da Associação Nacional de Pesquisa e Pós-Graduação em Turismo, São Paulo, September 2009.

Espinosa Castillo, M. (ed.) (2007) *Tendencias de la Investigación Turística a Principios del Siglo XXI*. Mexico: Instituto Politécnico Nacional.

Fayos-Solá, E. (1997) Educación y formación en la nueva era de turismo: la visión de la OMT, in World Tourism Organization (ed.) *Human Capital in the Tourism Industry of the 21st Century*. Madrid: WTO.

Formica, S. (1996) European hospitality and tourism education: differences with the American model and future trends. *International Journal of Hospitality Management*, 15: 317–23.

Gaspari, E. (2002) *A Ditadura Escancarada*. São Paulo: Companhia das Letras.

Gómez Nieves, S. (2008) Ciencia y desarrollo turístico en México. *Estudios y Perspectivas en Turismo*, 17: 272–90.

Gómez Nieves, S. (2010) La cientificidad en el discurso académico del turismo en México. *Homo Viator*, 1: 148–84.

Karapetrovic, S., Rajamani, D. and Willborn, W. W. (1999) University, Inc., *Quality Progress*, May: 87–95.

Leal, S. R. (2004) Is tourism education in Brazil sustainable?, paper presented at Association for Tourism in Higher Education Annual Conference 2004, Great Missenden, December 2004.

Leal, S. R. (2006) Madurez de la investigación científica en turismo en Brasil y en el mundo. *Estudios y Perspectivas en Turismo*, 15: 81–91.

Leal, S. R. (2010a) 'Panorama da produção científica em turismo no Brasil: Perfil dos autores, paper presented at the VII Seminário da Associação Nacional de Pesquisa e Pós-Graduação em Turismo, São Paulo, September 2010.

Leal, S. R. (2010b) *Quality in Tourism Higher Education: The Voices of Undergraduate Students*. Saarbrücken: Lambert Academic Publishing.

Leiper, N. (1981) Towards a cohesive curriculum in tourism: the case for a distinct discipline. *Annals of Tourism Research*, 8: 69–84.

Leme, F. B. M. (2009) Educación ambiental y turismo: Una formación holística, interdisciplinaria y de futuros educadores. *Estudios y Perspectivas en Turismo*, 18: 92–106.

Lohmann, G. (2004) CAUTHE 2004: Pesquisa em turismo e hotelaria na Austrália. E o Brasil com isso?. *Turismo em Análise*, 15: 250–3.

Matias, M. (2002) *Turismo: Formação e Profissionalização – 30 Anos de História*. Barueri: Manole.

Morosini, M. (2011) Internacionalização na produção de conhecimento em IES Brasileiras: cooperação internacional tradicional e cooperação internacional horizontal. *Educação em Revista*, 27: 93–112.

Panosso Netto, A. (2005) Publicações em turismo no Brasil, in L. G. G. Trigo, A. Panosso Netto, M. A. Carvalho and P. S. Pires (eds) *Análises Regionais e Globais do Turismo Brasileiro*. São Paulo: Editora Roca.

Panosso Netto, A. and Calciolari, G. F. (2010) Quantos são os livros teóricos de turismo publicados no Brasil? Uma análise da produção bibliográfica nacional (1990–2010). *Turismo em Análise*, 21: 668–86.

Rejowski, M. (1996) *Turismo e Pesquisa Científica: Pensamento Internacional X Situação Brasileira*. Campinas: Papirus.

Rejowski, M. (2010) Enseñanza e investigación en turismo: revelación inicial de estudios sobre la producción científica en Brasil, in M. Castillo Nechar and A. Panosso Netto (eds) *Epistemología del Turismo: Estudios Críticos*. Mexico: Trillas.

Rejowski, M. (2011) Panorama da educação e pesquisa em turismo no Brasil, keynote speech at the first Seminário Internacional de Estudos Críticos em Turismo, Universidade Federal do Rio Grande do Norte, 24–25 March.

Rocha Centeno, R. (1992) *Metodología de la Investigación Aplicada al Turismo: Casos Prácticos*. Mexico: Trillas.

Sakata, M. C. G. (2002) Tendências metodológicas da pesquisa em turismo no Brasil, unpublished thesis, Universidade de São Paulo.

Santos, B. S. and Almeida Filho, N. (2008) *A Universidade no Século XXI. Para uma Universidade Nova*. Coimbra: Edições Almedina.

Santos, B. S. and Paula, M. (eds) (2009) *Epistemologias do sul*. Coimbra: Edições Almedina.

Schlüter, R. G. (2000) *Investigación en Turismo y Hotelería*. Buenos Aires: CIET.

Teixeira, R. M. (2001) Ensino superior em turismo e hotelaria no Brasil: Um estudo exploratório. *Turismo em Análise*, 12: 7–31.

Teixeira, R. M., Fletcher, J. and Westlake, J. (2001) A educação superior em turismo: um estudo comparativo Brasil e o Reino Unido. *Turismo: Visão e Ação*, 4: 9–27.

Trigo, L. G. G. (2002) *Viagem na Memória: Guia Histórico das Viagens e do Turismo no Brasil*. São Paulo: SENAC.

Trigo, L. G. G. (2003) *A Sociedade Pós Industrial e o Profissional de Turismo*, 7th edn. Campinas: Papirus.

Vera Rebollo, J.F. (1995) Los estudios de postgrado sobre turismo en España. *Estudíos Turísticos*, 128: 11–21.

World Tourism Organization – WTO (1997) *An Introduction to TedQual – A Methodology for Quality in Tourism Education and Training*. Madrid: WTO.

13 Conclusions

Dianne Dredge and Gui Lohmann

There is no doubt that Brazil is a land of contrasts. It has been amply demonstrated in the chapters of this book that during the 1990s and the 2000s the country has been the subject of significant social, political, economic and environmental transformations. With respect to tourism, there are a variety of built and natural tourism landscapes, a large number of destinations at various stages of evolution, a multiplicity of stakeholders, and a diversity of issues and the challenges discussed in the chapters of this book. Underpinning many of these chapters there is also the subtext of government involvement in tourism, and the awakening and varied attempts by all levels of government to harness the potential benefits of tourism and manage its negative impacts.

The chapters contained herein have told the story of this tourism development in Brazil. They have employed various research methods and approaches, drawn variously from theoretical foundations and practical insights, and they have been told from a variety of perspectives. Importantly, this book gives voice to Brazilian researchers who are actively engaged in researching tourism from a variety of theoretical angles and pragmatic perspectives, and it gives them an opportunity to share their insights and understandings with an international audience.

The objective of this book was to expose the rich hinterland of tourism research in Brazil, and to encourage the predominantly English-speaking audience of global tourism scholars to critically engage with these insights and understandings so that cross-cultural fertilizations may follow. Not only does the size of Brazil (in terms of its land mass, population and economy for instance) provide a different context in which to consider tourism development and management, but it also challenges us to think beyond our own acculturated knowledge and experiences. The rapid socio-political, economic and environmental changes taking place in Brazil over the last 20 years, and explored in Chapter 1, provide the backdrop for the development of tourism. From a political standpoint, globalization and the embrace of free-market neoliberalism have transformed Brazil and opened up significant opportunities for tourism investment and development. There has also been a breakdown in the traditional centralized and heavily bureaucratic approaches to government involvement in many areas of policy, and tourism has flourished under these conditions. As a result, there is greater interconnectedness of social, political and economic spheres and an increased range of stakeholders actively involved in addressing the challenges of tourism product and experience development, investment attraction and institutional capacity building.

While the chapters of this book tell vastly different stories and interrogate various challenges and issues, a key contribution of the book is that it represents a systematic effort to bring to English-speaking audiences a snapshot of the diversity of tourism research in Brazil. The depth and breadth of tourism issues and challenges raised in this book tell only part of the story, with the complexities and challenges of doing research in Brazil left largely unexplored. In reflecting upon the chapters of the book in what follows, we also hope not only to expose the diversity of methods and approaches used to explore tourism, but also where opportunities lie for further research and cross-cultural collaboration into the future.

Significance and contributions

The introductory chapter (Chapter 1) provided an overview of Brazil, drawing attention to the rapid and sustained change taking place with significant implications for its social, economic, environmental and government systems. Between 1964 and 1985 the country was subject to military rule, and while much of the world was experimenting with globalization and neoliberalism, Brazil was very much characterized by a paternalistic bureaucracy, which limited opportunities for foreign trade and investment. With the fall of the military government in 1985, the doors opened and rapid and sustained change has washed over Brazil. It brought quite different levels of development, capacity building, expertise and support for tourism. Not surprisingly, in some parts of the country, the challenges and issues associated with tourism are similar to those experienced in the developing countries. In other parts of Brazil, tourism is a sophisticated and important foreign-exchange earner and regional development tool.

The role of governments in tourism, and the characteristics of the institutional arrangements and policy environment are central to understandings of tourism development in Brazil, so it is fitting that Chapter 2 explores this context. Chapter 2 has illustrated the significant shifts that have taken place in the institutional arrangements for tourism planning and policy development, particularly since the 1990s, which have broken down many of the traditional barriers to investment and product development. As would be expected, Brazil's organizational and public administration frameworks are heavily influenced by its colonial past, and the heavy-handed bureaucratic nature of Portuguese colonialism, and then later, by the authoritarian rule and paternalistic democracy of the military government. In other parts of the Western developed world, the potential of tourism began to unfold in the middle of the twentieth century. With the uptake of globalization and neoliberalism, economic management principles, and coupled with the growth in mass tourism and technological innovation, its potential unfolded exponentially in the latter part of the last century. Like many other areas of policy, the institutional arrangements and the development of clear strategic tourism policy in Brazil have been slow to emerge. Processes of political modernization, and the opening up of global markets have been instrumental in unlocking the country's tourism potential.

Chapter 3 picks up the thread of political modernization introduced in earlier chapters, exploring the increased community participation in tourism development. In particular, the chapter explores the implementation of community-based tourism (CBT) projects with four cases examined in detail. While the contributions of CBT projects to community well-being are evident, the failure of many projects can be attributed to a lack of communication around the benefits and requirements of working with tourism associations and co-operatives. Furthermore, monitoring and evaluation of projects would also assist in maximizing benefits.

Chapter 4 examines tourism transport in Brazil, highlighting significant challenges in the provision and management of transport infrastructure. In a country where resources and expertise are spread so unevenly there is a real risk that reallocating resources to more heavily populated areas, where aging infrastructure and overcrowding have exacerbated capacity issues, will only exacerbate inequitable provision. The distribution of roles and responsibilities of various government agencies and the private sector become paramount in addressing these issues. However, Brazil is still grappling with profound changes associated with processes of political modernization and decentralization that other countries have been dealing with for decades.

Chapter 5 highlights these implications from another angle: an exploration of the challenges associated with implementing sustainability measures in the staging of the 2014 FIFA World Cup and the 2016 Olympic Games. In this chapter, the authors discuss the drivers behind the staging of these elite events, raising issue with the requirements of the international agencies and the 'fit' and appropriateness of associated facilities over the long term. Such mega-sporting events are costly exercises that divert resources away from health, education and transport, and are not likely to fulfil claims of social, environmental or economic sustainability.

Social justice issues are woven through Chapter 6, which examines the challenges of empowering small business in and around protected areas. Through a case study of the Serra da Capivara National Park, the authors examine the different types of upgrades or innovations that can empower a local community co-operative to build a business and leverage off tourism. By implementing these changes, a local community was able to generate employment, improve household incomes and reduce resource extraction pressures on the adjacent national park.

In Chapter 7, the characteristics of adventure tourism development and its distribution channels are explored in a case study of Brotas. In this chapter, Carnicelli and Lohmann explore the very nature of adventure tourism, noting the importance of emotionally intense tourist experiences that involve risk-taking and uncertainty. While this sector traditionally attracts free-spirited adventure tourists, Brotas' tourism industry is re-orienting itself towards a family market on the basis of its perceived potential and proximity to the very large urban markets of São Paulo. Of particular interest, this chapter demonstrates that tourism has been effectively used as tool to stimulate economic development and that stakeholders are working collaboratively towards shared interests. Reflecting on past lessons and future directions, and understanding distribution channels are important in helping the identity address their future.

Chapter 8 explores the nexus between ecotourism and conservation in the fishing village of Praia do Forte, Bahia, where local beaches are important nesting sites for four species of sea turtles. In this chapter, Pegas provides an insightful and culturally rich account of the tensions between traditional reliance of the local population on sea turtles for meat and eggs and the need to protect and conserve these creatures and their habitat. The case study is optimistic in its findings and provides important insights for future projects of this kind. While there is still a long way to go, ecotourism has the potential to generate economic benefits for local communities marginalized in the broader economic context, and in the process deeply embedded cultural values around the consumption of sea turtles can be changed.

Rodrigues and Prideaux examine the challenges and opportunities for backpacker tourism in the Amazon region in Chapter 9. Interestingly, while the Amazon is perhaps one of the most iconic features of Brazil from an international perspective, the tourism potential in the region remains largely untapped. Even more surprising is the fact that even the intrepid and curiosity-driven backpacker market is largely absent from the area. In this chapter the authors find that the region has considerable potential but that there is little understanding of backpacker market characteristics and requirements and there is little interest on the part of governments to target the sector. However, their case study of the Ararinha Jungle Lodge reveals that there are considerable benefits for local communities and for local conservation efforts (reinforcing the findings of Pegas in the previous chapter).

Chapter 10 introduces the reader to Brazilian culture and a place of festival, music, dance and sensual tourism. It explores the experiences of participants in off-season carnivals or micaretas. For many international audiences, the Carnival in Rio de Janeiro conjures iconic images, but the off-season carnivals held around the country, and which principally attract domestic markets, can also have very large followings. Sensual behaviour at micaretas is highly visible, accepted and encouraged, whether subtly through lyrics or overtly by singers during the shows. In this chapter Moital and Gândara explore sensual encounters by tourists at *micaretas*, finding that there are different types of micareta tourists based on their motivations to attend, and that there are different micareta attendance careers which tend to be anchored in the sensual element. A key contribution of this chapter is to introduce and explore a particular type of domestic-event tourism which is little known in other countries outside Latin America. It not only provides an insight into one part of the domestic event tourism, but also provide a window to certain parts of Brazil's celebration of music and dance.

In Chapter 11, Grünewald provides an intriguing exploration of the vexed issues around indigeneity and cultural commodification in a case study of the Pataxó, an indigenous group living along the southernmost coast of the state of Bahia. In this case study the attractions most required by tourists were found to be commoditized handicraft or material culture, such as dances and other performances. The Pataxó have engaged in renovating these cultural elements and reconstructing their ethnicity as a response to these tourist demands. This work opened the way for social interaction and tradition-building, and the promotion of Pataxó ethnicity followed. However, although the Pataxó can commercially perform their indigeneity in the tourism arena, they do not possess the rights to manage the tourism market, and this creates a challenging negotiated environment within which they work. That said, a key insight from this case is that the negativity surrounding the notion of authenticity must questioned: new cultural configurations of traditions built through intensive processes of Indian 'cultural revival' are being exhibited to tourists and a contributing to a sustainable development project. Surely there are lessons to be learned and reflections to be made in many other contexts as a result of this case.

In Chapter 12, Leal, Panosso Netto and Trigo contemplate the evolution of tourism education and research in Brazil, making a very fitting final set of reflections about the state of education and research in the country. In many ways the development of tourism, hospitality and events education is characterized by similar issues, challenges and criticisms to those experienced in other countries. These include the growth in higher education as a result of it being linked more directly to economic development goals; the emergence of private providers; balancing liberal social science education and vocational education; and reconciling the demands of industry with academic rigour and critical thinking skills. That said, the academic workforce appears to have matured and built strong international links, which will only serve to improve the teaching–research nexus and inform policy practice into the future. The challenge for this nascent academic community then, is not only to build upon international research and literature by integrating a distinctly Brazilian perspective, but also to develop and enhance cultural awareness of the Brazilian context within the international audience.

Key issues and insights

Independently and together, these chapters explore a range of key issues for tourism in Brazil and draw attention to those aspects in need of further research and critical attention. In particular, three key issues underpin many of the chapters and which we seek to highlight here. First, an important undercurrent within this book is the extent to which changing approaches to tourism are driven by processes of political and economic modernization. In almost all chapters, the changes in tourism and impacts upon tourism have been driven by processes of globalization, economic modernization and the realization that tourism can be a force for community economic development, environmental conservation and cultural regeneration. There have also been transcendental shifts in the way governments operate and share power since the introduction of the new constitution. There is concern for community well-being, participatory planning is well advanced in some arenas and there is growing involvement in public–private partnerships. The literature from international contexts demonstrates that such changes are not without their problems (e.g. see Cartier and Lew 2005; Dredge and Jenkins 2007; Sharpley 2009), and as such, researchers have a myriad of opportunities to explore and analyse the impacts of these big societal shifts on tourism.

Second, the value and characteristics of leadership in the development and management of tourism underpin many of the successful case studies presented in this book, although it is rarely mentioned in any direct way. Few of the chapter authors would argue against the importance of good leadership and associated qualities including trust, communication, creative solution-building and negotiation in their case studies. Clearly, human resources and management expertise within the tourism industry are fundamental to the future success of the industry in Brazil, and researchers both inside and outside the country may focus attention on this area.

Third, despite the fact that private enterprise is becoming increasingly powerful in Brazil, the role of governments at all levels and their relationships with stakeholders provides a very important setting within which tourism development is either facilitated or inhibited. In each of the chapters, the role of government was discussed either directly or indirectly. While it emerges clearly in each chapter that the country still has a long way to go in terms of having clearly articulated roles and responsibilities for tourism, that policy has changed rapidly, and there are some issues around corruption, inefficient but highly embedded practices and so on, there is still much work to be done in creating a supportive institutional setting for tourism.

Fourth, despite the fact that the various chapters contained within provide a diverse snapshot of tourism in Brazil, there remains a lack of comprehensive, credible and accessible data and information that can be used to inform decision-making and policy development. For many international colleagues, this is an impediment they have confronted for many years. However, in the face of a rapidly expanding tourism industry, the need for good data and information should be recognized and the academic community has a role to play in such an endeavour.

Future directions

Tourism is a global and transformative activity and world-making in its orientation (Hollinshead 2009). From the chapters contained in this book, the call to action is clear. Tourism in Brazil is a rapidly changing kaleidoscope of initiatives, strategies, challenges, actions and reactions. Governments at all levels are experimenting with their roles and responsibilities, influenced not only by broader discourses about public management, globalization and neoliberalism, but also by the dynamic and culturally embedded reactions to this change demonstrated by stakeholders directly and indirectly affected by tourism.

The sheer size of its domestic and international tourism markets, recent decisions to host globally significant events including the 2014 World Cup and the 2016 Olympic Games, the increased focus on improving products, services and experiences and the increased profile expected provide exciting opportunities for research collaboration. Not only is further research needed, but research collaboration that is enriched by cross-cultural perspectives will become an increasingly important source of innovation and creative thinking.

However, not to recognize issues associated with the influence and dominance of the English-language research culture in this conclusion would be remiss of us. Many of the Brazilian academics contributing to this book have developed their research skills and critical thought processes within English-language universities. Some now have international posts while others have returned to and work for Brazilian institutions. Through their PhD study and training, which is socially and historically situated within a European (or US) context, these researchers construct their interpretations of tourism in Brazil. We have not attempted to deconstruct their interpretations, nor highlight these Western influences. However, the extent to which these authors become human agency in the reproduction of dominant (English) discourses about tourism is something for readers to reflect upon. In the critical turn that has taken hold in some quarters of the social sciences, we have become accustomed to questioning issues of power, subordination, democracy, and so on, but the effects of the saturation of research culture by Western developed perspectives and English language are less often acknowledged. In this book we have not attempted to address directly, but instead have given authors flexibility in their choice of methods, theoretical framings and presentation so that they may develop alternative knowledge about tourism in Brazil.

That said, we believe there are good opportunities, particularly for research that builds theoretical depth and improves methodological rigour of research activity. The chapters contained in this book reveal variable levels of engagement in theory and method, but what has become clear is that most chapters rely heavily on Western (English) dominated literature to provide the theoretical foundation and/or framing.

In sum, tourism researchers in the future should be aware of potential collaborations and perspective-enhancing opportunities available through research and research collaborations in Brazil. 'The compass of research and innovation is swinging more and more strongly to the east and south. Policy makers in well-established research economies need to understand what is happening and be prepared to engage with new research landscapes' (Adams and King 2009: 1).

References

Adams J. and King, C. (2009) *Global Research Report: Brazil*. Leeds: Thomson Reuters.

Cartier, C. and Lew, A. (2005), *Touristed Landscapes: Geographical Perspectives on Globalisation and Touristed Landscapes*. Oxon: Routledge.

Dredge, D. and Jenkins, J. (2007) *Tourism Policy and Planning*. Brisbane: John Wiley & Sons.

Hollinshead, K. (2009) The 'Worldmaking' prodigy of tourism: The reach and power of tourism in the dynamics of change and transformation. *Tourism Analysis*, 14 (1), 139–152.

Sharpley, R. (2009) *Tourism Development and the Environment: Beyond Sustainability*. London: Earthscan.

Index

Page numbers in italic refer to tables and figures.

For Product Safety Concerns and Information please contact our EU representative GPSR@taylorandfrancis.com Taylor & Francis Verlag GmbH, Kaufingerstraße 24, 80331 München, Germany

Batch number: 10725971

Printed by Printforce, the Netherlands